WHAT

★ ★ ★ ★ ★

*'Having read many footballers' autobiographies, this is by far
the best and most realistic of them all'*

'Great read about a superb player'

*'Good insight into the culture of footballers of that era before
sports science and clean living. Great times'*

*'Best read for a long time. Great player in a great team in
a great era. Good stories all through'*

*'Fantastic book, could not put it down, worth every penny.
Hope he writes another!'*

*'An immense level of warmth, humour and honesty that many
modern books lack these days. Highly recommended'*

*'Simply one of those books that you could not put down
until finished. I would certainly recommend to anyone
who wants to find out what the players got up to when
Liverpool were winning things'*

*'Good, honest, down to earth lad who tells it how it was and is.
Great insight into Terry's time playing and coaching'*

'Excellent read'

Reviews from Amazon.co.uk

Terry McDermott

TERRY MAC

Living for the Moment

the Moment

MY AUTOBIOGRAPHY

Sport Media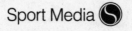

Terry collaborated with writer John Richardson on this book. John has spent more than 30 years on national newspapers.

He first met Terry in 1982 and they have been friends ever since.

A big thanks to wife Carole, sons Neale and Greg and daughter Rachel for their encouragement in helping me finally get around to putting my life into words. But more important for being in my life and making my life complete.

Terry McDermott

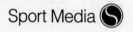

Sport Media

Written with John Richardson.

Paperback edition first published in Great Britain and Ireland in 2018 by
Trinity Mirror Sport Media, PO Box 48, Old Hall Street, Liverpool, L69 3EB.

www.tmsportmedia.com
@SportMediaTM

Trinity Mirror Sport Media is a part of Trinity Mirror plc.
One Canada Square, Canary Wharf, London, E15 5AP.

1

Hardback ISBN: 9781910335581.
eBook ISBN: 9781908319746.
Paperback ISBN: 9781910335871.

Photographic acknowledgements:
Mirrorpix, PA, Terry McDermott personal collection.

Design and typesetting by Trinity Mirror Sport Media.

Printed and bound by CPI Group (UK) Ltd,
Croydon, CR0 4YY.

CONTENTS

CONTENTS

FOREWORD

KEVIN KEEGAN

I'd never met Terry until our days together as Liverpool players. I had played against Newcastle with Terry in their side in the 1974 FA Cup final – but I never saw him! It's something I often remind him about because we won easily, 3-0.

When he first arrived at Anfield I think it was too much for him. It was nothing to do with his ability. I think it was because he was from Liverpool. He had this carefree attitude and probably didn't take it seriously enough. It took him 18 months to become a Liverpool player. Around the time I was about to leave, there was talk of Terry going.

But then the penny dropped and he worked it out that he could still have fun but be a top player as well. He was a very fit guy and one of the few who could keep up with me – despite his drinking, which I'm sure will get a mention!

In many ways, what helps our close relationship is that our

profiles are very similar. He started at Bury, I started at Scun-thorpe. His move to Newcastle was a big one, as was mine to Liverpool.

He was never taken on by a top club while nine of his Kirkby Schoolboys side were. The other one, as he will tell you, was Dennis Mortimer. The two of them went on to win the European Cup, a story to inspire any kid who is initially rejected or isn't given an opportunity. I was turned down by Coventry and Doncaster. My dad fixed me up for a trial at Doncaster. I didn't even get past the door because the guy guarding it said, "Sorry son, there are no trials tonight." He advised me to try the place opposite which was Doncaster Racecourse because I was small and looked more like a jockey!

So we're different in many ways but also similar in others.

We're good mates and I trust him with my life. That word trust is so vital in life, never mind football.

As a player, I would describe him as a great player with a capital 'G'. One who I feel at times has been very underrated. Recently we did a talk together in Hong Kong where they showed our goals. Yeah, they appreciated mine but when his were shown you could hear the whole audience going 'Wow'.

If you did a montage of the best 10 goals of anyone, including players like Alan Shearer, then Terry's would come out on top. He has scored more fantastic goals as a midfield player than anyone else over the last 40 years or so.

I'm not surprised it's taken him so long to write his book because he hasn't always had the confidence in himself for what he has achieved. That's what makes him such a great bloke and why his stories will be so interesting. He has some great tales to tell.

When I was persuaded to end my football exile by becoming Newcastle United manager in 1992 there was only one person I wanted at my side, Terry. He was always my first thought.

We're different, that's for sure. But I often think that's a good thing. You don't want someone as your right-hand man, assistant, 'buffer' – call him what you like – who is just going to agree with everything you say. Terry has his own opinions and isn't scared to voice them but he will never voice them in front of other people when it concerns me. So you can never get a division there. Our principles are the same.

He would just come and knock on the door and ask me if I had thought about this, that and the other. Terry is very worldly and that's what you want. He can tell you stories in the book that I wouldn't know because they never got to me.

When players come to an assistant manager they are doing two things. They are either trying to get a message to the manager through him or they are trying to get some advice that they don't want the manager to know about. Terry was fantastic at deciphering that.

When I arrived at Newcastle in '92, there were 16 games left. It was February and we were second bottom in the old Second Division, odds on to go down.

I trained with these bunch of players and thought 'oh my God, what am I going to do?' I needed somebody to bounce things off, someone who I knew well. There were other staff there but I wanted someone else who I knew I could rely on.

I phoned Terry up because I also knew he loved the club, having played there. I asked him if he felt like coming over and helping because it was a big job. He asked me when did I want him? I replied 'tomorrow'. He said 'I'll see you tonight then'.

FOREWORD

We met in the Gosforth Park Hotel, Newcastle, that night, and started planning. In fact, a lot of planning went on there over the next few critical months. At times it was hairy because it looked like the club was heading into football's third tier for the first time in its history. If that had happened, Terry and I would be remembered for taking the club down.

But the best decision I made was bringing Terry in. I remember after training sitting in the same bath we had known years previously as players. He had been playing for one side during the training session and I had been on the other. We were now in our forties. I asked him something about the next match coming up on the Saturday and he said 'you know, the first names on the teamsheet should be yours and mine!' He said we were still the best two players there and then we killed ourselves laughing.

That was what was great. We're second from bottom and having a serious conversation and then he comes out with something like that which eases the tension.

We had a time when the chairman Sir John Hall wouldn't put the money up and I was all for calling it a day. We drove away from the ground and got to Haltwhistle on the A69. Terry said we should go back, play the game on the Saturday and then go home. He was right.

Anyway, we came back, sorted things out and started moving in the right direction once the board agreed that we never wanted to be in this situation again. Terry was very important in all that at the beginning.

Terry as a player had always been his own man – completely honest and up front. I remember Arthur Cox, our manager at Newcastle, saying to me 'what about your mate out drinking last night – on a Thursday night?' I asked Arthur why he was telling me, I hadn't been with him. Terry was in the room, heard this and piped up: 'I drink every Thursday night!' I couldn't believe it, he hadn't tried to deny it or anything. He said he'd done it all the time he was at Liverpool.

Coxy told him to read the club rules which said you couldn't do that if we had a game on the Saturday. But it never did Terry any harm.

Peter Beardsley loved chocolate and all the fitness manuals say you can't eat loads of it but Peter did and had more energy than anyone, so who cares?

Terry was breaking all the rules on drinking but it was like a fuel to him. Give him a few pints and he'll run for ever. It was like his gas.

I just love his character, his honesty. He can't just have half a pint. What I love about him is what you see is what you get. He doesn't try to be anyone he isn't. There's a lot of things he has done that I wouldn't have but he would never advise any player to do what he did.

He is also, like myself, a huge family man. I can remember the day he brought his now wife Carole to the North East for the first time. He told me he had met this girl and thought this was the one for him. I'd heard that before.

But Carole has been great for him because until her arrival, you could never see him settling down. You couldn't see anyone putting up with him in marriage. Now our families are very close.

We even decided to have a vasectomy on the same day although I couldn't resist playing a little trick on Terry. After arriving home following the procedure I was sore and tired and told my wife Jean I was going off to bed for a lie down.

But I also told her that if Terry rang to tell him I'd gone out for a four mile run.

Sure enough, later on Terry called confessing he was in sheer agony and obviously wanted to know to ease any worries that I was also suffering.

Well, you can just imagine the look on his face when Jean announced I had gone out running!

On a serious note, you couldn't have anyone better than Terry to bounce things off.

I think if he hadn't have got around to this autobiography he would have been doing the public a disservice because there are things in the following pages that people can learn from as well as being entertained.

Like me, I know you can't wait to read them.

Kevin Keegan, 2017

PROLOGUE

EVERY DAY COUNTS

THERE is little chance of me ever forgetting the day I officially became a pensioner – December 8th, 2016: Terry McDermott, super-fit one-time footballer, now at the mercy of the medics.

Just a couple of weeks earlier, I had been in Liverpool preparing to go out to meet someone and I was talking to my wife Carole. Out of nowhere I could feel my speech wasn't right and there was a little tingle in the corner of the bottom of my lip. She also noticed my speech was a bit peculiar. After two or three minutes, the feeling disappeared and my speech was back to normal.

Later that day, I experienced the same feeling. I didn't really want to talk, just hoping it would go away again. That night, we drove back to our house in Newcastle. There were no further problems and I just put out of my mind what had happened, not thinking it would return.

A few days later, just a couple of days before my 65th birthday, I was speaking to my big Liverpool mate David Johnson on the phone when I could feel my speech going again. I was starting to slur and there was nothing I could do. I didn't have any control over my actions. He couldn't have noticed anything, so I ended the conversation, went over to Carole and told her that my speech had gone again. She agreed it still wasn't right, so she said: "Right, Terry, you need to see a doctor." But it was 6.30pm and the doctors wouldn't be open.

She rang 111 (the non-emergency service) and they started asking questions on the other end of the phone.

"What are his symptoms?"

She replied: "His speech is a bit slurred and there's a bit of a tingling sensation in his mouth."

I was put on the phone and the person at the other end told me: "I want you to go straight to hospital."

I couldn't believe it. "Manchester City are playing Barcelona on the TV tonight," I uttered. "Can I go tomorrow?"

"No!" was the firm retort.

She told me she would ring back with an appointment to see someone at the Newcastle RVI hospital. A minute later, I was booked in at 8.40pm. I'm now starting to worry, asking myself why am I being rushed in to see someone that night? When I arrived at the hospital, I started undergoing blood tests and having monitors attached. I'm now really thinking there must be something wrong.

Everything is going through my mind. I'm feeling very vulnerable. I hate hospitals at the best of times but now I'm the one in the spotlight. Someone who has always been naturally fit over the years and as a player had a reputation for having immense stamina and exceptional running power. What really freaked me out was when they wanted me to have a head scan. I entered the tunnel-shaped machine.

What can they be looking for? What the hell is wrong with me?

Despite all the drama, there had been the odd moment of amusement. While I was waiting to see the consultant, I was lying on top of a bed with curtains drawn around for privacy. There were two Geordies in two of the other beds in the ward.

One said: "Howay man, Terry McDermott was here before."

"No man, it was someone else. Someone who looks like him."

I was behind the curtains killing myself laughing.

They still hadn't come up with any conclusive results by the time they decided to send me home with a tablet to take and orders to return the next day for some Ultrasound tests. At least when I got home I had a good sleep because I was worn out by then. Carole and I didn't leave the hospital until 5am.

The next afternoon, I had the Ultrasound tests on both sides of my neck. They weren't able to get a conclusive reading from one side so I had to go to The Freeman Hospital in Newcastle the next day because they have a better and more sophisticated machine.

So, instead of having a few celebratory drinks with my family for my landmark birthday, I would now be in a hospital undergoing more tests. It was a good job that we'd celebrated my birthday the previous weekend, watching *Simply Red* and *Motown The Musical* on two separate nights in London.

When I went to the hospital, the first person we bumped into to ask directions was a doctor called Mike Wyatt who said that he had been assigned to look after me. He said that I was booked in for Monday.

"Monday? For what?" I asked, puzzled. "For an operation."

Everything started to become clearer. I'd had a mini-stroke and one of the arteries in the neck was between 62 per cent and 69 per cent blocked. If this hadn't been detected in time I would have had a fully blown stroke. I might not have died but I could have been in a right mess. He told me that in some ways I had been lucky because some people don't get a warning. It just hits them. He assured me that the operation would sort things out.

I rang a few people for assurances about what I was going to go through, like my former Newcastle United club doctor Ian McGuinness, who is now in Qatar. "Listen, Terry, they do these operations every single day. You will be fine," he insisted. He told me a story about a Qatari lad of 22 who even had the same problem. It can happen to anyone, no matter how fit you are or what your lifestyle is like.

But this was happening to me and I couldn't really believe it.

The operation was a complete success and I want to thank the wonderful people who looked after me: the surgeon James McCaslin; Craig Nesbitt, who assisted him and loves his football; anaesthetist Stephen Hillier and Justin Joyce, the recovery nurse who woke me up every hour. It makes you proud to know we have an NHS that works.

The biggest problem after the operation was trying to smuggle myself out of the hospital to avoid the newspapers getting hold of the story.

Someone had the bright idea to wheel me out with one of my legs lifted up, making any onlookers believe it was an old football-related injury that was getting fixed!

The good news is that I can still enjoy a drink. I'm going to enjoy life even more and go to more places around the world, explore more. Instead of saying 'we might do this and that', we *will* do it.

I suppose an experience like this does make you look at life differently. I've been lucky, I know that.

It was great the number of people who got in touch to see how I was after news filtered around about my op. Great mates like Kevin Keegan, Kenny Dalglish, Graeme Souness, Alan Hansen, Phil Thompson, Ian Callaghan, Ray Clemence, Alan Shearer, Lee Clark and David Johnson, who has been there all the way with me. It's a reminder of the amazing football life I've enjoyed and the many great memories I've had along the way.

If I'm honest, I've never really wanted to do a book but now I have, I couldn't be more pleased. People were always coming up to me and asking why hadn't I retold some of the football stories in print so that they could enjoy them. In the past, I've come close to recounting the tales but never taken the final step. It's great to know they are now finally out there.

I know my mum and dad would be proud of this book. My dad saw my career unfold but the biggest pity for me was that my mum died so young – at the age of just 55 – and she never really saw me at my peak as a player. It would have been great if she could have shared more of those big game moments, especially our great European nights. Well, hopefully you are sharing now, Mum...

I hope you enjoy my book and get as much enjoyment as I have in revealing the various episodes in my life – which, as you imagine, hasn't been dull.

Terry McDermott, 2017

CHAPTER 1

TALE OF
TWO CITIES

LIVERPOOL and Newcastle. Scousers and Geordies. The Reds and the Magpies. The Mersey and the Tyne.

My footballing life was destined to be torn between these two great cities. Two cities that are so identical. The people share so many characteristics: friendly, opinionated, funny and most of all, football-mad.

I'm very proud to say I've played in front of the two best sets of supporters in the game. Both are so fanatical and they both understand football. They will accept players who are trying but won't have anyone who pulls out of a tackle or doesn't give their all. I couldn't choose one set of fans above the other.

The main difference, of course, is Liverpool fans have enjoyed loads of success. No-one will forget the Red army that travelled to Rome to watch us win our first European Cup in 1977. The Kop speaks for itself. From the moment I saw it at Anfield, I was mesmerised and wanted to be a part of it.

Newcastle's fans are just as special. They never give up on their team. Can you imagine what it would have been like on Tyneside if the Toon had experienced just a percentage of the Kop's great days? Those fans deserve better.

A few times over the course of my career, these two worlds have collided.

In 1974, I was a Newcastle player coming up against a Bill Shankly team inspired by the rising superstar that was Kevin Keegan. We were well and truly beaten 3-0, which left me cutting a forlorn figure on the Wembley turf, watching Emlyn Hughes going up the steps to lift the FA Cup for Liverpool. Little did I know that I would soon be sharing an Anfield dressing room with Emlyn and Kevin.

Perhaps the most famous encounter of more recent years came on April 3rd, 1996 – a match that has gone down in history as arguably *the* most entertaining game of the Premier League era.

I was now assistant manager to Kevin, who had taken over from Ossie Ardiles in February, 1992. After avoiding relegation from the Second Division that year, we had taken Newcastle up to the top flight as champions and transformed the club into title challengers.

We made a great start to the 1995/96 campaign, but going into the match against Liverpool, the 12 point lead we once held at the top of the table had gone. We were three points behind the leaders Manchester United with two games in hand. Liverpool were five points behind us in third but still in the title race. This was being billed as a game we had to win to keep the heat on.

As usual, we had travelled down the night before and stayed in a hotel. Kevin was calm. If anything, inside he was more excited than worried. He knew we had a good team.

Kevin and I had been back to Liverpool as Newcastle players before. We got drawn at Anfield in the FA Cup 12 years earlier. It was, at the time, the worst draw we could have got. We ended up losing 4-0 on a Friday night – and in front of 11,000 Geordies who had taken over the Anfield Road end. It was a night that would make Kevin's mind up that his playing days were coming to a close.

The difference then was we didn't have a team capable of competing with Liverpool. Under Kevin as a player, and Arthur Cox the manager, we were just evolving with a lot of work still to do. This time around, with Kevin as manager and me as his buffer, we were a really good side.

Some people used to think that I would get upset to be called Kevin's 'buffer'. Far from it, especially with the term going back to some of Liverpool's greatest days under Bill Shankly and Bob Paisley.

For Kevin to regard me in that way was a compliment. I was his Bob Paisley. Bob always referred to himself as Shanks' buffer when Bill was the manager. Shankly was louder than Bob. Shanks used to walk with steel toe caps so people could hear him coming along the corridor; Bob would be in slippers.

Kevin had so much trust in me. When he first asked me to come and join him as Newcastle manager I made a conscious effort never to disappoint him because, as you will discover, I had been a bit of a boy in my time. I said to him: "Kevin, I will never let you down." He replied "Do you think you would be here if I felt that could happen?"

TERRY MAC

This was the fourth time I had returned to Anfield in my role as assistant at Newcastle. But being back at Anfield on this night, it felt special when I stepped on to the grass in a stadium I had known so well over the years. I always used to go out on the pitch before games and have a knockabout with the lads. I had tingles going down my back when I walked out of the tunnel that night. All the memories of what I had achieved as a player came flooding back. The goals. The famous games. The trophies. The Kop. So many great friends and happy times.

The place was virtually full when we went out for our warm-up around an hour before kick-off. Most of the Geordie support was already in full attendance. The atmosphere was already incredible. I had never known anything like it before or since.

A look back at the two starting line-ups brings the memories flooding back. Pavel Srnicek, Steve Watson, John Beresford, David Batty, Philippe Albert, Steve Howey, Rob Lee, Peter Beardsley, Les Ferdinand, David Ginola and Faustino Asprilla for us; David James, Jason McAteer, Mark Wright, John Scales, Neil Ruddock, Rob Jones, Jamie Redknapp, John Barnes, Steve McManaman, Robbie Fowler and Stan Collymore for them.

Before the game, I was told by someone from within the Liverpool camp that they were going to go easy on us because they didn't like Manchester United so much. I passed that on to Kevin. "They're going to let us win," I told him. I hadn't believed that for one minute and he just said 'shut up, don't be so stupid!' – and he was right. The game proved that – they didn't want us to win. You must be bloody joking!

As soon as the ref Mike Reed put the whistle to his lips, it was thrilling stuff – unless you happened to be in one of the dugouts, then it wasn't so comfortable!

Seven goals later and it's sheer bedlam inside Anfield. Kevin and I are both slumped over the advertising hoarding, hardly believing what we had just witnessed. It's one of football's most poignant images. I smother my face in the manager's coat I had been holding, burying the sickening reality of a 92nd minute Stan Collymore winner for Liverpool in a match we had led twice. I can't believe what has happened.

Within 30 seconds, the referee blows the final whistle. 4-3.

With my mind in a complete whirl, I had to somehow go through the football tradition of shaking hands with the opposition. At least the Liverpool manager was Roy Evans, a brilliant bloke who, as you will read, was a real help to me during some difficult days I had as a player at Anfield.

Being a born and bred Liverpudlian, of course, on any other occasion I would have wanted Liverpool to have won. I had played alongside the likes of Ian Rush. There was Robbie Fowler, Steve McManaman, John Barnes. I admired them because they were Liverpool players but they had just done us – it felt like they had shattered the dream, even though we still had seven games left to play.

I also had a lot of my family at the game including two brothers, uncles and so on. For one night, even though they were Liverpool fans, they had been supporting Newcastle. For me.

Looking back now, I'm in no doubt about the impact of that night at Anfield. It wrecked us. If we had won that game, I believe we would have gone on to win the Premier League that season and make history for Newcastle United.

How poignant that the cruellest blow I've suffered in football happened at the club I supported passionately as a kid and where I went on to win league titles and European Cups.

It hurts more now than it did then – that we didn't do it for the Newcastle fans. It's what Kevin always says. Fans pay their hard earned money to watch us and that season was our big chance to give something back. Kevin will admit that this defeat at Liverpool took a lot out of him.

Because of his passion and the way he cares for people, I think it killed a part of him for many years. If he was asked which game hurt him most, I am 99 per cent certain this is the one – as it most definitely was for me. It's 100 per cent for me. No doubt about that.

A little while ago, I did a talk in front of around 500 people alongside Peter Beardsley, John Beresford, Steve Howey and Keith Gillespie, all involved on that night. There was footage of all the goals for and against us during the 1995/96 season.

When the Liverpool 4-3 came up I immediately felt sick and had to look away – and it wasn't anything to do with the food we were eating!

There's hardly a day passes when I don't think back and wonder 'how didn't we win the Premier League?'

I have had many great days in football but sometimes it's the bad experiences that can leave just as big a mark. We were so close that year but it just wasn't to be. That's fate and you have to accept there will be sad times as well as happy if you're going to devote your life to football.

At least league titles were a little easier to come by when I was a Liverpool player, fulfilling my boyhood dream of pulling on the famous red shirt.

CHAPTER 2

WALKING
THE LINE

10 KRAMER Walk, Kirkby – home for the McDermott family for many years, including most of my time as a Liverpool player. As an overspill from Liverpool and full of high-rise flats, Kirkby wasn't exactly pleasing on the eye but it gave me everything I needed, especially when it came to learning my football skills.

As the third eldest in a family of six, raised by mum Maggie and dad Peter, it was a hard upbringing but the lack of money in the family was more than made up for by how close-knit we all were.

There was Peter, Charles – who tragically had no real life, as I'll explain later – Robert, Irene, Mary and me. Kirkby was at least a step up from our original home, a three story tenement containing just two bedrooms off Scotland Road. With six kids and just two bedrooms we couldn't have stayed any longer and so, in December 1957, it was off to Kirkby.

The newly-built house had a front parlour, four bedrooms, a back living room, a big hallway and a kitchen leading out to a coal hole in the back garden, which was often turned into a cricket pitch for me and Peter.

When we arrived there was no heating of any sort, no cooking facilities and no open fire. We all went up with the removal men and the foreman on the site promised there would be a fireplace by the end of the day. A neighbour, Mrs. Mulrooney, who had lived nearby in Liverpool and had moved to Kirkby just a few months previously, made us chips to keep us all warm until the workmen fitted the fire. In the meantime, we had to make do with two electric heaters, one on the landing and the other in the hall. For most of the winter we were freezing, there would be ice on the inside of the windows. There were no radiators at first.

Despite all that, we were considered quite posh because we had an inside toilet – although that's where any pretensions of grandeur ended! We had holes in our socks and there were bits of cornflake packets covering up holes in our shoes because there wasn't usually enough money to buy any new ones.

On a Sunday, you knew there would be a decent Sunday roast waiting for you. But it was first come, first served. Those there first would get the best and the rest the left-overs. It was hard for my mum but you always knew if she was around there would be food put on the table for you.

After Sunday dinner, my dad would find us a movie on the telly to watch with someone like Alice Faye, the actress of the day starring. There was no live football or football highlights in those days. Sometimes it was more interesting because it could be John Wayne in a big film. Then, later on, we sometimes had Sunday tea. Tea was cakes and biscuits and treats my mum made, like rhubarb and custard.

Any aspirations of being a footballer were almost wrecked before I had barely started walking. At around 18 months old, it was discovered I had a worrying amount of fluid in one of my knees and that unless they could successfully drain it, there was a fear that I might lose my leg. Thankfully, they were able to treat the knee but they must have taken too much liquid out because over the years I've had to replenish it through the help of Heineken, Carlsberg and any other lagers you would care to mention!

Once I was back on my feet, I couldn't wait to kick a football with my elder brother Pete, who was already hooked on the game. We couldn't afford to buy a proper football so we used to snatch one of our younger sister's dolls, unscrew the head and use that as our ball. The hall was our football pitch, the living room door being one goal and the front door the other.

If I wasn't playing football then, like most kids from the area, I would be up to no good. I was a real daredevil and it's a wonder I'm still around to tell the tales. Peter would often get hit by other lads because he looked like me. If I'd caused a bit of trouble, the lads would come looking for me but pick on Peter. It was often a painful case of mistaken identity. He got a couple of smacks.

Near our home they were building some 15 storey-high flats. We used to run up the stairs and get right to the top, trying to dodge the security guy who we called the Cocky Watchman. To avoid getting caught, we would climb down from the top via the balconies which meant swinging like monkeys from one to another. If you missed, that would have been it – certain death. But you never think about these things when you're a kid! The flats are still there to this day, about 400 yards from where I used to live. Every time I go past them now, if I'm visiting in the area, I look up and remember with some trepidation what I used to do. I have palpitations. I was mad at the time but if anyone dared you to do something – no matter how dangerous – then you would do it. That's just the way it was.

One day, one of my high-rise stunts cost my mum and dad money they couldn't afford to part with. When a school was being knocked down, I climbed on the roof and started throwing tiles off, watching them smash on the ground. I didn't realise they were still worth a bit of money because they were going to be used again. The police caught me in the act and frogmarched me back to our house where Mum and Dad were forced to pay 17 shillings and sixpence. They weren't happy but Dad never laid into me, he accepted there was no malice intended.

My dad worked at Tate and Lyle, the sugar factory – a big employer in the area. Somehow he had to feed six kids with his wage. My mum would help with the income by getting a job wherever she could, cleaning floors or whatever. If they didn't work, there would have been no food for us, it's as simple and as stark as that. But we didn't know we were poor growing up because everyone we knew lived the same kind of hand-to-mouth upbringing, living from one payday to the next. We were all in the same boat.

Our holidays were trips to Southport – if we were lucky – or New Brighton and Wallasey. A big highlight was getting on the Royal Iris, the famous ferry that took you along the Mersey to

New Brighton. It only took 10 to 15 minutes to get there but it was exciting and we enjoyed our holidays, even if they were never lavish. We'd take a few bottles of water and some jam or maybe sauce butties and we were as happy as could be.

Of course, wherever we went, we couldn't wait to get the football out – and it was a real one by this time.

Pete and I were now mad-keen Liverpool supporters. We were six and seven and couldn't wait to go to our first game. I vividly remember a few years later when the club changed the shorts from white to red after Bill Shankly decided his players would look bigger, more intimidating, dressed in all-red for a European Cup game against Anderlecht in 1964. We couldn't afford to buy any new red shorts so my mum used to die them – but they would come out pink – not the best for kids being brought up in Kirkby!

We got into the usual scrapes that kids did back then. All harmless really. The pic 'n' mix in Woolworths was always vulnerable to kids like me looking to help themselves. I didn't see myself as a thief, it was just what all the kids seemed to do; pocket a few sweets when no-one was looking. We would go after school if we were feeling a bit hungry. Someone would be the lookout and the rest of us would fill our pockets and scarper. I wasn't fussy about what we made off with. You were grateful for anything, although the Lovehearts had a great taste.

I wasn't the brightest at school. I liked going because you could play football and you had a laugh. I didn't get one GCE – I left with nothing. The only subject I was any good at was PE. That's what I lived for.

When I was at Sacred Heart Junior School, I was supposedly the cock of the school – the best fighter – but I never had to have one scrap to prove it. For some reason they accepted I was the hardest.

Little did we know that we had a future world boxing champion in our midst. John Conteh, who went on to become world light heavyweight champion, was in our school. He was a year older than me. Looking back now, I don't know how he wasn't cock of the school because even then you wouldn't have picked an argument with him! I was more friendly with one of his brothers, Robert, while our Pete was quite friendly with John because they were in the same year. There were never any real signs then that he was going to develop into a world boxing champion – but that was the same for me as a footballer.

It was a great school for football because most of the teachers were avid fans. I remember we won a cup in a two-legged final. John played right back. I scored the winner in the first leg and Pete scored the winning goal at home. I was a year below and played again the next year when we won the same cup again. John was just getting into his boxing by then but at 10 and 11 he was more into football.

When I moved on to St. Kevin's Secondary Modern School in Kirkby, football took over my life. I used to go to and from the school kicking a tennis ball. We were playing during every minute of every break from lessons; it was totally and utterly in our blood – there wasn't a minute when we weren't thinking about running around with a football. Then, back home, it was off with the doll's head and another game of impromptu football with our Pete.

At the bottom of the road was a power station with a big wall. You would find me there most evenings heading a ball against it with another lad, John Flanagan. We used to see how many times we could keep heading it without a break – sometimes we would get to 200. Maybe that headed goal I scored for Liverpool against Spurs many years later which many people still go on about came from hours spent at the back of the power station. We'd play anywhere we could – even in the road, although you had to stop all the time for cars coming through. It was just football, football and more football.

There was no homework back then and to be fair, the teachers never got on my case. They knew I was thick and just lived for football. I just wanted to be a footballer – probably like just about everyone else in the school. It would also have to be for Liverpool, the sporting obsession of my dad and most people we knew.

My dad would go to watch Liverpool all the time, mostly with my Uncle Charlie. He eventually started taking my brother Peter and me to watch the reserves at Anfield.

One of the biggest thrills as a young starry-eyed kid was seeing the great Billy Liddell in the flesh. He was coming to the end of his days as a Liverpool hero and was often in the reserves, which was great for me.

I was first taken to watch Liverpool in the January or February of 1958. For my eighth birthday, I also got my first pair of football boots, complete with wooden studs. I remember my first game wearing them playing with Peter on the walkway just outside the house, not the best surface for wooden studs!

One of the first games I remember was Liverpool Reserves beating Newcastle reserves 7-1 and Billy Liddell took a penalty. It hit the post, allowing Willie Carlin to score with the rebound. We thought Billy had done it on purpose.

TERRY MAC

He was my dad's hero – for many years he *was* Liverpool or 'Liddellpool'. He naturally became our hero and although his best years were behind him, it was still great to see him in the flesh in the reserve side. It was the equivalent of a young kid in recent times watching Steven Gerrard, being mesmerised by what he had achieved.

Liddell could play all along the front line but usually was employed as a centre forward or out on the left wing. He was also the scorer of *the goal that never was*. A couple of years before we started watching him, he had sent a shot into the Kop net against Manchester City from around 30 yards but the referee blew his whistle when the ball was still in the air for the end of the game. It ended up knocking Liverpool out of the FA Cup.

Back then, you could stand up and there was nothing stopping you walking from one end of the ground to the other. Reserve games were watched by crowds of between 2,000 and 3,000. If Liverpool reserves were kicking towards the Anfield Road end, we would stand behind the goal there and then move on to the Kop for the second half, which was a huge thrill in itself.

While Dad would always pay for Pete and I to watch the reserves, he made us save up our pocket money if we wanted to start seeing the first team. We would get one shilling and sixpence and put it away so we could go every fortnight to support them.

We started watching the first team from the boys' pen. Our dad used to take us down on the 92B bus. We'd get off down Scotland Road, walk up through Everton Valley and he would drop us by the pen which was up at the back of the Kop on the left hand side as you looked on to the pitch. It was sixpence to get in. He'd walk around to the Anfield Road End and after the game we'd wait for him to pick us up. What my dad didn't know is that sometimes there was a gap in the railings to escape from the boys' pen so we'd end up in the Kop.

The stink of stale piss often would waft in from the Kop. There was also a lot of bullying in the boys' pen. A policeman would often be in there trying to stop fights between local gangs. We were eight or nine at the time and the hard lads were 13, 14 so they came looking for us.

Being on the Kop was an experience. Most of the blokes had knocked back a few pints before the game and because the Kop was packed, they couldn't be bothered trying to make their way to the toilets – so a rolled up *Liverpool Echo* was often used as a filter which allowed them to relieve themselves.

We let Dad down once, although I don't think many people would blame us. Liverpool were playing Preston in the FA Cup. It was when Peter Thompson was playing for Preston before his move to Liverpool. My dad sent Peter and I down to Anfield to buy some tickets. It was a freezing cold Sunday and all we had on our feet was a pair of plastic sandals with thin socks. The rest of our bodies weren't much better, being protected by a tee-shirt and thin jumper. We had to give up queuing in the end because we were in danger of getting frostbitten, so Dad didn't get his tickets!

To this day at Liverpool, where I'm one of the ex-players on hosting duties, we do tours of the ground. I still get a tingle going into the players' lounge and into the dressing rooms but most of all going on to the Kop. There can be up to 50 punters and as we move towards the Kop at the end of the Anfield tour, they always play *You'll Never Walk Alone*. I never fail to get a lump in my throat. Then we do a bit of a spiel and I always mention how I used to climb over from the boys' pen into the Kop. "The minute the policeman turned his back we were over!" I tell them. The fence was quite high but I was used to heights going back to my escapades on the unfinished flats in Kirkby.

Once, after getting into the Kop during a European Cup game against Inter Milan in 1965, I was wedged against a barrier and could hardly see a thing. It got too much. At times there would be massive surges and swaying which, for a young lad, was frightening. If it got too bad, the older fans would lift you over their heads to a safer area. At the beginning of the Inter game, it got too much and I was passed over the heads of other fans; big men, many of whom were tough dockers easily capable of picking up scrawny kids like me and plucking them out of trouble.

We were taken to the front at the side of the pitch where the St. John Ambulance or the police were waiting for us. I thought they were going to put me in the paddock but they took me to the Anfield Road End and led me out through the gate to the road outside. I had only seen 10 minutes of what turned out to be one of the most famous, atmospheric nights in Anfield history with Liverpool winning the first leg of the European Cup final 3-1 against the Italian champions. The Kop were singing 'Go back to Italy' to the Inter players, but I was going back to Kirkby instead!

During Liverpool's first season back in the top flight, 1962/63, we beat Burnley in the FA Cup in a replay at Anfield when they were a top Division One side, finishing third in the table that year. Ronnie Moran scored the winning penalty in extra-time in front of the Kop after Ian St. John was brought down – the noise that night was phenomenal.

A few seasons earlier, we were the poorer relations of the city, Everton being in Division One while we were scrambling around in Division Two. Our family were devout Liverpool fans as were all the relations and although Everton were in the top flight, there was no way my dad was going to take me to Goodison Park. Once a red always a red. It's in the blood. It was never even up for discussion.

Things started changing for Liverpool with the arrival of Bill Shankly in 1959, although there were still some memorable moments in the Division Two days. Liverpool had some decent players. We had Bert Slater in goal, Ronnie Moran at left back and there was Alan A'Court. Ian St. John was also emerging as a real star.

Liverpool won the Second Division title in 1962 after beating Southampton in the pouring rain at Anfield. Pete and I raced on to the pitch at the final whistle to celebrate. Shanks had turned the club around. It was only the start of a wonderful couple of decades for the greatest club in the world.

As me and Pete danced around the Anfield pitch that day, along with thousands of others, eager to try and grab a hold of our heroes, I could never have believed I'd some day be out there under my own steam, helping create new memories and helping make the Kop louder and prouder than ever.

It was the first time I'd ever been on to the hallowed Anfield turf, but it wouldn't be the last.

CHAPTER 3

WHERE'S BURY?

ALTHOUGH I have introduced most of my family, I haven't told you about my younger brother, Charles. He was a twin with one of my sisters, Irene.

While Irene was born without any problems, poor Charles was damaged from birth and was later discovered to be mentally and physically handicapped.

It became evident there was something seriously wrong with Charles when he was around nine months old. Irene and Charles shared the same cot but while Irene was bouncing around, anxious to take her first footsteps, nothing seemed to be happening with Charles. Within a few days he was diagnosed with cerebral palsy, something medics are now more prepared for than they were in the 1950s and 1960s.

It turned out that a lack of oxygen during the birth process had cost Charles an ordinary life. Both Irene and Charles were born as 'blue babies' and were told that they needed a blood transfusion from birth. My parents were told that their daughter Irene was strong but there was a chance that Charles could die during the procedure. They gave permission for the transfusions. It was only years later they discovered that Charles wasn't given a blood transfusion after all.

To make matters worse for my parents, they couldn't see him too often because it was a major trek to the hospital on the Wirral. Having no car, it was a case of a bus from Kirkby into Liverpool. Then a train to the other side of the Mersey, followed by another bus. Then, of course, there was the journey back. They would leave at around 8am on a Sunday and not be back before 6pm. It was too much to go every weekend.

My mum tried desperately to cope with the situation by bringing Charles up at home, but with everyone else to try and look after as well, it became impossible. Eventually, although it was painful, she was forced to place him in a special care home on the Wirral. It had become too stressful and she struggled to physically cope with him too as he grew bigger. Later on, he was transferred to another special needs centre in Widnes.

I used to go and visit him when I was growing up but, to be perfectly honest, it wasn't something I looked forward to because seeing him was heartbreaking. He recognised my face but that was about it. I'd end up in tears, though I tried not to break down in front of him. You had to put on a brave face, but inside I was in bits. He was bedridden. I don't even remember him being placed in a wheelchair to take him somewhere, to give him a break from what must have been a living hell. There was no conversation. You would get to the bedside with a "Hello Charlie" but that was it. His eyes would light up but there was nothing there. You might get a little grin, but even that would go through you. Imagine what it must have been like for Irene, his twin. Most twins have a close bond but she could never properly connect with Charles. She's had a life, Charles hasn't.

In a strange way I probably got strength from his predicament, realising just how lucky I was. I sometimes looked at him and thought 'that could have been me'. Perhaps that's why I've been able to get on with things and not take myself too seriously, looking to have fun when I can. I knew that whatever my circumstances, Charles would have happily swapped with me, just to have the chance to live a healthy life. Charles had nothing. It was just an existence for him. He wouldn't have had a clue about my career.

That career didn't look at one stage like it was going to take off at all.

Liverpool Boys could select their squad from around 200 schools while Kirkby only had three to choose from and St. Kevin's was one of them. Even though there was a smaller pool of Kirkby kids, we had a top team. But when the Football League clubs came knocking on the door offering schoolboy forms, I was overlooked.

Most of the other lads in our team got fixed up pretty quickly, including team-mates Chris Duffy, Jimmy Redfern, Chris Dwyer and John McLaughlin. Redfern was our star and he was off to Bolton as was Chris Duffy while John McLaughlin was scouted by Liverpool. Gerry Farrell went to Wolves and Kenny Swain to Chelsea.

Although I missed out, I was in good company because the only other one in my age group not signed up at the time was Dennis Mortimer and we both later went on to win the European Cup!

Obviously no-one fancied Dennis and I while the rest were dreaming of a golden future. I was gutted as I saw player after player getting signed up. The families were also being looked after with financial incentives to put pen to paper, money we could obviously have done with. I couldn't have stood out enough, just like Dennis. It probably spurred me on even more to be a professional footballer.

Our Kirkby team went on to reach the quarter-finals of the England Schools Trophy, eventually losing to Seaham Boys from the North East. Their big player was Richie Pitt who went on to play for Sunderland, a top centre half.

Soon my chance did arrive, although again at first I thought I had missed out.

Liverpool were playing Burnley on a midweek night, November 9th, 1966 and as usual, we'd all gone to Anfield. I remember the game clearly, Liverpool were winning 2-0 with goals from Chris Lawler and Peter Thompson in front of 50,000 fans. St. John was my favourite player and to this day I can rattle off the usual side at that time: Lawrence, Lawler, Byrne, Milne, Yeats, Stevenson, Callaghan, Hunt, St. John, Smith, Thompson. It hardly ever changed week to week. Tommy Smith wore the No.10 but played alongside Ron Yeats at the back.

After the match, I returned home and was told that a Mr. Colin McDonald from Bury had knocked on the door asking to talk to me.

My immediate reply was "Where's Bury?" I didn't honestly

know where it was. I asked what division they were in, only to be told it was the Fourth Division.

He'd left a contract for me to sign as a schoolboy. I didn't need asking twice. He'd also been to Dennis Mortimer's house but Dennis didn't want to know – he had no intention of going to Bury and eventually signed for Coventry instead.

I couldn't wait to sign my forms. It was a case of 'get it done before they change their minds'. No-one had wanted me. It was sheer relief. My mum and dad were the same. They wanted me to join a club. They knew what it meant to me. They couldn't have predicted the things that were going to happen to me over the years as a footballer. The alternative was to work in a wood factory or a paint factory. With them, it wasn't a case of 'Oh, Terry is going to earn decent money'. They knew I would just be happy playing football, it was all I had ever wished for. They were proud I had a club and I was at least on the bottom rung of a ladder.

It meant that the whole of that Kirkby Boys team had been signed up for league clubs, Dennis and I being the last. After sending the forms back, Bury were quickly on the phone wanting me to play for their 'A' side on the Saturday. There was no looking after us with a signing-on fee. In fact, we were out of pocket when I started playing for them. You would get a few expenses to get the train because we didn't have a car but that was it – no rich pickings for the McDermott family.

On matchday, we had to get the train on a Saturday morning at 8am for a noon kick-off. My dad and cousin John usually came with me. Things didn't always go to plan. One time the train broke down at Wigan station and I had to find a telephone kiosk to ring Colin McDonald and tell him we weren't going to make it on time.

"Well, just get here as soon as you can," he told me, clearly not happy. We eventually made it but the game had kicked off. "Terry, get changed, and hurry up!" Colin told me. So I rushed into the dingy dressing room, with bits of kit scattered everywhere, and opened my kitbag.

Oh shit. I'd forgotten my boots. I kept turning the bag upside down, again and again, hoping they would magically appear but I was knackered. I'd left them in the phone kiosk at Wigan station. Thankfully someone found some, ones which were were riddled with holes, but at least I could play.

We kept making this journey for the next few months. My dad even gave up watching Liverpool to take me to Bury every Saturday. Back then I was a number four, a right half and in those days I was great in the air, really brave – probably going back to the days of heading that heavy ball as a kid at the power station.

It was such a great learning curve. Some weeks you would be going to play Liverpool or Manchester United, yet one day it all nearly came to an end.

"Son, you can't keep going to Bury," Dad announced. "It's costing us too much – it's too big a journey. And we're not even sure they're going to sign you, are we?" I was only on schoolboy forms so nothing was guaranteed.

With a heavy heart, and with little idea where my future lay, I left school and had to get a job. I had three different jobs in a matter of weeks. One was stacking wood, where I lasted about four days; probably the first and last person to ever be sacked at this place. You just had to move one plank of wood from one spot to another so only the lowest skilled workers would apply for a job there.

One day I went outside the premises when I should have been still stacking because I knew some of my mates were having a laugh at me working.

Being completely bored and fed up I went to talk to them. We were having a bit of a laugh when the foreman spotted me and told to me to clear off and collect my employment card.

I wasn't bothered. I just wanted to be a footballer. As kids, you would go potato picking and pea picking for extra pocket money but this was for real – and I hated it. You certainly appreciate things more when your luck eventually changes.

I was still going to Bury but, as time went on, Dad gave them an ultimatum: was I in or was I out? It was time for them to make their mind up, for his sanity as much as mine, I suppose.

Then the good news came through. I was to be taken on as an apprentice. The relief and pride this brought was immense; as memorable now as it was then.

It also proves you should never give up. I loved being at Bury and I wasn't disappointed in the slightest that Liverpool hadn't come in because I didn't think I was good enough. Our house might have been covered in red rosettes and scarves and we might have been the biggest Liverpool fans in the world – but that doesn't give you a right to play for them.

Looking back, I learned so much at Bury. We used to train on the car park which was made of concrete with holes everywhere. You also had to be as handy with a paintbrush or broom as you were with your feet. One day we had to paint the stand at Gigg Lane. Nobody at Bury got anything for free; everything was fought for – and that makes for tough footballers and good men. It was about as far removed as can be from the Academy upbringing most kids get these days, but it made us hungry. There is a certain pride to be had from working your way up from nothing to the top.

During those early days at Gigg Lane, I tried to travel from home every day but it became too much and I found digs – and that's when the temptations kicked in. I very quickly began drinking and gambling! But I was also driven by the fear of having to return to life as an ordinary worker. I was desperate not to have to do any ordinary jobs and once I had a taste of playing at Bury for the 'A' team, I didn't want it to end. I wanted it badly. I would have been happy to be a player anywhere. I would work my socks off.

Being at Bury gave me mental strength. The worst thing in football is having to tell kids they are not going to get a contract. I've been there and seen kids cry when they are told they're not being taken on. It's terrible. Your dreams are shattered. I was determined that mine wouldn't be. It helped that Bury were such a tiny club. They had to give you your chance. If I'd have gone somewhere like Liverpool, Everton, Manchester United or Tottenham, I would probably have been discarded but a club like Bury needed to bring kids through.

I actually lived in two different digs. The first one was with a Mrs. Smith in Walmsley Road and she was great. There was another lad with me, a Scot with ginger hair called Jimmy O'Connor.

We then went into digs right opposite the main gate at Gigg Lane. I could see the stadium from my bedroom window. It wasn't long before I made my first team debut, although it needed a great big lie from the reserve team coach Billy Urmston to make it happen.

One of the players had got injured and the manager Tommy McAnearney rang Billy.

"Is Terry ready?" he asked. "Can he do a job for us?"

"Ready," Billy said. "He's been brilliant for us. He's been our Trojan. He won't let you down if you put him in."

That really wasn't the case but I was extremely grateful – in reality I had been crap!

My debut was a thumping 8-0 win against Tranmere Rovers. It was January 10th, 1970 and it remains Bury's biggest ever league win. Not a bad way to start, eh? But guess what? I was left out of the next game! I'd done well but the captain Dave Lyons had to come back in after injury and I was the one to make way. That's the reality of football.

Even though Bury were flitting between Division Three and Division Four, they could attract some really experienced players who had done it at the very top – like Bobby Collins, who had played for Leeds United and John Connelly, who was in England's 1966 World Cup winning squad. There was also a young Alec Lindsay who went on to to play for Liverpool.

Sadly, old pros are not at clubs as much these days. Once upon a time, players who had performed right at the top floated around in the lower leagues when they were past their prime. You could learn as a young player just by watching them and seeing how they went about the game.

I was still only a kid about to leave my teens behind and plenty of players let me know that I still had a lot to learn. There were some wily old campaigners in the Third and Fourth Division, players who would scare the life out of me. They would think nothing of going over the top on a snotty-nosed kid from Kirkby. Often we would train on the dreadful car park and some of them would go for a slide tackle on the concrete, leaving you on your arse, covered in gravel with hands and knees bleeding. Imagine that these days!

The other thing about training with the first team was they would let you know in no uncertain terms if you weren't at it. The minute you made a mistake, one or two of them would always bollock you. They blasted you so much, you would think your ears had been perforated.

That helped me in later years because when people had a go at me at Newcastle or Liverpool I listened, but it didn't frighten me – not after Bury.

Bobby Collins was a great player but a dirty little so and so. I've not seen a smaller player – he was like Ronnie Corbett; the difference was Bobby was no laughing matter! But he was a top footballer and his passing ability was incredible, plus he always had time to help you, which was great for a young player like me.

Having John Connelly at the club was also fantastic. Others, like Alf Arrowsmith, big centre back George Heslop – who had played for Manchester City – and little Paul Hince, who became a journalist with the *Manchester Evening News*, were also in the team and I learned so much from them and their experiences.

One thing they did not have to teach me, though, was drinking. I was a student of that all on my own. I started on that road as soon as I had broken into the team on a regular basis. After an away game we would come back and go into the social club by the side of the ground. There would be a bit of music on and all the girls would be in there, throwing us long glances and flirting like crazy. What young man wouldn't be in his element in that position?

There was a fella in the team called John Murray who had played for Burnley and he would always encourage me to have a few pints before he pulled out a cigar, the biggest one you have seen. I would join in. We thought we were real Jack the Lads. We used to come out of there, absolutely pissed, and I had to stagger home – which took about a minute. Having my digs across the road from the ground turned into a bit of a master-stroke! Before knowing John, I stuck to Coca-Cola and nothing stronger but he introduced me to drink and I suppose I've never really looked back.

I was good company with a few drinks inside me. I was never one who, when full of ale, wanted to fight everyone. Dafter than usual? Yes. When you've had a drink you become more brash, more outgoing. I've never been one who really likes being the centre of attention, I'd rather be in a corner with my family and friends.

I wasn't loud. I was very shy at the time. People might laugh at that now considering what I've got up to, but it was a fact. I've grown more confident over the years. Even as a player at Liverpool in the early years I used to dread being asked questions in front of the other players. I suppose drink was an escape.

John also got me into betting – not surprising when he lived in a flat over a bookies. Our wages were paid in cash at the time. He loved a bet and I soon caught the bug too. There was many a time I would go to the bookies with my wages on a Thursday and come out later that afternoon following the last race with no money, not even enough to give the landlady for my rent.

I later actually brought John to Newcastle United when Kevin Keegan took me there after becoming manager the first time around. We brought him in to help in the academy.

I had met him at Goodwood Races and he was working as a debt collector. He ended up staying at Newcastle for years after we left. And, yes, he was still a drinker and a gambler – a bit like me!

CHAPTER 4

CALLING THE TOON

I FELT playing for Bury I had made it as a footballer. In truth, I hadn't.

Looking back I was Billy Big Time, drinking and smoking cigars, just because we'd managed to get a draw at somewhere like Exeter, but despite all this, it was my football – and not my drinking – that was starting to get noticed by bigger clubs.

In the 1972-73 season, we had a great run in the League Cup, our biggest scalp beating Manchester City in October, 1972.

City had a great side. Colin Bell, Neil Young, Mike Summerbee and Franny Lee were in the team that came to Gigg Lane but we won 2-0 and that made a lot of people sit up and notice me.

We then gave Chelsea a hell of a fright in the next round. I did well against both City and Chelsea and that's when I realised I could get better. Sometimes it's easier playing against quality teams because they give you more time on the ball whereas in the lower leagues I was used to players being up your backside all the time, kicking lumps out of you.

My mum started to keep some newspaper cuttings because I was now starting to make some headlines and I heard that Liverpool were watching me. I found out later that the famous Geoff Twentyman, Chief Scout at Anfield, had recommended me. There was speculation about different clubs but I never took that seriously; I was relaxed and happy to see what happened. If you let it go to your head, then you usually try too hard to impress.

I didn't help myself by being a complete lunatic on the field. I was constantly being sent off, I was naïve and easily wound up. I would punch people, mouth off at referees and could be nasty as a youngster. My logic was that if some bastard was going to go two feet over the top of the ball, I'd go three feet and do him before he did me! Back then, because you were allowed to get away with loads, you could chop someone in half two or three times before the referee would even think about booking you.

I was with Roy Evans recently and we were talking to a group of people asking him who were the hardest players he had known. He said there was Graeme Souness, Jimmy Case and then pointed at me adding 'and this fella 'ere'. I wondered who he was looking at!

"Terry was a nasty piece of work when he had to be," Roy said. "He'd think nothing of going over the top."

My record at Bury was so bad that eventually the FA dragged me down to London with the manager at the time, Tommy

McAnearney. They rattled off what I had done and it was time to take my medicine.

"You know what, Mr. McDermott," the suits said, "you've got the worst disciplinary record of anyone I've seen."

I apologised. It wasn't nice to hear as they dished out a big suspension, something the boss did not like, but accepted because I deserved it.

Despite my disciplinary record, as the 1972-73 season progressed, it became clear that Newcastle wanted me. In fact, Joe Harvey, the manager at St. James' Park at the time, bought me without even seeing me in action.

On the recommendation of his scout, Len Richey, he was due to come down to watch me play for Bury against Reading at Gigg Lane but after driving down from the North East, the game was postponed when the fog suddenly descended. He had a wasted trip and I thought that's the end of that, at least for a while, but the next week Newcastle agreed a fee with Bury for me.

They had suffered an injury to one of their top players, Tony Green, and they were hoping that one day I would be able to emulate him. He was a great player for Newcastle and so it was some compliment to think they thought I might be able to fill his boots.

Allan Brown was now the Bury manager having taken over from Tommy McAnearney but I told him I didn't want to go. I liked it at Bury and it suited me.

His response was simple. "Are you mad? Newcastle are in the First Division while we're in Division Four." That summed it up but I really loved living where I did and enjoying the social life that came with it.

I then told a few of the Bury players about what had happened and in particular, Ben Anderson, who was a big strong centre half. He and Ray Parry confirmed to me that I would be crazy to stay when someone like Newcastle had come calling. "This is your chance," Ben said. "Teams like Newcastle don't come calling every day. You better take it."

In the end, after these chats, I changed my mind. It was the right move for everyone because this was also a chance for Bury to make £22,000, which was not a bad return for a lower league club in those days – especially when I hadn't cost a penny.

Billy Allen was the chairman. He would always be in the social club when we were getting tanked up on our return from games and would more often than not get blitzed at the same time. But he was really committed to the club. He later sadly died while shovelling snow in the car park in an effort to make sure a home game went ahead. He just keeled over and that was that.

Before going up to sign for Newcastle I asked him for a payment because I had cost nothing, so Bury were making a 100 per cent profit on me. "We can't really do much," Billy said. "But come to the social club on Friday and I'll see what I can do."

After that, I popped in for a few weeks, on time, and he'd stuff a brown envelope into my hand, containing £100 in cash. This continued for a while until the Newcastle paperwork was finished. So I didn't do too badly in the end.

The same couldn't have been said about my introduction to life in the First Division.

Allan Brown himself drove me up to Newcastle and en route to the North East we got a puncture. We had to ring and tell them we were going to be late. Luckily, everything went smoothly after that and I quickly became a Newcastle player.

The first time Joe Harvey actually saw me play was for the reserves at St. James' Park. I discovered at one point during the game he had turned around to Len Richey and demanded to know why they had bought me! Maybe it was because I had spent most of the game going around kicking people, trying to impress, thinking that I had made it as a First Division player.

Playing for Newcastle was a far cry from Gigg Lane – and it was hard to come to terms with. It was a huge step up and there was no escape off the pitch either. I quickly found out that the main topic of conversation on Tyneside, even amongst the women, was about Newcastle United. If you weren't doing the business, they weren't slow to tell you. Deliver and hero status was just around the corner.

Despite Joe Harvey's first impressions, within two or three weeks I was in the first team – and stayed in it. Joe was absolutely magnificent once I had got into the team.

He was so supportive of me. He was my type of manager. He would walk around the place with a fag in his mouth, puffing away, smoke everywhere. You'd even see smoke bellowing out from the side of the pitch from Joe's cigarette. Terry Hibbitt was another smoker. He would dive into the toilets at half-time for a crafty fag. You would look towards the cubicle where he had bolted himself inside and see smoke coming out from over the door. You don't see that now!

Keith Burkinshaw, who went on to manage Spurs, was the coach and although he was a good fella, he could be a bit abrupt with you at times.

One day in training we were having a five-a-side game. On some occasions, these could get a bit heated as everybody took them seriously. This day, Keith was on refereeing duties and one decision he made got me really wound up. He gave a free-kick against me. I just went, "Oh, fuck off!" It was just the natural reaction of someone frustrated – there was nothing more in it than that. Keith shouted back, "Don't you swear at me!" and he sent me off, forcing me to make my way to the changing rooms.

Coming the other way as I was walking across the field was Joe Harvey. "Hello, son, what are you doing?" he asked me. "That big idiot over there has sent me off!" I replied and when he asked what for, I told him it was over nothing.

"Get yourself back over there in the game," Joe immediately shouted – and that was the end of it – it was an example of how much he understood what made his players click.

Joe was a fantastic man-manager and the players loved him. Having his support was incredible for me because after playing in front of 3,000 at Gigg Lane, I was now being watched by more than 40,000 at St. James' Park which always bubbled with excitement. They were in the top half of the First Division and although we rarely threatened the top places, we were still a good team with plenty of star players.

We had Malcolm Macdonald and John Tudor up front; Stuart Barrowclough on the right, with pace; 'Jinky' Jimmy Smith, one of the most skilful players I've ever seen and Terry Hibbitt on the left, who was phenomenal. I always remember thinking I wish I could be as good as him. His left peg was like a magic wand but he was also a moaning so-and-so. He would never shut up and that annoyed a lot of players. What really got them going was if he threaded a ball through and they couldn't control it. He would be gesturing to the fans *'look at that great ball and how it's been messed up'*.

You shouldn't do that, but he was a great player.

There was also Pat Howard, an uncompromising centre half alongside Bobby Moncur, while Frank Clark went on to win two European Cups with Nottingham Forest. Add to that the likes of David Craig, Tommy Cassidy and Willie McFaul in the side, and we should have done a lot better in the league.

However, Newcastle did win the Anglo-Italian Cup in 1973 and the Texaco Cup in 1974 and 1975 so we had some silverware on the shelf!

Winning the Anglo-Italian Cup was no mean feat because with all the tricks the Italian teams got up to, you never had any easy games.

They were horrible to play against. Their players would always be pinching you or pulling at you. They weren't averse to spitting at you either, which was terrible. It didn't really affect me – especially not after my experiences at Bury where you would be kicked from pillar to post every week.

The Texaco Cup, a competition featuring English, Scottish, Northern Irish and Irish sides that hadn't qualified for Europe, was more memorable for our two-legged semi-final against Birmingham in 1974/75 in which Tommy Gibb had his leg broken in a challenge. A few minutes later, Jimmy Smith extracted revenge by a crunching tackle of his own on the player who had committed the Gibb offence. It broke the Birmingham player's leg.

We then had to play the second leg at Birmingham where Jimmy got physically battered. But nothing fazed him because he had so much skill that he would just nutmeg their players and wind them up even more. He suffered a lot of injuries but also liked his drink too much and so he never became the star he should have with all the natural skill he possessed.

In the end, goals from Kennedy, Nattrass, Cannell and Barrowclough secured us a final spot against Southampton, who Newcastle beat 3-1 on aggregate over two legs after I'd moved on to Liverpool.

It might have been the Texaco Cup but the Newcastle fans couldn't care less. It was silverware, something that the Fairs Cup win of 1969 had whetted the appetite for. Joe Harvey certainly took the competition seriously. There was no talk of resting players and it remains the last cup competition they have won.

It wouldn't be right to say there was a drinking club at Newcastle at this time but we all liked a good night out. We would often frequent some of the city's night clubs, Greys Club being the main one at that time. I would often go with Jimmy and Tommy Cassidy. We were in an era where every single top football club would have some hardy drinkers on the books. There were a few bars around Eldon Square and then we moved on to Greys.

I had a relatively short stay as a Newcastle player – around 18 months – and it was good fun, although it might have ended even quicker following an impromptu drinking spree on the New Year's Eve of 1973, just hours before a game in London against Arsenal.

Manchester United were staying in the same hotel as ourselves as they had a game against QPR and after we had eaten, most of the players had gone to bed.

Tommy Docherty was the Manchester United manager at the time and when he spotted Terry Hibbitt and me, he asked if we fancied a beer. "We can't," I told him. "We've got a match tomorrow." "Half a pint won't do you no harm lads," he said.

He was right. Half a pint didn't. The other seven and a half did.

Four hours later, we were still at it. Terry was the main man at the club. He told me the odd one would be okay, so I just followed his lead. Two pints led to four, then to six and then to eight!

We finally staggered off to bed but when we came down for breakfast the next morning, who was waiting at the bottom of the stairs? Joe Harvey.

"You little cunt," he snarled at me. "You pair of bastards," he added. Of course we knew what we had done and so when he asked for confirmation that we had been drinking, we had to admit it.

He told us that if he had any extra players down in London to put into the team he would have booted us out and sent us back to Tyneside on the first train out of the capital. Now he wanted us to get out on the pitch that afternoon and help Newcastle win the game.

We were bang to rights but wondered how the hell Joe found out about our illicit drinking spree, and so quickly?

Well, it turned out that next morning Tommy Docherty rang Bertie Mee, the Arsenal manager, and told him that the Gunners should win that day because he had got Terry Hibbitt and Terry McDermott pissed the night before.

Joe quickly got to hear that and had rightly put us on the spot. I was frightened out of my wits wondering what the hell I'd done but I needn't have worried as we beat Arsenal 1-0 and the two Terrys were the best players on the pitch. Terry even scored our goal!

That was it, we never heard another thing about it. To make it even better, United ended up losing 3-0 at Loftus Road.

Cheers Tommy!

CHAPTER 5

IF YOU CAN'T
BEAT 'EM...

S ADLY, we didn't have a happy ending in that same
1973/74 season when we reached the FA Cup final and
came up against Liverpool.

There was little to suggest that we were going to go all the way
to Wembley, especially with the club almost having another
Hereford on its hands. The memory of that ignominious defeat
against the non-leaguers – when Ronnie Radford scored THAT
goal against Newcastle back in 1972 when I was at Bury – would
have haunted many of the players when we were drawn at home
in the third round to Hendon.

The Newcastle fans went absolutely ballistic as we were held
to a 1-1 draw in front of a disbelieving St. James' Park. I had
signed the season after the Hereford debacle but Hendon was

shaping up to be just as bad an experience. It was embarrassing but fortunately we got the job done in the replay and saved ourselves from another humiliation by winning 4-0. I honestly don't know what would have happened if we'd lost.

There was another struggle in the fourth round as we could only draw 1-1 against Fourth Division Scunthorpe United, Kevin Keegan's old side, on Tyneside. Again, as in the replay against Hendon, we managed to avoid any further trauma, easing through 3-0 in the second game.

At least we got going in the fifth round and turned it on at The Hawthorns to beat West Brom 3-0. Then it was Nottingham Forest at St. James' Park in the sixth round – a game that ended up having to be replayed because of a crowd riot. It became known as 'The Battle of St. James' Park' and for good reason.

The atmosphere was unbelievable. I've never experienced anything like it. There were 52,551 in the ground that day, and you could hear every single one of them.

During the match, we were losing 3-1 – and had had Paddy Howard sent off – when suddenly you saw Newcastle fans coming on to the pitch from the Leazes End. They just charged through, looking to get at the Forest fans who were standing in the Gallowgate End.

The referee, Gordon Kew, told us all to get off the pitch because the situation was becoming dangerous, more so, of course, for the Forest players. I wasn't that fearful because they were our fans but I'd still never seen anything like it. It certainly wasn't pleasant for the Forest players. Many of them looked frightened to death and couldn't wait to get off the pitch. I don't blame them for looking panicky.

We trudged back to the dressing rooms for 10 minutes while

the police regained control and, to be honest, this saved us. At 3-1 down with 56 minutes gone, we looked down and out and our cup run appeared to be coming to an end.

Eventually the police cleared the pitch, there were 39 arrests reported and many fans were taken to hospital with injuries. Considering all this, it was a wonder the game restarted but everyone thought it would be in the best interests of safety for it to resume.

We were quickly awarded a penalty and it was down to me to try to settle things down by converting the spot-kick. It was a hell of a responsibility, especially in such a fevered atmosphere, but I slotted it home. I was just a kid in comparison with my team-mates, but they didn't want to know.

That transformed the game and John Tudor grabbed the equaliser with a fantastic diving header from a typical Hibbitt cross before the captain, Bob Moncur – of all people – volleyed in the winner. It was no surprise Forest had ended up losing after all that had gone on

Yes, a Newcastle 4-3 which we actually won...

Well, not for long. The FA demanded a replay after ordering an investigation into the crowd invasion. It had been a hell of a comeback for us and we were disappointed when we had to replay it but the FA wouldn't budge and the match had to be played at Everton's Goodison Park. The first match ended in a goalless draw so we had to return three days later when a goal from Malcolm Macdonald saw us through to a semi-final with Burnley.

The trip home after the win was amazing. The Geordie fans kept passing the team coach blaring their horns and waving their scarves out of the windows. It was like a black and white escort. We were heroes and that just showed how desperate they were for success.

The 'Battle of St. James' Park' was in some ways typical of the time. The 1970s and 1980s always carried danger for football supporters It was a time when you were forever looking over your shoulder. I would often be panicking about my brother Peter who was still a mad-keen Liverpool supporter. I'd be worried he had found himself caught up in it.

Even as players, we would witness the fighting outside grounds. Largely, though, we were in a bubble being escorted to and from games. Sadly it seems to be starting to creep back in. There have been incidents in the stands at some games, including West Ham. You'd hoped the bad days had gone for good. I worry about my two lads, Neale and Greg, who go to games. Football has got to get a grip. It's driven fans away. I always tell them to be careful. Watch where they are walking, don't go down the wrong road.

Back in 1974, we were in the semi-final at Hillsborough and Malcolm Macdonald was simply unstoppable. Super Mac was on fire in that game, although sadly those black and white flames were doused in the final. I think someone must have directed a water cannon on him he was so bad at Wembley – but more of that later.

Super Mac and Terry Hibbitt won the semi-final for us. Malcolm was a great goalscorer, he was strong, quick and good in the air and that day Burnley couldn't get near him. Terry was also a fine player, supplying the ammunition. When Hibbitt hit a great ball over the top, Malcolm didn't need any cajoling, he was on to it in a flash. Just for good measure he scored again after that. He was simply unplayable that day.

It suddenly dawned on me that just two or three years earlier I had been playing against the likes of Exeter and Gillingham and now I was going to be facing Liverpool at Wembley in the FA Cup final.

In the days before the big day at Wembley, we could have done with Malcolm shutting that big mouth of his. He certainly wasn't shy. To be honest, he was all for himself. The worst thing he ever did in the build-up to the final was say what he was going to do to the Liverpool defenders. In the papers, he boasted how he was going to worry the life out of Emlyn Hughes, Phil Thompson and Tommy Smith. He was going to destroy them and win the FA Cup for Newcastle. Not the wisest thing to do.

When I read it, I thought 'what has he done?' I was just a kid, what I thought didn't matter but I know the older players thought it was a huge mistake.

When I eventually joined Liverpool, the FA Cup final came up in conversation and players like Phil Thompson told me Malcolm did the team-talk for them in what he said. Shanks evidently just pinned Super Mac's bragging words up on the wall. He just told the players 'read that' and walked away. The damage as far as we were concerned had been done.

I always found Malcolm a bit flash for the North East. For a start, he had a boutique and he liked the jet-set lifestyle. If you're like that, you have to back it up with trophies. I would like to know how many he won? I don't feel bitter towards him at all, but what he did in the build-up probably cost us the FA Cup. Without a doubt he wound Liverpool up.

At Wembley that day, my family were there with their black and white scarves and rosettes – loads of them. They had mostly travelled down with the Liverpool fans, some of whom they knew, but for one day they had given up their allegiance to the Reds and were supporting me and Newcastle.

In those days, you could get up to 100 tickets and you would always want all of them because if you didn't have a huge family like me there was always a fella called Stan Flashman. Ticket tout Stan was the man. He boasted he could get tickets for any event in the country, including the Wimbledon final in the Royal Box and I wouldn't have bet against him. Players looked upon Stan as their big pay day because – remember – the wages weren't massive in those days. You were finished at 33 or 34 and there were a lot of years ahead, so some money for extra FA Cup final tickets would go down nicely. The same thing happened at Liverpool and no-one could blame players cashing in. For some it was an opportunity to make money.

The game itself was an utter embarrassment and it could and should have been worse.

All those hopes and ambitions we had nurtured when we came down to London a few days earlier were destroyed. Kevin Keegan, who was to become a huge mate, scored twice, with Steve Heighway grabbing the other in a one-sided game.

It was Bill Shankly's last game in charge. It might have been sentimental on the Liverpool side but I was utterly devastated after the game. People were thinking I couldn't lose because of my Liverpool roots. You must be joking, I felt physically sick because we were well beaten.

After being utterly stuffed like we were, no-one wanted to talk in the dressing room. You just wanted to get showered and get the hell out of there.

Before the game someone had sent me a Kermit the Frog figure for good luck. Well, he got booted to shreds in the dressing room afterwards. Poor old Kermit came in for a right hammering. I'd carried it proudly into the dressing room before the final.

For the occasion we'd had special black and white jackets with wide lapels designed, which was the fashion of the time. The lapels wouldn't have looked out of place on Elvis Presley. We'd walked out on to the pitch in this gear. After the game you still had to wear these suits, so there was no hiding place. Everyone knew you played for Newcastle United.

I went outside to meet my family near where the coach was situated. Some fans were still there and they had every right to shout out 'you were shite!' or worse.

They never did. Instead they clapped you. Many of the players didn't deserve that because they hadn't performed.

Joe Harvey was Joe Harvey. He got his cigarette out and didn't blast anyone. He knew no-one ever goes out on the pitch and doesn't try. Some people could have been a bit cuter than they were – especially in the press.

All in all, it was a terrible experience. Losing an FA Cup final is a sickening, sickening feeling.

After the game we had a do at The Russell Hotel in London because a banquet had been organised, win or lose. I couldn't wait to get out of there so me and Tommy Cassidy could go out clubbing and get lashed to try to erase the memory of that horrible afternoon.

The next day we got the train back to Newcastle in time to board the coach for a tour around the city – which was hugely embarrassing.

I couldn't believe that they were having one. We had been shocking at Wembley and yet the Newcastle fans turned out in their thousands to greet us as if we had achieved something.

I just wished we could have given them something to shout about.

We ended up at St. James' Park which was rammed. That tells you everything about the Newcastle supporters. It must have been very difficult for them to go all the way down to Wembley and for the team not to show up.

To make matters worse, what did the fans see the next day at the parade? Some drunken footballers who hadn't done themselves justice – it was another pathetic showing on our part.

Reporting for pre-season a couple of months later came with growing speculation that other clubs were watching me, hoping to take me away from the North East.

One of the interested parties was rumoured to be Liverpool. To be honest, I thought it was all a load of crap and wasn't bothered by it. The season was about to start and that was all I was concentrating on, especially after the disappointment of the FA Cup final. Yet the Liverpool interest was genuine.

Geoff Twentyman, who had been keeping an eye on my progress at Bury until Newcastle nipped in, was back on the scene updating his reports on me. But it wasn't until the October that they made their move.

The first I knew Liverpool were genuinely interested in signing me was when I got a call from Phil Thompson, a lad like me from Kirkby, who had become an established top defender at Anfield. He just asked me if I fancied playing for Liverpool. He had to be joking. I honestly thought it was a wind-up.

Now, whenever I see Thommo, I tell him that he could still get done for poaching!

When I was with Newcastle I stayed with a young defender

called Alan Kennedy who was coming through the junior ranks – someone, of course, who would end up following me to Anfield. I was only supposed to stay at his place for a couple of weeks while I sorted myself out but I ended up there for all my time at Newcastle.

We were well looked after by his mum and dad. His mum worked in the local chippy so there was never any shortage of fish and chips. On matchdays, she would give me a three course meal. I would start with soup, a full dinner – roast beef, cabbage, carrots, potatoes, gravy…the lot! – and finish off with apple pie and custard. I'd then be playing three hours later in front of more than 40,000 people!

There was none of this sports science or special pre-match diet for me, no pasta or stuff like that. I still don't believe in it anyway. They say it's good for this and that but everyone is different so how can it work for every player? I could run forever and so my three-course meal didn't do me any harm. I would have that every single home game. And that came after fish and chips on the Friday night.

When Liverpool came in for me I was lying in bed because I had been out the night before as we'd played earlier in the day. Alan had gone in to train because he hadn't been involved and Joe Harvey had called him in and told him to get me to come to the ground.

When Alan relayed the message, my first thought was 'oh no what did I get up to after the game last night?'

I got in the car and drove to St. James' Park to meet Joe. He told me Liverpool wanted me. I could hardly believe it. I didn't have an agent. The only person I knew who had an agent then was Kevin Keegan.

Liverpool – the team I had idolised as a kid – were in for me. My first thoughts were: 'I don't want to go'. At the same time, I thought I could make some good money. I didn't know what they had offered for me but I knew it would have been a substantial amount to tempt Newcastle into selling.

I eventually told Joe I'd go, but because Newcastle had only paid £22,000 for me, surely I was due something from the club because of the huge profit?

"You're not getting a penny," Joe told me. "No-one is forcing you to go and if you wanted to, you could stay put."

By now, my mind was made up. I was going and that was that so I told him to give me the envelope he was holding. I'd been requested to carry the envelope with me to Liverpool where they were waiting for me at Anfield.

After setting off for Merseyside in my car, a Ford Capri, that was blue – not the best colour for a Liverpool fan! – the contents of the brown envelope started to intrigue me and my curiosity began to get the better of me. I kept looking at the envelope lying on the passenger seat. I thought it must include the transfer fee and as I drove past Leeds, the temptation got too much.

I decided to put my knee on the steering wheel to control the car while I opened the letter.

There it was – Liverpool were paying Newcastle £166,000.

I continued the journey and the first stop was at my mum and dad's house in Kirkby. I picked my dad up and then went to Anfield to meet the manager Bob Paisley, secretary Peter Robinson and the chairman John Smith.

They first guided me into a room for my medical. They looked at my knees, had a little squeeze of this, a squeeze of that and within five minutes I'm out again – that was my medical.

Now I couldn't wait to sign the contract. I didn't ask how much I was getting. It must have been the quickest Liverpool signing ever. There were no negotiations. My dad was there but he wouldn't have had a clue. Maybe I should have asked for more because it wasn't that much better than my deal at Newcastle, but really I didn't care.

My dad was made up. What a day it had been for him. What must he have felt? He had been watching Liverpool all his life and now his son was about to play for them. I'd picked him up to meet people like Bob Paisley. He was working at Tate and Lyle which employed thousands, including many Liverpool fans, so imagine the pride he would have had the next day, his lad having just signed for the club. He wasn't one to shout from the rooftops – that wasn't the way any of us had been brought up. It's why we all get on. There is no boasting or bragging. My dad knew he couldn't change in front of his workmates. Inside he would have been elated but outside he was his normal, humble hard-working self.

Playing football was the pinnacle for me but I still didn't think I was anything special, any different from other blokes. I was just lucky that I was a professional footballer.

After signing, there was no big fanfare because I wasn't a big name. I wasn't an international. The only fanfare was in the McDermott family. There was a big fuss made by everyone, including aunts, uncles and cousins that ran into the hundreds.

There was also a photographer outside my parents' house the day after I signed. We let him in to take photos of some of the family. It was then I realised that maybe I had arrived as a professional footballer.

In many ways though, the hard work had barely begun.

CHAPTER 6

THE LIVERPOOL WAY

I'D never met Bob Paisley before I signed for Liverpool but when I did, as usual, he didn't say very much. Before becoming the manager, he had been used to remaining in the background as Bill Shankly's right-hand man. Bob had only been in charge for a few months when I arrived because Shanks had departed after the FA Cup final. Bob's first signing had been Phil Neal and I was the second.

I was disappointed, of course, at missing out on the Shankly era, but I still used to see him quite regularly at our Melwood training ground.

Often he would turn up in his tracksuit and most mornings he would join in the five-a-sides. The players were still calling him 'Boss' and to Paisley, who should have been known as 'Boss', it was 'Bob'. You could see that was becoming an embarrassment because Shanks still seemed to hold the power as far as the players were concerned. He was naturally a lot louder than Bob and was still looked upon as a god-like figure.

No-one had a bad word against him. On matchdays, he used to wait outside the changing rooms, watching the opposition players file in one by one. He looked them up and down and couldn't wait to disappear into the Liverpool dressing room to tell the players: "Aye, they are all scared of you boys. You've got to beat this lot today, they are frightened to death!"

It was in his blood. He didn't want to quit. A lot of the older players told me that there were many times when Shanks threatened to leave, saying his time was up. But he would always back down. A few months after he did finally decide to end his reign, he couldn't keep away from Melwood. Maybe he thought it was a mistake. We were all still mesmerised by him and you had to feel for Bob. Shanks was like a great big shadow lurking over his shoulder.

One day I had been out drinking the night before and, unlike today, there weren't bottles of water or rehydration drinks laid out on the side of the pitch. My mouth was feeling like the bottom of a budgie's cage.

I went into the toilets and had my head under the cold water tap when I heard this voice boom out, "Jesus Christ, son, you don't do that! It's not pure." It was Shanks. He gave me a lecture on water and why not to touch the taps. "You don't see lions with their heads under taps, son," he told me.

After a while, Bob obviously had had enough. It must have cut him like a knife, but he asked Bill not to come in. So Bill was forced to stop his daily excursions to Melwood and instead started going to Everton's Bellefield training ground. It was great while it lasted for me, seeing the great Bill Shankly, someone I had idolised, at close quarters every day.

My debut shortly after signing was in the Merseyside derby against Everton in November, 1974 – no pressure, then!

I had an idea I would be playing. Phil Neal made his debut on the same day. No-one pulled me to one side. Bob read out the team like he always did and I was in it. It was an incredible feeling, something I had dreamed about as a young fan. It seemed an impossible dream when I was being left behind by my Kirkby Boys team-mates who were signing for clubs, including Liverpool. Even at Bury it seemed a million miles away but here I was, ready to make my debut for the team I had spent my pocket money on supporting.

Bob Paisley's instructions were to stay out wide on the right and drive the ball low into the box because John Toshack wasn't playing. It was Kevin Keegan and Phil Boersma up front.

The game, though, was crap and I was even worse. It ended a 0-0 draw, the most boring game you could ever be involved in. To be honest, I was overawed, I couldn't handle it. I suppose it was all too much emotion crammed into 90 minutes, too much expectation, a local lad trying to make an impact with the club he had watched from the terraces. Sometimes it's what is going through your head which can rule your legs. Just over two years previously I had been playing against teams like Chester and Wrexham. It was too much for me.

If I thought I had made it in the First Division with Newcastle, I was about to endure a rude awakening. I hadn't made it – nowhere near. I played in the first six games and then I found myself out of the side. I understood because I was still only 22 and I was at a big club. I had to learn quickly. I didn't and so I was in and out of the side all season.

I remember the groans in one game when I tried a long ball up to John Toshack but it went straight to the opposition. It makes you decide not to hide but not to go looking for a pass. The early games passed me by.

My first home game was against West Ham. I did manage to flick a high ball back to Phil Neal for my first touch which got the crowd going. That was as good as it got for a few weeks.

There was also plenty of competition for my midfield role. There was Peter Cormack trying to get in the side and Ian Callaghan sometimes dropped into midfield. Ray Kennedy also had the same problem at first, he didn't play in every game, and there was Jimmy Case also trying to break into the side. John Toshack was up front with Kevin Keegan and Brian Hall was also involved. There were good players everywhere you looked.

Cally was and still is a legend. I never look upon myself as one but when you've been at a club for 15 or 16 years and played 800-odd games for the club then that's legendary status. Also, it's appropriate in the way he has conducted himself on and off the pitch over the decades.

Looking back now, I think I was overawed by who was in the Liverpool dressing room when I joined. I found myself shaking with nerves before my first training session. Back then, we would get changed at Anfield before getting on the coach to Melwood. I walked into the dressing room for the first time absolutely bricking it. I'd watched some of these players and as a fan had been in awe of them. I knew who they were and now I was alongside them. Ronnie Moran took me in. If you hadn't quite made it, you went into the away dressing room while the first team squad utilised the home dressing room. Up and coming players like Jimmy Case were in the away dressing room.

Ronnie led me into the home dressing room and introduced the players but I knew who they were anyway! I went around each one shaking their hands. Emlyn Hughes was great. He put his arm around me and tried to settle me down. Kevin Keegan just acknowledging me was enough. I was frightened to open my mouth because I wasn't the most eloquent of fellas.

The changing room itself was unspectacular. Somewhere like Barrow was probably better. But it's what you win in that dressing room which is more important. It's hardly changed at Anfield over the years. They only moved into new improved facilities in 2016 after the building of the new Main Stand. There was a big communal bath and four showers. I loved getting in the bath – providing no-one had peed in it! Some of the players preferred showers.

The players never shut up on the coach to Melwood, banter about things they had done the night before or chatting about the game that was coming up. There was no-one funnier than Kevin and he always talked to me, kept me involved.

Half of them probably didn't know who I was, except maybe that I had played in the FA Cup final against them for Newcastle back in May.

You also have to remember that I'd been brought in to eventually replace someone in that room who may have been playing for Liverpool for years. You can imagine what they're thinking. 'He's not good enough to take my place'.

I sat with Phil Thompson on the coach to training and because he was another kid from Kirkby we immediately had something in common – he had also been the first one to tell me I could be on my way to becoming a Liverpool player. On that first day, I went everywhere Thommo went. I just followed him, like a faithful sheepdog.

At training, after a few sessions, I imagine Bob must have wondered what had he bought, just like Joe Harvey had done when I first signed for Newcastle. It was difficult trying to concentrate on my game when I realised I was playing with players I idolised.

All in all, I think it took me two years to realise what it meant to play for Liverpool. During that time I was in and out of the side and it was not easy.

I was wearing the number 5 shirt when I scored my first Liverpool goal against Burnley at Turf Moor in March, 1975. To be honest, I couldn't care less what number was on my back as long as I was out there on the pitch.

Two weeks later, I scored my first ever goal at Anfield and ironically it came against my former club Newcastle. It couldn't have been better because it happened in front of the Kop. We were 3-0 up and then came my moment, firing in our fourth, a low shot – not spectacular, but thankfully it ended up in the back of the net. I didn't go berserk celebrating because I had loved playing for Newcastle in front of their fantastic fans.

Inside, though, I was delighted and so proud to have scored at the Kop end – it doesn't get much better than that for a boyhood Liverpool supporter whose family are mostly staunch Reds. I couldn't wait to read the Sunday papers the next day and I was delighted to see that I was man of the match in some of them.

But it wasn't always plain sailing. At times I thought it was unjust that I'd been dropped and sometimes I was brought off just when I thought everything was starting to go right. There was a standard joke during those early years that when the numbers came up for the substitution – they were just one to 11 – there would only be two number boards in the box, kept next to the touchline. One was 8 and the other was 10, the numbers me and Jimmy Case used to wear. It was us all the time. But I suppose we were learning our trade.

It was hard being in and out of the team. For me, it's not about money. It never has been. All I wanted to do was to play. It was even harder being out of the first team because the reserves would play on the same day. If Liverpool were at home, I would be in the reserves at somewhere like Aston Villa, playing in front of two men and a dog.

When I wasn't playing it was heartbreaking, especially when we won the First Division title at Wolves in 1976. It was my first taste of championship success with the club, yet I wasn't even on the bench and that killed me. I didn't get a medal because I'd not played enough games. I played nine league games and one in the League Cup against York City. Although people say I won five league titles with Liverpool, in reality it was only four in terms of medals.

It was unfashionable QPR who were chasing us all the way to the title with Gerry Francis pulling the strings. We needed a good end to the season to see them off. We were unbeaten in the last nine games, only conceding four goals – three of them in one game, a 5-3 stormer against Stoke at Anfield.

We went into the last game at Molineux knowing only a win would guarantee the title. We managed it with three goals in the last 15 minutes from Kevin Keegan, John Toshack and Ray Kennedy. But when the party started I felt it was going on without me. I had watched the game from the dugout. There I was wearing my fashionable leather bomber jacket rather than the famous red shirt of Liverpool.

The place was packed with Liverpool fans, some of whom had managed to sneak in without tickets. In the dressing room before the game, Phil Thompson famously asked Bob Paisley whether he would help get his brother into the ground because he didn't have a ticket. Back then at Molineux, there was a door near the changing room where he could get him in, so Bob agreed and opened it only to see around 30 other Liverpool fans charge in.

There was a real buzz going back on the coach. There were fans on the motorway celebrating and when we later got stuck in a traffic jam on the M6, some of the fans got out of the cars and started playing an impromptu game of football.

All this was incredible for the club itself, but it still didn't feel as good as if I was a regular in the team.

On numerous occasions I went to see Bob and told him I just wanted to play. He would always listen very intently, nod and then say, "Son, all you have to do is to play The Liverpool Way." "If I'm not going to play Bob, I might as well leave," I would tell him, but he always insisted he didn't want me to go.

Sometimes I'd go to see our coach, Ronnie Moran, and I'd ask him exactly what Bob meant by The Liverpool Way. "Work it out for yourself son," would be the reply.

It was the same for everyone when they first joined the club. I remember when Graeme Souness first signed for us in 1977. He went up to Joe Fagan and said, "Joe, I've been here four days now and no-one has told me what to do." Joe said, "We've just paid bloody £500,000 for you and you're asking me how do I play? There's a football, so go and play!"

The Liverpool Way meant keeping hold of the ball, making simple passes and not overcomplicating things. Just pass, move; pass, move. Don't stand and admire your 30-yard balls.

As I tried to get into the team on a more regular basis, there was one person who kept me going – without him I would have snapped and told Liverpool to stick it up their arse – Roy Evans.

Roy was the reserve team coach and he kept reassuring me. "Keep training, do the right things week in, week out and you'll get back into the first team," he'd say. And he was right. When I got the opportunity I had to make sure I took it. Roy was always supportive of me. When I did break into the team regularly he was still great and if it wasn't for him I would have left Liverpool before I'd made any real impact.

There would be decent players in the reserves at different times. Quite often, Jimmy Case would be alongside me and there would be players coming back from injury like John Toshack and Brian Hall, as well as youngsters like Trevor Birch and Brian Kettle.

We would often win the Central League by January because we would be so far ahead of everyone else such was the class in our side. But I didn't want reserve medals. And I haven't kept any – I threw them all away. I hadn't come to Liverpool to play for the reserve side. I wanted to win trophies for the first team.

I learned from a documentary a few years later that Brian

Clough wanted to sign me for Nottingham Forest. He told a story about Bob Paisley and how he phoned him asking if he could sign me. Bob never even mentioned it at the time. Nowadays, an agent would have found out and let you know – but not back then.

To be honest, I don't think I would have joined Forest anyway. I couldn't have put up with Cloughie's mannerisms, even though I speak regularly to Garry Birtles who loved him. It was a hard time but obviously Bob still had faith in me and that's why he told Clough I was going nowhere.

During this time, I was back living with my mum and dad in Kirkby – in fact, I stayed there for most of the eight years I was with Liverpool.

I had a house near St. Helens, but it was sometimes used by certain other Liverpool players more than me. Some of my team-mates would often ask to borrow the keys for, let's say, 'entertaining purposes'. Now and then I would go there but mostly I would be in at home, surrounded by family, mates and those I knew best. I was happiest there.

I eventually started playing more games in the first team.

The next season, 1976/77, we won the League again – and this time I did get a medal, having started 36 matches in all competitions.

Everything was happening in those hectic few weeks at the end of that season with another League championship secured, an FA Cup final to play in and then a few days later the chance to make club history by winning the European Cup for the first time.

It should have been the happiest time of my life.

CHAPTER 7

ROME TRUTHS

I WAS absolutely flying during that 1976/77 season. I felt accepted in the dressing room. Everything was going well. I was playing for my boyhood team regularly, the fans were singing my name and I was living every kid's dream. But amidst all this, my life was being turned upside down.

Not by football, but by cancer.

During that season, it became clear that Mum did not have long to live. She was spending most of her time in the special Clatterbridge cancer hospital on the Wirral.

When I visited her, I would often see the great Liverpool comedian Ken Dodd because his long-term partner was also having treatment there. Doddy's partner was in a private room, but my mum was in a general ward.

It was so hard seeing Mum the way she was, watching the life ebb away from her on her hospital deathbed.

One day it became too much. I just couldn't handle the situation and I had to walk out of the ward because she looked so gaunt and frail. It wasn't the mum I knew, there was nothing on her – she was just skin and bones. It was probably the most important time of my football life so far but I also knew my mum was going to die and, looking back, I don't know how I got through it.

In a strange way, though, the starkness of the situation imbued me with greater inspiration to be successful. It brought my own life into clearer focus and made me realise how lucky I was. I wanted to be successful for her – I wasn't going to pull out of any matches. That's not what she would have wanted. That's not the way she brought me up. She had already made me go the extra mile in life, so I wasn't going to stop now.

There had been a real belief in 1977 that after winning the League, we would clean up with the FA Cup and European Cup to claim an unprecedented domestic treble.

In the FA Cup, we were drawn to play Everton in the semi-final at Maine Road and I scored one of my favourite goals. Luckily you can still see it on YouTube!

It was a left footed chip over David Lawson, the Everton keeper, in the 10th minute. To be fair, I worked on shooting with both feet during training. In my early days at Bury I used to practice volleying with both feet a lot. I was decent with my left foot.

I'd noticed against Everton that the keeper was on the penalty spot, which I felt was a bit bizarre, so when Kevin Keegan played the ball into me, I pretended I was going to shoot with my right as Mick Buckley tried to close me down, quickly switched it to my left to unbalance him and then chipped it into the net. The keeper had no chance because it sailed around three or four feet over him before dipping in. I'm proud of that goal.

The only thing was I should have worked on my goal celebration routine. I just went hurtling back towards the half-way line with the rest of my team-mates chasing me. But just as in training when we went on runs, they couldn't catch me!

I wince now when I see my reaction after scoring other goals. Usually I'd just jump up in the air with one hand raised, pathetic.

Many people have probably forgotten that goal in the FA Cup semi-final because that 2-2 draw is always talked about as the match in which famous referee Clive Thomas disallowed a late Everton 'winner'. Bryan Hamilton put the ball in the back of our net and there is still conjecture over why it was disallowed. It was either for handball or for offside, no-one has ever come up with the definitive answer.

To be perfectly honest, I don't know why it was disallowed, even after seeing the controversial incident many times over the past years – although obviously at the time I was glad it was because it meant a replay, one we won comfortably 3-0 at Maine Road. It was a lucky ground for me, Maine Road, we always seemed to beat Manchester City there.

We were by far the better team going into the Wembley final against Tommy Docherty's Manchester United, who had finished 10 points behind us in sixth place.

Kevin Keegan was our main man, even though everyone knew he was leaving us at the end of the season. The fans were fine with that, though of course they didn't want him to leave. Some people couldn't understand why he wanted to leave a successful side like Liverpool, but that was Kevin – he has always wanted to challenge himself. By telling the club early about his plans, it gave them time to look for a replacement. Kevin is always honest with people, something he took into management too.

It didn't affect anything on the pitch during that season because you always knew what you were getting from Kevin, 100 per cent in every game. He wasn't distracted.

With him in our side, how we didn't win the FA Cup I still don't know. All the goals came in a mad five minute spell not long after half-time. United went ahead through Stuart Pearson, then two minutes later Jimmy Case hooked the equaliser past Alex Stepney. We would have been expected to go on and win the game and maybe we would if it wasn't for a freak goal just three minutes later that came off Jimmy Greenhoff's chest from a Lou Macari shot.

We were absolutely gutted to be beaten by United, considering the age-old rivalry between the two clubs. We were the better team over the 90 minutes and should have won, but we didn't. That's football sometimes. You could hear a pin drop on the coach taking us to Watford, where we were due to catch the train back up to Liverpool.

On the station platform, we were all moping around, the wives just as miserable as us. Suddenly Ray Clemence decides to start up his own singing and dancing routine. We couldn't believe what we were seeing, our goalkeeper thinking he was on stage at the London Palladium. It broke the ice, Clem belting out some songs from musicals – at least that's what I thought they were – he wasn't exactly in tune! Within minutes, we were joining in, singing and laughing.

Once we got on to the train we got the beers out and were

partying again all the way back home. As soon as we got back, I went to the Continental nightclub in Liverpool – even though we were back in training the next day to prepare for the European Cup final.

On Monday, we were off to Rome to try and write club history as the first Liverpool side to win Europe's biggest prize. As soon as we arrived Bob Paisley famously announced, "If any of you want to go out for a walk, well, there's nothing to see because I've bloody well bombed it all." That was a reference to Bob having been involved in the Second World War in Italy with his tank division.

By now, although it had hurt, the FA Cup final was forgotten. We had work to do.

People ask me now what was my favourite Liverpool game? What was your favourite goal? I always say the 1977 European Cup final. Borussia Moenchengladbach had a good team, players like Uli Stielike, Jupp Heynckes, Rainer Bonhof. Walking out into the Olympic Stadium sent a shiver down your spine – even an hour and a half before kick-off. There was a sea of red and white all around the ground. The Moenchengladbach fans were squeezed into the corner, completely outnumbered by our fans. We had 35,000 supporters there – absolutely staggering.

The fans had also forgotten the FA Cup. In fact, some of them had made their way to the Italian capital straight from Wembley. They didn't want to miss this. They got there by coach, train, car, whatever they could manage, to ensure they were in Rome for what we all hoped would be an historic night.

There wasn't much money about because of all the strikes that had afflicted the era. The fans weren't bothered. They would have sold anything to get to Rome. On the trains, some of them were sleeping wherever they could to make the long journey more bearable, even on top of the baggage racks. When we saw the fans, we just knew we couldn't let them down. I'm convinced that was the inspiration for us to win the European Cup.

Kevin was absolutely magnificent that night. Some people had a go at him after the FA Cup final accusing him of not being bothered because he was leaving at the end of the season. Well, he gave his answer in the only way Kevin can in Rome. He tore Berti Vogts, an experienced German international, to bits. No-one, even Berti, could live with Kevin, who was darting here, darting there. He was like an electric eel. You couldn't get near him.

I scored first to give us the lead and, for my goal, Kevin took Vogts away to the other side of the penalty area. It gave me around 20 yards of space for me to run in to – something you don't normally get in top class football. Berti should have been in the area trying to block the danger but he was so obsessed with trying to stick with Kevin, he was way out of position.

When Steve Heighway released the ball, I was in. I saw their keeper Wolfgang Knieb coming out. He must have been about 6ft 8in, a real giant. I just sensed this huge shadow zooming in on me and I thought 'I'd better get rid of this before he gets any nearer' so I just hit it and it flew into the corner of the net.

That was it, we were 1-0 up. They came back and equalised through Allan Simonsen, a decent player who ended up at Charlton, but 12 minutes later it was 2-1 with an incredible header from Tommy Smith. It was Heighway's corner and Tommy met it beautifully and it soared into the net. He's never scored a better header.

But it was Kevin's run to win the penalty which really sealed the victory. Heighway slipped the ball to me and I found Kevin racing forward. I then burst to the right which meant one of the Borussia defenders came out with me. That left Kevin one-on-one with Vogts and there was only one winner, Kevin turning him and accelerating into the box. Vogts made the challenge and Kevin went crashing to the ground – penalty. Saying that, I honestly didn't think it was because I'm certain Vogts got a touch on the ball. To the naked eye it looked a penalty but in slow motion Berti seemed a bit unlucky.

Phil Neal took the spot-kick. If he hadn't taken it then I would, because I went on to take a few for Liverpool although that would have been my first in a red shirt!

When he put it away, you could see Bob Paisley, Joe Fagan and Roy Evans celebrating in a big huddle. They thought the job had been done. The whistle went and that was it. We had created history and I was part of it – just a few years after turning out for Bury in the Fourth Division.

As soon as we got back to the dressing room, the celebrations started. Clem was singing and dancing again. Ronnie Moran – as usual – said: "That's it for this season, lads. It's what we do next season now that counts. Next season starts tomorrow." Cheers, Ronnie!

There were so many people in the dressing room you could hardly move. The chairman John Smith went around everybody congratulating them. The other directors were there. Jack Ferguson, who we knew from the Liverpool Holiday Inn which we used for pre-match meals, joined in the celebrations. Roy Evans, who had done so much for me, was also there, of course.

Bob just stood there with little emotion, sipping a lemonade. Joe and Ronnie would like the odd whisky. When we won the League title Joe was there with a bottle of Scotch asking if anyone wanted a nip of it. But in Rome, we had to wait until the reception before getting a drink. Amidst all the party atmosphere, I spared a thought for my big mate Phil Thompson, who missed the game through injury. He was a mad Liverpool fan like me. It doesn't get much better than touching the gleaming trophy which is the European Cup. If anyone deserved to get hold of it, it was him. It must have broken his heart missing out on that unique night.

At least, for me, it had been an escape from reality and what was happening to my mum.

At the hotel afterwards, a big banquet was laid on for us. We were going to have one, win or lose. We all got changed, came down and started celebrating with a few drinks, getting stuck into the food. There were a few fans knocking around so we invited them in and before you knew it the place was full of happy Liverpool supporters. They were like a plague of locusts. Within five minutes, all the food had disappeared.

The next morning, Kevin was going around with a black eye. The word got out that it was Jimmy Case who had left one on Kevin over a row about Kevin not having played well on the Saturday – that he hadn't tried. That was a load of bollocks. It was Phil Neal who had actually caught him with his elbow. What had happened was some of the lads, including Kevin, had been messing around in the swimming pool in the morning, trying to push each other in. Phil caught Kevin accidentally in the eye with his elbow and he was left with this shiner.

We left the hotel for the airport in the afternoon to fly home and the drinking started again on the plane. Soon plied with drink, I was on the plane's intercom and started taking off Bob Paisley with his North East lilt, his sayings and his mannerisms.

"Clem in goal, then doings and Joey and that…" I was saying, mimicking Bob announcing the team before the game.

I had been sitting next to Alec Lindsay, who told me not to do it. But I wasn't bothered. I was told Bob had a little giggle. He wasn't bothered either. The press lads loved it too because they all knew about his sayings. They would try to take him off as well – but all in good humour. We all loved and admired him.

By the time we got off the plane we were all pissed. And when we got back to Liverpool we were in a terrible state! Not long after, I found myself in Benidorm with my big mate Thommo.

I didn't know whether to go away or not because Mum was still very ill and I wasn't sure how long she was going to last – but I was told I needed a break after a long hard season, so I took the advice and went.

I rang home every day to see how she was from the hotel room and then one day I received the news I was dreading – that she had died. She was only 55 years old.

That was it, I packed my things up and got a flight home. Thommo was great and came back with me. He could have stayed and had a jolly, but wanted to be with me.

As soon as I got home the house was full with relatives and my dad was crying. It was terrible.

At least I hoped she realised that I had helped Liverpool make history by winning the European Cup.

CHAPTER 8

THE CLASS OF '77

MY team-mates in that famous 1977 Liverpool team weren't just great players, they were big characters too.

One of the main men in the team was Ray Kennedy. Ray has been struggling with Parkinson's disease for a long while now and sadly is a shadow of his former self. It's heartbreaking and makes you appreciate more what you had – and still have. He has had to put up with it for more than 30 years now. I still see him but, if I'm honest, I don't see him enough. I always ask Jimmy Case how Ray is because I know Jimmy talks to him on a regular basis.

There were no early signs of the terrible disease which Ray was to later succumb to. I think it surfaced for the first time when

Ray was at Swansea under John Toshack. Jimmy Case has said that he had noticed Ray being a bit slow in discussions but I hadn't noticed anything. At Swansea, Tosh started having a go at him for not putting it all in but obviously that was the start of it. Unbeknown to Ray, he didn't have the same energy levels.

At Liverpool, Ray was quick-witted and always had a story to tell. I used to change next to him and he would often be winding me up about my drinking. "I can smell the fumes from here," he'd say!

We all loved a night out and Ray was no different. He was a big, smart, handsome man, a really smashing guy, always the best dressed, someone who loved the fashions and a magnet for any wandering eyes from girls looking for a marquee bloke on the arm. Usually, though, like the rest of us, it was a pint that he craved.

Ray was a great player. He came in as a centre forward from Arsenal but Bob Paisley switched him to the left side of midfield. He was someone who still had an eye for goal and would often race into the box from a deeper lying position and score crucial goals. What he didn't get enough credit for was his incredible passing ability. I knew that when I made a long run into the box and Ray Kennedy had the ball at his feet, he would deliver the perfect pass for me to get on the end of. He could deliver with both feet, but especially if it was on his left I knew he would be able to find me.

Despite being able to do anything on the pitch, he still got stick from a certain Liverpool fan in the Kemlyn Road stand who used to give me grief as well.

He would batter both of us. It depended on which way we were kicking because I'd be on the right and Ray was on the left. If we were kicking towards the Kop in the first half, then Ray would be right in this guy's firing line. When we were walking in at half-time I'd ask Ray, "Is he there?" Ray would often reply that he was and that it had been a nightmare hearing him deliver the insults.

In the second half, it would be my turn. When there was a lull in the game, suddenly you would hear this voice boom out. "McDermott, you drunken bastard! You've been drinking again!" This would go on all the time. I remember in one game I scored and when I celebrated I headed towards where I thought this guy was and told him where to go with a victory salute in his general direction. You get these fans who are quick to single out certain players at most clubs. Obviously this fella didn't like me or Ray.

Ray's big mate Jimmy Case knew how to handle himself when the flak was flying. Jimbo was the silent assassin. You would get players during games shouting this and that to you – that they are going to break your leg and so on. It's all talk, hot air. Jimmy wouldn't say anything. Instead, he would just snap a player in half – and then help them up. He was also a little bit deaf and would use that to his advantage. If the referee was shouting at him, he would cock a deaf 'un!

Jimmy was a tough, tough guy. It was the way he was brought up on the hard streets of South Liverpool. There was a lot of unemployment, plenty of hard-up families. He finished his apprenticeship as an electrician while he was on Liverpool's books. He would train in the day and go off to learn to become an electrician at night. So, any time we had a problem with the lights or anything electrical, we would give Jimmy a call.

Jimbo must have been one of the unluckiest players not to have collected a single England cap. It must have been desperate for him seeing nearly everyone else disappear from Melwood on international duty some weeks. If anyone deserved at least one cap, it was him. He had a shot like a mule. Every game he would give 100 per cent. He knew like me if he didn't put it in or got an injury he might find himself out of the team. So he often just played through the injuries.

When you talk of hard men, no-one came tougher than Tommy Smith. Tommy got on very well with Jimmy. It's probably where Jimmy learned some of the black arts of the game!

I looked up to Tommy. He was the elder statesman of Anfield and at the top of his game when I arrived. We were younger than Tommy so he didn't usually come out socially with us.

Tommy was nicknamed the 'Aintree Iron'. I remember him confronting Leighton James once, who was playing for Burnley. Tommy was right back and James was on the left wing. Leighton tried to go past him and you could hear Tommy snarling at him 'Try and go past me again and I'll break your ruddy neck!' Then there was Paul Mariner, who became a great friend of mine. Paul could look after himself but I've never seen anyone more frightened after Smithy scythed him in half. After that he moved to another position to get out of Tommy's way.

I know Tommy didn't particularly care for Emlyn Hughes, which happens at football clubs. Not everyone is going to get on with everyone else. They had a respect for each other.

What seemed to cause the fall-out was the fact that, at the time, Tommy was often playing at right back and the rumour was that Emlyn went in to see Bob and told him we needed two fast full-backs. It appeared Emlyn was trying to hasten Tommy's

Early shots: From a kick about on Southport sports field to a teenager playing for Kirkby Boys in 1966/67 (below)

School champs: With my St Kevin's school team (back row, second from the left) after becoming champions of Lancashire

First Gigg: Winning an aerial battle with my first professional club, Bury

Big move: Joe Harvey signed me for Newcastle in 1973

Magpie hero: This fresh-faced 21-year-old soon developed great affection for the North East and I gave my all for the black and white shirt

Out on the Toon: I loved life on the pitch and off it, enjoying some great nights out with the likes of Tommy Cassidy and Pat Howard – even if it doesn't look like I'm having fun here!

Wembley woe: I may have been a Liverpool fan growing up, but losing to them in the 1974 FA Cup final really hurt. I swapped my Newcastle shirt with Phil Thompson

Family pride: When I signed for Liverpool in November '74 my family, including my mum and dad (front), were delighted. Less than three years later, Mum was tragically no longer with us

Red letter day: The most successful period of my career came when I joined Liverpool. I was greeted at Melwood by skipper Emlyn Hughes and immediately hit it off with fellow Kirkby boy Phil Thompson

Spectacular strike: It took a while to earn a regular place in the team but by 1977, when this photo was taken during a 2-0 win over Arsenal at Anfield, I was able to show what I could do

King of clubs: Winning became so commonplace at Liverpool, we used trophies as card tables!

Weigh the lads:
The airport
scales wouldn't
have registered
much with Phil
Thompson sitting
on them!

Yes we can-can:
Some of the
lads were more
happy to pose
than others!

Goal rush:
A trademark
celebration of
mine, sprinting
away after
finding the net

Euro glory: I scored the opening goal in the 1977 European Cup final in a 3-1 win against Borussia Moenchengladbach and won a further two winner's medals in 1978 and 1981

Eyes on the ball: A picture of concentration as the ball comes towards me

Champagne Charlie: Drinking in the bath with Graeme Souness after our title success in 1980

Hamburg with relish: A hat-trick against SV Hamburg in the Super Cup final in 1977 put an extra spring in my step

Perfect goal: This header rounded off a 7-0 win over Spurs in 1978 – a goal Bob Paisley described as the best ever at Anfield

Red mist: I was shown the red card – as was Everton's Garry Stanley – during the derby match in October 1979, but I wasn't the only one throwing fists!

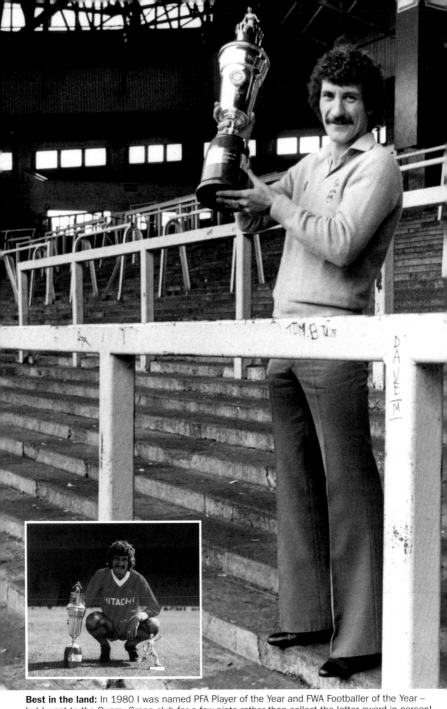

Best in the land: In 1980 I was named PFA Player of the Year and FWA Footballer of the Year – but I went to the Quarry Green club for a few pints rather than collect the latter award in person!

departure – definitely not the wisest move. That was it as far as Tommy was concerned, but it never escalated into a physical confrontation. Even though they weren't close, there was no evidence of that out on the pitch. There was no 'look at them, they're not talking'. They were professionals, so on matchdays they were the best of friends in a playing sense. They would look out for each other. Off the pitch they would revert back to not being so chummy.

I personally loved Emlyn. I was in awe of him, as I was a lot of the players. They called him 'Crazy Horse'. He was so powerful and his work-rate was incredible. He could play anywhere after starting off as a left back at Blackpool. He had that lovely smile. Most people liked Emlyn.

He took me under his wing when I arrived and used to take me to Cartmel for the horse racing. I think it was also to get me used to the local brew! He was a big racing man and we later teamed up together to buy a horse. Ginger McCain, of Red Rum fame, was the trainer. It was called 'Simmering'. I don't know why.

I remember we were away with England when it was having its first ever race at Wetherby. We had £2.50 each way on it at 16-1. We were in a hotel abroad and Emlyn was listening to the commentary on the phone in the hotel room, relaying the commentary to me, getting more and more excited as the finishing line got closer and closer. The next moment the phone has come off the wall socket and it's in the air as he celebrated our horse coming first. What a start to life as horse owners! We quickly acquired a second horse 'More For England', but I don't think it ever won a single race for us.

We would go to Cartmel every bank holiday. It would often be a two-day meeting so we could travel up there complete with a picnic even if it was the drink we were more interested in. We would get mullered as the day wore on. It was brilliant.

I wasn't surprised when he did so well on *A Question Of Sport*, with that cheeky smile. I even appeared with him on one of the shows. It was really enjoyable. Everyone still remembers him having his arm around Princess Anne who was a guest on the programme. He was so full of life and it broke my heart when he died of a brain tumour in 2004.

Apparently, the first sign there was something wrong was when he was riding a bike and just fell off it. Then he went to the races a few weeks later with a mate of mine, Mike Dillon from Ladbrokes. Emlyn suddenly just fell against Mike after losing his balance. Mike could hardly keep him up on his feet. Later he was sadly diagnosed with an inoperable condition. I'll never forget him. He looked after me so well.

When he came to do talk-ins after finishing as a player, if he was in the North East he would come to the house and have a quick sandwich before he shot off to the venue. We also played in the Emlyn Hughes XI for charity games. If the game was on a Sunday we would travel on the Saturday, stay over and have a great night out. We would be out until 4am and we'd be playing at 11am. There were ex-players and people from TV and show-business. It was Emlyn who was the leader in all that – a great bloke. He had been one of my heroes and I would put him up there as one of Liverpool's greats.

As I've said, one of my biggest friends at Liverpool was another great captain, Phil Thompson. Like me, he was a lad from Kirkby. I already knew about him with it being such a small community. We became big drinking mates. Thommo was a great player who maybe didn't get the adulation he deserved. You don't become an England captain without people giving you respect.

At first, no-one had thought of Thommo as a centre back because he was a midfield player. It was Bill Shankly who switched him to defence and he was a revelation. There he was, stick thin, but nothing much got past him. He could read a game, he was strong in the tackle, could head a ball and also scored a few goals. Like Phil Neal, he was another Mr. Reliable. Another seven or eight out of 10 every game.

We used to go out all the time together, to Liverpool pubs and working men's clubs. Phil was more sensible then me, although that wasn't hard! The week was a right mix with the lads: Toad Hall, Southport on a Monday night. Tuesday could be a place called Uglies and then the rest of the nights would be shared between places called The Continental, Shorrocks Hill, Benny's and, of course, Quarry Green.

Then, of course, there was no social media, although there were times when we came close to copping a bollicking. Every now and then, you would get spotted by a fan who wasn't happy seeing you drink, so they would write in to the club to tell Bob Paisley.

The letters, though, would only get as far as Karen who worked as a secretary. Karen would simply put them straight in the bin. Bob never saw one of those letters! Nowadays you can't really go out and let your hair down. Mind, I suppose being boring for 10 years and picking up £20 million isn't too bad.

There was a regular group of us who took advantage of the cheaper drink in the working men's clubs – Thommo, myself,

Alan Hansen and Alan Kennedy. We were known as the Four Musketeers. We'd either go for a few beers in the afternoons or enjoy a night out together.

Thommo was the first to fall when he met his eventual wife Marg. I didn't go out one Sunday night – I must have been ill or something! – so Thommo went out with my brother Pete and a few of the lads to a working man's club in Kirkby. The next day at training, Thommo said he had met a brilliant girl and he was going to see her during the week. He ended up marrying her – the first of the faithful Musketeers to drop! From that day, Thommo and Marg were inseparable – his first love and they are still together now, a great couple. That was the beginning of the group's numbers starting to dwindle. Hansen fell soon after when he met his girlfriend.

They say that goalkeepers are always big characters and Ray Clemence was one of the funniest guys you could ever meet. A real genuine bloke (believe me – quite a few footballers in the game are not as genuine as you would like them to be). Clem was the life and soul of the party. Wherever we went he would always have a smile on his face and was always up for a laugh.

He was a joker in a dressing room full of jokers. The only time I ever saw him get really annoyed was in training when we had shooting exercises and someone tried to chip him. He would come out to block your shots and some of us would try to catch him out by dinking the ball over him and into the net. He would retrieve the ball from the back of the net and kick it as far as he could! There was many a time you would see it sail over the wall towards the pub which was just outside Melwood.

When we had the five-a-sides in training, he wouldn't go in

goal. He always wanted to be the centre forward, the striker. To be fair, he was pretty decent up front. He really enjoyed it. All left foot, but pretty good.

I was shocked when he decided to leave in 1981. I remember him sitting in the dressing room in Paris after we had just won the European Cup for the third time. Normally he would be jumping up and down celebrating and although he was obviously delighted that we had won, he was just sat down. He wasn't his normal effervescent self. It transpired afterwards that he had decided to look for a fresh challenge. He'd won the European Cup three times and needed to test himself somewhere new.

I was devastated when we knew he was leaving. We were losing a great goalkeeper and a great guy. He was so unlucky not to get more England caps than he actually did because of Peter Shilton. Ron Greenwood decided to rotate the pair of them

David Johnson was another great character. He is still a big, big mate of mine – we've remained great friends and there's hardly a day goes by without a phone call. He's always great craic and someone I love being with.

He was nicknamed 'The Doc' because every morning he would come into training with a wash bag and it would be full of tablets and potions – if you had a hangover or weren't feeling well, he always had something that could help you. We never knew what we were taking. It could have been marijuana for all we knew!

David was a really good player. He was brave, he scored some great goals, was brilliant in the air and could run all day. I bet some teams now wish they had someone like him. He came from Everton and ended going back there. I know he wished he hadn't gone back because it became a nightmare for him.

As an international, he scored two goals at Wembley for England against Argentina, who were then the reigning world champions. Maradona played. But he says to me now that people don't recognise him in the street – in fact, in general I think he doesn't get the recognition he deserves. He was well respected by the players.

When we played in an FA Cup semi-final against Arsenal, he got smashed in the face and had to be taken off. He hadn't been playing well. When he came back on after a bit of concussion he was absolutely brilliant. I say to him now he should have got concussed more often! There he was with a great big bandage on his head and playing like Pele…

One story The Doc loves to tell happened when we went on that end-of-season 'Gulf Tour' in 1980. After the flight over, on which we'd obviously had a skinful, we were invited to a palace to meet a prince, only to find even more drinks laid on for us.

We then had to go into a giant hall for a banquet and at the end of the meal the doors opened and in walked six chefs carrying a giant cake shaped like a football pitch. It had 22 players on it, corner flags, goalposts with nets – the lot. We were asked to gather together with the prince for a group photo next to this cake and I found myself stood behind one of the nets.

The ale had got the better of me at this point and, as you do, I undid the zip on my pants and balanced a certain part of my anatomy on the crossbar. Bob Paisley took one look and shouted, in his North East accent, "Tuddy Mac, put it away!"

I'm not sure how I got away with that and hopefully the photo didn't end up on the walls of the palace!

Of all the players I've known from that era, I've never heard anyone criticise Ian Callaghan. He is so respected throughout the football world. He comes in now on matchdays and is still Mr. Nice Guy. Cally had been another of my idols. He was quiet but still enjoyed a laugh. You would think at first that he was too nice to be a footballer, but what a player. He was non-stop action, always swinging balls into the penalty area. Eventually he moved to the centre of midfield.

Cally is Liverpool through and through. He has not changed in more than 50 years. Having said that, he was a dirty little sod! He wasn't slow to put his foot in. He was like a little Johnny Giles, not as nasty as him but he wasn't frightened. He was tough but the referees liked him so he didn't get punished. I think he only got booked once.

Cally was the Marathon Man, Liverpool's record appearance maker. Another man in the same mould was Phil Neal. He was Mr. Reliable. You don't play 400-odd games on the trot for Liverpool without being a bit special. He's the most decorated player in Liverpool's history with all the medals and trophies and he deserved all the plaudits which came his way.

I came to Liverpool just after Phil and although I arrived at Anfield after playing in the First Division with Newcastle United, he came from Northampton from Division Four and he really got thrust in for his debut at Everton – the same as me. He'd been nowhere near that standard for Northampton.

I played in front of him because I was right-side midfield. He was phenomenal. He might get injured, but Phil would play through the pain barrier. You won't get that now with some of the players. He just wanted to play all the time. Many of us felt in that Liverpool period that if you picked up an injury and you were out of the team you might not get back in again. We would all play with dead legs, twinges of all sorts.

Phil was a good communicator and he would always be talking through games. You could see quite early on that he was captaincy material with all his cajoling. As he started winning things, his experience over the years proved invaluable and it was inevitable that his time as the team's skipper would come. He deserved it.

To this day, he's still Mr Reliable. When the ex-players like myself do tours of the ground he still never misses one! Some of us might be absent through illness or other commitments, not Nealy, he's there all the time, a 100 per cent appearance record. He loves being part of Liverpool.

I would be with him and some of the other Liverpool lads for England games. After a midweek Wembley game we would have a chauffeur-driven car waiting to take us back to Merseyside. But before getting into the motor we would disappear for a few beers in a hotel near the ground. Everyone knows what I was like, I would always want a few more before taking our leave. Phil would keep at me, telling me it's getting on for midnight and we all had a three hour journey back home. He was right, I was wrong. He knew the importance of trying to get a good night's sleep because we would always be at Melwood the next morning for massages and recovery. Phil was the ultimate professional and I certainly wasn't! But he was still good to be around. He loved some of my stories and was up for a laugh as well as being the absolute professional.

We were all different characters and it's fair to say I didn't have too many conversations with Steve Heighway. He would come out with the big intellectual words and there's me with no GCEs or other qualifications! But we did team up before most games. We would disappear into the toilet area and aim a ball at the shower control. The first one to hit it 20 times was the winner. That became a tradition, although I don't think it did the shower unit any good! We would do this every home game and it turned into a bit of a superstition.

Steve didn't really come out with us much socially but that didn't matter – he was a decent fella and very much part of the squad. I can probably thank him for helping make one of my stand-out goals for Liverpool. It was in the now famous 7-0 hammering of Spurs at Anfield in 1978. David Johnson played a great ball in front of him but instead of taking his defender on at speed, he somehow sent in a great cross for me to head in at the far post. It was an unbelievable ball, I don't know how he picked me out. I'd made the run from the other end of the pitch, where we had been defending a corner. We were 6-0 up and I'm leaning on the post talking to Alan Hansen and Alan Kennedy about where they fancied going that night. The next thing, Ray Clemence grabs it and he has thrown it to Kenny Dalglish and I've set off running at breakneck speed towards The Anfield Road end. It carries on to Steve Heighway who set me up for the header. Steve, a really bright guy, went on to coach at the Liverpool Academy and has recently been back working with the young Liverpool players in Kirkby alongside a new coach by the name of Steven Gerrard.

Steve Heighway would also supply great service to a certain Kevin Keegan. It's fair to say Kevin was a superstar not just in England, but in Europe. I remember looking at him on the pitch and thinking how small he was. But he was great in the air and built like a brick outhouse. If you knocked into him you knew about it. Not many players got the better of him physically.

TERRY MAC

I played against him when I was at Newcastle and soon I was in the same dressing room as him. I was overawed at first. I think when me and Kevin started to get close was when I broke into the England squad. We would travel together and watch games. During the 1980 European Championships in Italy we would often play tennis together. I wasn't bad but Kevin was good at everything. He was a great golfer. Excellent at tennis. He could swim well.

Kevin was funny in the dressing room, cracking jokes and always winding people up about their clothes. You might have a new shirt and you walk in thinking you're the dog's you know what and suddenly you hear "what the hell have you got on there?" bellowing out from Kevin. Then he would batter the shoes you had on. That was the banter and soon everyone would be at it like little kids. But it was great for team spirit. There was laughter all the time and at the heart of it was Kevin.

The only time he got serious was on matchdays. It was like someone flicking a switch. The jovial mood from training had disappeared to be replaced by a committed game attitude.

In training, Kevin was always regarded as being the fittest. We used to do this run at Melwood, a long run in between the pylons – at full speed. We're doing the run and I'm just behind Kevin who would always get to the front. For once, I stayed at his side and then, with the end in sight, went past him. He couldn't believe it. I think that made the coaching staff see me in a different light, thinking I could make more of those lung-busting runs in matches. It proved that I could get up and down the pitch and find myself in the penalty area more and more. If anyone was fitter than Kevin you were doing okay. I knew I had to maintain the same fitness, otherwise I would be history.

Kevin had originally joined Liverpool under Bill Shankly and absolutely adored him. He liked Shanks as much as you would like your own father. Kevin's own father was a top man. He used to come to all the home games. He would be in the players' lounge. He was a miner from Hetton-le-Hole.

If Kevin was a one-off then so was Joey Jones. Joey was and is unique. Everybody liked him. You couldn't dislike Joey, but at the same time, you wouldn't want to get on the wrong side of him. At times he could be frightening and got involved in a few skirmishes in training. He was a hard, hard player. If you were in a war, you would want 11 Joey Jones' in there with you.

Joey wasn't the most gifted of players – and he would be the first to admit that – but what he didn't have in ability he made up for it in effort. Absolutely crackers, but a joy to be around every single day. I remember when he left Liverpool for Chelsea he used to drive every day to the south and back from Wrexham with Mickey Thomas beside him. Who else would do that?!

I remember when we were playing Barcelona in the Nou Camp, we were leading 1-0. The Barcelona fans had seen enough and were flinging cushions on to the pitch aiming at their own players.

I was on the bench with Joey in the dugout. The next thing, Joey is up and throwing them back at the supporters. You could hear Bob Paisley shouting out, "Bloody hell man, you'll get us all shot. Sit down man."

Another man who made an impact is David Fairclough. I know he doesn't like being labelled 'Super Sub', but David still called his book that! He was a great goalscorer and I don't just mean the European Cup goal against St.Etienne, which everyone goes on about. He was better than that. David played a lot of first team games and was a decent player. He didn't like being on the bench, but there were good players ahead of him. He felt at times he was hard done by. Once he scored three in a game and got left out of the next one, so no wonder he felt aggrieved. Also, you look at his scoring average and it was very good.

He won't appreciate me saying this too much, but it was good to have someone with an eye for goal coming on as a substitute. Someone who could change the outcome of a game and often did. It's cruel, but true – I couldn't care less who was playing as long as I was. You had to look after yourself at Liverpool, especially with so many good players there. You just wanted to see your name on the teamsheet.

If the names were read out I didn't really listen after I'd heard mine. Don't forget I'd had my own moments as a substitute – for instance, I was the other sub on that famous St Etienne night, but I didn't get on! – so I could sympathise with David to a certain extent. I don't think David ever felt of himself as a regular, but he certainly contributed to the cause.

So, as you can see, it takes all sorts to make up a team and we certainly had that at Liverpool!

CHAPTER 9

GOING OFF
THE RAILS

AFTER the European Cup final in 1977, it really had been non-stop drinking from the minute we got to the hotel after the game.

But for me it was an absolute release in the knowledge that my mum was on her deathbed. I had been traumatised by that and the drink was helping.

From the airport we clambered on to an open deck bus for the celebratory tour around the city, complete with the trophy we had won in Rome. We soon got on to discover more beers were on offer. The problem was, after all this drink, where do you go to relieve yourself?

Going along Queen's Drive, one of the main thoroughfares in Liverpool, the bus was going so slowly that you could dive off and knock at someone's door, pleading to use their toilet. You'd get back on and start all over again. How I didn't fall off the back of that bus, I don't know. I was hanging over. Everyone was warning me to be careful.

We went around the city and the scenes were incredible, fans decked in red and white everywhere. We got off at St. George's Hall, where we were due to be presented to the Mayor and all the city's dignitaries. We ended up on the balcony overlooking the crowd facing the Liverpool Empire Theatre. There must have been close on 100,000 around the area – fans as far as the eye could see. Then Emlyn lifted the European Cup up to show the fans.

We were all looking a bit bedraggled. Emlyn, who had had a few as well, started singing 'Liverpool are magic, Everton are tragic' which later got him into trouble. He later had windows in his house smashed, obviously by incensed Evertonians.

I was at the front of the balcony and I couldn't move. By now I'm desperate for a piss. I felt there was nothing else I could do but to unzip my trousers and relieve myself over the balcony. I was blissfully unaware at the time but my stream landed all over a nurse who was standing in the line of fire. She was amongst a group of St. John Ambulance people.

The next night we were due to play in Tommy Smith's testimonial at Anfield. I got a telephone call from a reporter from the *Sunday People* informing me that his paper had a photo of me urinating over a nurse.

I was honestly completely unaware of what I had done and so denied it was me. He said they were going to use it and I just put the phone down on him. But I thought to myself 'I'm in trouble here' so I rang the elder statesman Tommy Smith and asked him what I should do. I told him the story. His advice was simple. "Phone the fella up and tell him to fuck off," was Smithy's take on the issue. So I did just that.

We played the testimonial on the Friday night and on the Sunday I picked up the *Sunday People* and saw the picture of me urinating off the St. George's Hall balcony. There was a cross obscuring you know what – a big one as it happens! I thought I was going to cop it now from the club. I feared after this they were going to get rid of me. There were also quotes from the nurse. I managed to find out who she was and I sent her some flowers, but I still thought I'd be in serious trouble.

As it turns out, the club never said a single word. The nurse could have gone to Liverpool and demanded that they sack me, but she was absolutely brilliant and forgave me. To this day, I'm extremely grateful. If she's still out there, a very big thank you.

It was ridiculous what I did but you tend to do stupid things in drink. One mischievous fan even sent me an incontinence bag through the post!

After my mum died I've got to admit I went off the rails a bit because I had this attitude that I couldn't give a toss about anything.

What is worse in the world than losing your mum?

Her selflessness in helping raise a large family, with the added burden of regular trips to see poor Charles, must have made it at times almost impossible. But she never moaned and why she was taken away from us at such an early age, I'll never know to this day. As you can imagine, Dad was never really the same person again. None of us were.

I went out drinking every night. The only night I didn't was

Friday. On a Thursday night, when the Liverpool rules said you should be at home, I would be nightclubbing. In fact, the club rules said you shouldn't be out after Tuesday! I knew I was wrong, but I didn't care.

I would be out all day Sunday. Monday night, as I've said, I went to a place called Toad Hall. Tuesday into town. Then Wednesday another club and out again on Saturday, after the game. This would be if we didn't have a midweek game. I would also go back to Bury and meet up with my drinking mates Peter Reid and Bryan Robson, although they would never go out on a Thursday. I think Bob and Ronnie Moran knew what was going on, but never said anything.

The players certainly knew because they could smell it. David Johnson would often lead the ribbing pretending he was going to pass out but at least no-one could ever complain about my stamina. I'd still be out in front. Maybe, deep down, Bob thought all the players could do with a few drinks down them!

As a club, we also had to deal with the fallout of losing Kevin to Hamburg.

Even though we were still celebrating winning the European Cup, everyone was devastated seeing Kevin leave during the summer of '77. He had been so charismatic; everyone had got on with him brilliantly.

We were all upset because you wondered just how we could replace him. He had been the best player in England for the previous three years. At least Kevin had given the club advance warning so they could plan ahead. And what a bit of planning they did, securing one of the finest players Britain has ever produced.

Most of us were aware of Kenny Dalglish because if you play

for Rangers or Celtic you are going to get exposure, but I thought when he first arrived at Anfield that there was no chance of him ever being as good as Kevin.

Kenny was quieter, but he was funny. He would tell jokes, tell stories, maybe about some of the players he had known at Celtic. Some people who have never known Kenny, still to this day, portray him as being a dour character. That couldn't be further from the truth.

I looked over at him as he got changed for his first training session. He didn't say too much and must have felt a little inhibited because, after all, he was sitting with players who had just won the European Cup. I think at first he just sat there listening and taking it all in. He is a very shrewd person – someone who picks things up quickly.

Kenny didn't seem too bad in training, but really you can never tell a player's abilities until you see them in match action. It's alright being decent five-a-side players in training. I can name a million of them. It's what they can do out there on the big pitch that matters.

Replacing Kevin had been a major decision for Liverpool. They knew they had to get it right. Geoff Twentyman had been up to Scotland to watch Kenny a few times and Tom Saunders, another of Bob Paisley's trusted aides, also went up to run the rule over him.

There had been little bits of speculation in the press about who was coming in, including stories about Kenny, but as players we didn't have a clue about Kevin's replacement. We weren't informed until the deal had been done. That was the way Liverpool always worked. They never mouthed off about who they were going to sign to make sure other big clubs didn't sneak in on their targets. Most of us were on our summer holidays when it was announced that Liverpool were signing Kenny Dalglish. He had been a big fish in a smaller pond. Would he be able to swim amongst the sharks of the First Division?

His first game was against Manchester United in the Charity Shield at Wembley. Within 10 minutes we realised what a player we had. He was unbelievable. Everything he did in the opening few minutes was bang on. He was so physically strong and would stick his backside into everybody – that was his forte – but no-one could have forecast that he would be held in the same high esteem as Kevin, that he would be adored so much by the Kop.

Later on in the season we signed another great Scot by the name of Graeme Souness. That completed the trio, as Alan Hansen had also come in during May, 1977.

The first thing any of us really knew about Alan, or 'Jocky', as we called him, was learning he had been arrested by the police for running naked on Blackpool beach! He had been with Scottish mates – the Scots used to and still do come down in their masses to the seaside resort during certain weeks – and had been dared to run into the sea without anything on.

Unluckily for Jocky he had been spotted by the police and escaped a charge following a good telling off.

He signed without any fanfare from Partick Thistle while all the focus had been on Kenny. Alan was brought in as one for the future – and what a future he enjoyed.

What really made Jocky a success in my opinion was he joined our team – our drinking squad.

Much of our boozing took place in Quarry Green, which was a working men's club in Kirkby. It was within walking distance from my house, just ten minutes away. The same people would be in there. Many of them would go to games, but wouldn't pester me just because I played for Liverpool.

It was a fairly big place. You could get 200, 250 people in it. It had a stage where they would put shows or acts on. My brother Pete was the man on the microphone. He was the master of ceremonies and did a bit of singing to get us all going.

We'd go in the lounge. There was also a snooker room which is still going to this day. I go back there occasionally because it holds some great memories.

The bars would shut at 10.30pm on the dot and we'd line up the drinks so we could carry on after closing time. We'd wait for everyone to go and then sneak back into the lounge. The doors would be locked and we'd often stay on until 3am.

I never had a hangover. I was fine getting up after a session. Occasionally I would oversleep if I'd forgotten to put the alarm on, but that was rare.

My drink has always been lager although I've sometimes gone onto Southern Comfort and dry ginger. I had a spell on wine but that didn't last for long especially when it was Liebfraumilch and Blue Nun! They were toe curlers (and sometimes leg openers…)

I'll have the odd glass of wine now but it's still usually lager. I didn't like every lager going. For instance, Grunhalle was a non-starter for me. I would avoid a pub that sold that or Stella Artois. I preferred Heineken, Carlsberg or say, Harp.

Some of the Liverpool players were the same. Sometimes on a coach going to an away game, Jocky Hansen, Alan Kennedy, Phil Thompson and myself would have a little league list of favourite beers and lagers.

TERRY MAC

It might be an important game but we'd be compiling this league table of drinks beforehand. Carlsberg could be top, although it might take 30 minutes to get to that decision.

Definitely in relegation trouble was Grunhalle.

Alan was on the pints with the rest of us and was just good fun. None of us got lairy, although of course sometimes it would affect the loins. Well, we were young and mostly single at the time. Alan became one of us, a fantastic guy. He had been a bit shy when he first came in. That quickly changed. Instead of listening to the conversation, he started making it and loved the banter. You could see even then he was developing a real understanding of the game and was quick to analyse incidents from our games. He was living in digs but was a cracking golfer, which we quickly discovered.

On the pitch, even though we had won the League and the European Cup in 1977, the hunger remained to win more trophies. There was no chance of resting on our laurels. If anyone did that, they would find themselves out of the team. There was also the financial aspect to consider. These days you get loads of money before you've really achieved anything. Then you had to play the games, not just for medals but for the cash incentives. The wages were good, but not spectacular. Where you made the real money was in winning things and being a regular in the team. If you were injured or out of the team through a lack of form, your wages would dip considerably. Everyone just wanted to play every single game for both reasons.

There were also fresh challenges emerging during the 1970s. Nottingham Forest had developed under Brian Clough to become a real force in the English game. Aston Villa were also coming to the fore.

When you think what Brian Clough did in building a team from the depths of the Second Division with many players who had been cast adrift by other clubs, it was a truly amazing feat. John O'Hare, Martin O'Neill, Archie Gemmill, Larry Lloyd, Kenny Burns, Frank Clark, the list of great players goes on. Then there was Peter Shilton in goal.

They had some tasty characters, people who could look after themselves. We had a number of meaty games against them and in 1977/78, they ended up beating us in the League Cup final after a replay at Old Trafford.

I still don't know how to this day. Well, to be fair, much of that was down to brilliant goalkeeping from Chris Woods, an unknown teenager at the time who was thrust into the game with Peter Shilton ineligible and John Middleton having left for Derby County.

I remember John Robertson saying after the Wembley game – which ended up goalless – that we could have won 7-0. That was being very kind to Forest. It could have been 17-0 because we just pummelled them. I did manage to get the ball in the back of the net, only for it to be disallowed because Kenny had wandered into an offside position. But everything else we hit at goal, Chris Woods stopped. It was the best performance I've ever seen from a goalkeeper, especially for someone who was just 18. He went on from that to have a really decent career.

It was on to a replay at Old Trafford – another game we should have won – but instead ended up losing 1-0.

I scored another goal but this time it was ruled out for handball! To this day, I know that the ball never hit my arm and TV replays of the game back me up. There were very few complaints from their players at the time but referee Pat Partridge disallowed it.

—

I was just over the halfway line and knocked it forward with my chest, ran on and stuck it in the top corner of the net. But my big moment was snatched away by a bad decision. I've seen Pat over the years and each time I mention the disallowed goal telling him that there was no way the ball touched my arm. He usually apologises and it's all gone now. We just have a bit of fun over it – but I wasn't laughing at the time.

The disallowed goal also cost Ian Callaghan his first booking in 856 games for moaning about the decision! Just to make matters worse, Pat ended up awarding Forest a penalty for a foul on John O'Hare which was a yard outside the box. Phil Thompson brought him down but everyone except Pat could see it was well outside the penalty area. You didn't need TV replays to tell you that. That cost us another winners' medal.

Probably the nastiest confrontation between us and Forest took place a week before our European Cup final against Bruges. Forest had already beaten us to the League title and were coming to Anfield. They seemed desperate to wind us up. Ian Bowyer kept coming up to me during the game, screaming, "Come anywhere near me and I'll snap your leg in half. You won't be playing in any European Cup final." I kept goading him, telling Bowyer he would have to catch me first. Everywhere I went, he followed, or tried to. I even pretended at one point that I was going to pay a visit to the toilet. I called him over. "Come on we're off to the loo," I shouted.

Our team was changing with Kenny involved, Jocky getting a few games and Graeme becoming more involved after he signed. When he moved to Merseyside, Souey was staying at first in the Holiday Inn in Liverpool.

One night, myself, Thommo and Jocky thought we'd pop into the hotel for a drink and to see Graeme.

We met him in the bar and I asked what everyone was having.

Thommo said, "pint of lager." Jocky said the same, "pint of lager" and I was a pint of lager too.

"Graeme?"

"Half a pint of lager," he answered.

"You what?!"

He got absolutely battered. He had to quickly up his order. We stayed with him for a couple of hours. He learned quickly.

'Charlie' has never been quiet. That was his nickname after 'Champagne Charlie'. I still call him that to this day. When he sends me a text message he always signs off 'Charles'. It was just the way he was. He wasn't being clever or cocky in any way, he would just rather have champagne than pints of lager. We accepted that because he mucked in and was a great lad.

I had a couple of nicknames by the way. Most people call me Terry Mac, but at Liverpool the boys nicknamed me 'Ledge'. It had nothing to do with my footballing skills either! We used to play a card game on the team coach called seven-card brag and on one occasion I had to take one of Emlyn Hughes' seven cards unseen and then, after he'd turned his three cards over, slot it back in in the hope it complemented the hand.

According to Kenny Dalglish, as soon as I said "there you go son," the lads knew I'd picked the perfect card and it turned out I had. Call it luck, but this kept happening again and again whenever we played, earning me a few quid and the nickname 'Ledge' which they still use to this day.

Anyway, back to Graeme. He moved in different circles when it came to the opposite sex. While we may have had our eye on some girls who worked in Tesco, he was going out with Miss World, Mary Stavin. She was with him for the 1978 European Cup final. She made an impression alright!

We'd known Graeme at Middlesbrough and knew he was a good player. What we didn't realise until we saw him up close is that, actually, he was a brilliant player. On the field he had great determination. He wouldn't exactly bollock you for a mistake but he had that withering look, a horrible glare so you knew not to do it again. Graeme would be amongst the top three mid-fielders I've played with. For me, it was Souey, Bryan Robson and Glenn Hoddle.

Charlie was tough but you had to be able to mix it, other-wise you were dead in the water. I didn't really have any regular bust-ups. You knew which players to avoid. For instance, Peter Osgood of Chelsea might have been a striker, but there were few players better at looking after themselves than Ossie. He might have been the *King of Stamford Bridge* but it didn't stop him putting it about with the so-called paupers.

Souey didn't need a little black book of people to do, like Jack Charlton was rumoured to have. He had a good memory. He could give it but he would take it and not complain, which is how it should be. Some of the tackles when he was player manager of Rangers make me wince to this day. But he would always look after you on the pitch. If someone did you – and it was allowed then – he would make sure he gained revenge. Souey never used words, just his studs. He was our midfield enforcer – the best in the business.

Every player in our era would have been sent off. There was no protection from referees.

Now you can't touch anyone.

It was a big let-down for everyone at Anfield not retaining the title that season, but Forest were worthy champions. The only way to compensate for the loss of the First Division championship was to try and win the European Cup for the second season running.

Despite not winning the title, personally, this was the season when I felt I had become a real Liverpool player.

What really changed it for me was the realisation that I could score goals. I never used to score many. It would be just five or six over the season. The turning point came, ironically enough, against Kevin Keegan's new team, SV Hamburg, in the Super Cup, a game between the European Cup winners and the European Cup Winners' Cup victors over two legs.

We'd drawn in Hamburg 1-1 and it was the return leg with Kevin back at Anfield. Before the game I was urged by Bob Paisley to get forward more and link with Kenny Dalglish. On this night, the penny dropped. I scored one during the first half and then in the second half, kicking towards the Kop, I struck another two to complete my hat-trick, including one from 25 yards. I was awarded a trophy for man of the match and the next day John Toshack said in the media that this was me at my best, scoring goals after long deep runs. We ended up stuffing Kevin's new side 6-0.

My confidence soared and after that I was usually amongst the top Liverpool scorers at the end of the season. It just dawned on me that I could do more in the opposition box.

The season ended with the European Cup final at Wembley against FC Bruges.

To be honest, it was a horrible game. There was Kenny's winning goal in the 1-0 success – and that was about it. I played my part in the goal, chasing the ball before it was clipped into Kenny by Souey before our number seven dinked it into the net.

The rest of the game wasn't pretty. From the first minute, Bruges played for penalties. I had a chance to score with only the keeper to beat after running from the halfway line. I should have played it for Jimmy Case to tap in, instead I shot. Even now I get annoyed with myself. What the hell was I thinking? I blasted it and hit their keeper on the leg.

The game was crap, but we won the European Cup again which was what really mattered – and for the second year running. I suppose it doesn't matter how you've won it.

Nothing was going to dampen the celebrations. With it being at Wembley the Liverpool fans were everywhere. It was brilliant going around the edge of the pitch with the fantastic trophy. Red everywhere.

The celebrations were better. There was another magnificent banquet which, like in Rome, was gatecrashed by Liverpool fans. Once again, the food didn't last long!

We stayed in the bar until around 4am. We weren't too clever when it was time to travel home for the victorious procession around Liverpool, although this time there was no repeat of the St. George's Hall incident. I was still blitzed though and I can't remember how I got home!

Bob Paisley, as usual, didn't let his hair down. He was already preparing for pre-season training. "Well done, see you next season" was about as gushing as he got. He wasn't one of the great speakers. In fact, he didn't like speaking much.

When managers go on the TV nowadays, they will be dressed up in the latest suits. Bob would just have his smoking jacket and slippers on as he talked to the cameras. I don't think he was ever comfortable with the media. He was okay with the local reporters but seemed to be threatened when the big hitters from London came up. He would open up more to the local lads.

Bob would rather watch the horse racing on the telly with me before games. He loved horse racing and even ended up owning a few horses. He was close to the trainer Frankie Carr and jockey Frankie Dare. While everyone got on planes to go abroad for their summer break, Bob would go across the Mersey to Frankie Carr's stables and ride out some of the horses.

He would often come into the dressing room and declare: "Frankie fancies a horse to win."

Back would come the reply: "Which Frankie?"

"You know, Frankie doin's! He's got a good horse."

You were often none the wiser.

Despite winning the European Cup, you wouldn't get any medals until the start of pre-season training. Even then there was no ceremony. They would be in a box and Ronnie Moran would just come around at Melwood and hand them out. No sooner had they been around your neck than they were being collected and put away by the club.

Ronnie would dole them out saying: "There's yours, there's yours. Now forget about them, it's a new season starting from today. Thanks boys."

He would go around to each player. "How many games did you play?" "Nine." "Oh, you don't get one." He would then move on to the next player.

Ronnie was hard at times, he liked a shout. If there were any arguments between players and staff they would involve Ronnie. Often a player would be confronted with the statement from Ronnie: "You need to buck up, you're bloody useless!"

TERRY MAC

I'm certain Bob and Ronnie didn't agree on everything, but you would never see them disagreeing in front of the players. That would undermine the leadership as far as the players were concerned.

Ronnie was hard as nails as a coach and as a player. It's tragic to think he is now in a care home suffering from dementia. He was a great person at Anfield. It's beyond belief when you see how vulnerable the likes of Ronnie, Ray Kennedy and Tommy Smith have become over the years.

But someone like Roy Evans looks like he is still in his twenties. Roy has hardly changed a single bit.

CHAPTER 10

INVISIBLE MAN

WHEN it comes to the Liverpool teams of a certain era, people will always mention those 'trendy' haircuts of the time! I'm talking of course about the famous Anfield perm.

We got our hair done at a place in Kirkby called *The Chopping Block*. Kevin Keegan had been the first to go for the permed look which was to become the fashion for many of the footballers of that era. Getting on the coach for an away game if you had just visited the hairdressers was horrendous. The first time I did mine I was absolutely crucified by the others, but we all knew we'd get stick. The only consolation was I never thought mine was the worst. Thommo can lay claim to that, he quickly got called Shirley Temple!

The fact that we all went for the permed look, allied to the later 1990s shell suit fashion craze, was obvious fantastic material for the comedian Harry Enfield who created 'The Scousers' with their permed hair, shell suits and moustaches shouting 'Calm down! Calm down!'

Half of the team must have had moustaches. There was me, Graeme Souness, David Johnson, Alan Kennedy, Ian Rush. Even Thommo tried to grow one. I wasn't offended by Harry Enfield at all, even if one of The Scousers was called 'Te', short for Terry!

Back on the pitch, it was a great start to the next season for me, Bob Paisley calling the goal I scored in the 7-0 thumping of Spurs in August, 1978, the best he had ever seen at Anfield. You don't get higher praise than that. Most of the fans believe it was my finest goal, although I have other memorable ones, the Rome goal in 1977 as well as my FA Cup semi-final goal against Everton in the same year and a volley at Tottenham in 1980.

What was also great about the 7-0 victory was Spurs had in their ranks that day two of Argentina's World Cup winners, Ossie Ardiles and Ricky Villa. They had a fantastic team which also included Glenn Hoddle and Steve Perryman, so to lose like they did was incredible. I don't think Ossie and Ricky had ever seen anything like it and for me to score the seventh goal to place the seal on a great day was incredible.

I saw Ossie a few years later and in his broken English he told me "Bloody hell, when we went to your place and lost 7-0, bloody hell!" He obviously hasn't forgotten it to this day – a game I'm sure he would love to forget.

For Bob to say what he did made the hairs stand up on the back of my neck. He might have eulogised about the goal to everyone else but all he said to me after the game in the dressing room was, "Look, Terry, you can do that all the time. You can score goals like that if you are prepared to work."

That was part of another successful League campaign in which we won the First Division title with a record points total, amassing 68 when it was two points for a win. We only conceded 16 goals, four at Anfield. Clem weighed in with 28 clean sheets from 42 games. That told you everything about what a good side we were. What was amazing, especially when you compare it to today's football, was the fact we only used 16 players. That is beyond belief, especially when you remember some of the tackles that players got away with.

Some of them weren't really tackles, they were full blooded assaults! That was the way it was. You might get up to three warnings and then you would get booked. Now in many cases you get a yellow straight away.

The worst thing for me now is seeing the play-acting which goes on, players pretending they are hurt. It's sickening considering what used to happen. Okay, sometimes you do get caught with a nasty challenge but there are players out there who will dive at the first opportunity to try and get an opponent sent off. They know who they are. It's disgraceful.

Francis Lee had a bit of a reputation during our days of going to ground easily. He was known as 'Lee Won Pen', but he was the exception rather than the rule. It's an epidemic in today's football and to a large extent you have to blame the foreign players because that's the way many of them have been brought up, to dive. Any contact, go down.

The worst foul against me came from Spurs' Terry Yorath, who had a reputation for taking no prisoners.

It was a game at Anfield and the ball had come across into the penalty area only for Terry to fly at me with both feet and smash me to the ground as he collided into the back of my legs. I was splattered all over the floor, but he didn't even receive a booking.

Another was at home to Swansea in 1981, the day after Bill Shankly's funeral, when John Toshack was player-manager for them. I'd just stuck away my second successful penalty of the game, a 2-2 draw, and was picking the ball up to take it back to the centre circle when their keeper Dai Davies just booted me after telling me where to go, leaving me sprawling in agony in the back of the net. Ronnie Moran ran on to the pitch screaming at the referee before he eventually turned his attentions to me and treated me in his role as a physio. It was a hard, hard game.

Looking at those stats from the 1978/79 season reminded you how good we were at defending as well as going forward. In effect we had eight defenders, the four at the back and the four midfielders. When we needed to, we would get behind the ball and defend for our lives.

Then, in goal, Clem was the original ball-playing goalkeeper. He was at it long before Pep Guardiola insisted his keepers were good with the ball at their feet. Can you imagine just four goals conceded in 21 home games? Incredible. He was the best. Peter Shilton was good, but I would take Clem any day of the week.

We might have been successful in the First Division that season, but Forest put us out in the first round of the European Cup.

We went to their place in the first leg and weren't too bothered when we went a goal down. In fact, Emlyn and Thommo kept reminding the Forest players of that. They certainly let them have it back when Colin Barrett, of all people, made it 2-0 with a spectacular volley near the end. The second goal really killed us because it meant in the second leg at Anfield, Forest could afford to sit back and absorb the pressure with the cushion of a two-goal lead. We were out after a goalless second leg at our place.

As well as Chris Woods emerging, Forest unearthed another unknown, Garry Birtles, who cost Clough just £2,000 from non-league football. Garry has become a good mate of mine over the years. He became a really good striker and, of course, went to Manchester United, although things didn't really work out for him at Old Trafford.

Cloughie and his sidekick Peter Taylor were the masters of psychology. They were always meaty affairs against Forest. Players left their foot in during tackles. Forest had some tough characters like Larry Lloyd, Kenny Burns (who would kick his granny!), Archie Gemmill – another tough so and so – and John McGovern. Most of them came from teams who didn't want them, so they all had something to prove, a siege mentality which served them well.

They would be taken by Brian Clough to pubs the day before games at times. I don't think I even did that!

It was never going to last because the players who Cloughie moulded into this top side were all getting on in years and could never really be replaced. At Liverpool, we were able to keep on bringing in top players.

Every season, two or three players were brought in who would eventually improve the team. Mostly they became regulars. Players like Alan Kennedy joined us. He was quick and had followed the same route to Liverpool as me, having played first for Newcastle United. He also had the job of replacing Joey Jones who was a massive fans' favourite. They loved him. That was difficult for Alan, but he ended up winning them over. He certainly did when he scored the winning goal in the 1981 European Cup final.

The 1979/80 season got off to a great start with me scoring twice at Wembley when we beat Arsenal 3-1 in the Charity Shield. I had all my family there. I was looking for them each time I scored but couldn't see them in the 100,000 crowd.

A full Wembley is something else, a ground where it never stopped being a thrill to play at. The stadium was showing its age, even back then, but to play there – for club or country – was the ultimate ambition. Scoring goals at Wembley never got boring. My first was a long-range effort that summed us up at the time; we only needed half a chance and when I was put through on goal early on, I just pulled the trigger with my left foot from outside the box and Pat Jennings stood no chance.

We were unstoppable that day. Kenny scored a wonderful weaving goal and then set me up for a third – proving again why he was the Footballer of the Year.

After the match, I was given permission by Bob Paisley to stay behind in London for the weekend with my family to celebrate. We were up until around 4am downing the beers, although the next morning wasn't so clever. A lot of people might have let it go to their heads, scoring two goals at Wembley. I just took it in my stride and wanted to be with my family and close friends.

This was just the start of things to come in an amazing season which saw me win the PFA Player of the Year and the FWA

Footballer of the Year awards. I was the first to win the two in the same season, although I was also involved in a Merseyside derby controversy in the October.

It's not exactly something I'm proud of, but I made a bit of Anfield history by becoming the first Liverpool player to be sent off in a Merseyside derby in the 20th century. My big mate Garry Stanley joined me by replicating that fact with Everton.

There was a big melee, a right free-for-all after Garry had gone through David Johnson. The usual suspects were soon on the scene, Jimmy Case, Graeme Souness for us. Everyone quickly dived in, punching and pushing.

I joined in and ended up hitting Garry in the mouth – I still think I've got the indentation of one of his teeth on my knuckle. It was ridiculous because the pair of us must have been the softest players on the pitch when it comes to being physical, but we were both dismissed.

One thing it didn't do was alter our friendship because that night we met up for a drink in Liverpool. In fact, when we were going down the tunnel after being sent off, we were arranging where to hook up later for a good night out. We ended up having a few beers.

It was a shock to read the newspapers the next day and learn that no-one else had been sent off that century in a derby. That was incredible when you think of all the hard knocks who have been in combat down the years then two wusses like myself and Garry have to make the walk of shame down the tunnel.

Even on that day, you had the likes of Mick Lyons and Souey weighing in. Probably the referee was too frightened to send them off.

Bob Paisley didn't say a word afterwards to me because he

knew the referee could have sent 10 players off following that bust up. We were the scapegoats. The game ended 2-2 and I think there was even a female streaker on the pitch that day!

The PFA dinner was later that season and I got the call from Cliff Lloyd, who was secretary of the PFA, that I was amongst the six nominees for the award. The talk in the papers before had been that it would end up being between me and Glenn Hoddle for the trophy.

Shortly before, I hadn't done my cause any harm by scoring a really good goal in a victory against Glenn's Tottenham at White Hart Lane in the sixth round of the FA Cup.

To be honest, it didn't bother me if I won the award or not. I wasn't going to lose any sleep over it. I actually thought that maybe Glenn deserved to win it because he was such a great player, skilful, with a great passing game. He was a god at Spurs. Kenny Dalglish and David Johnson were also deservedly in the top six. Kenny had had another season to remember, a player who continued to develop towards legend status.

They wanted us to all go down for the presentation in London on a Sunday night, but that was a problem. Sunday is one of my big nights out. I would always go out to Quarry Green with my dad and family members. I'd be missing my 20 pints! I know I drank too much but that's how it was and it kept me sane mixing with the people there. They were just down-to-earth characters who wouldn't go running to the papers with stories.

So I thought 'I'm not going to London'. I've never wanted to be the centre of attention. Awards were for other players, not me. I've never ever felt special. It's why it's taken until now to write my book.

I spoke to the Liverpool secretary Peter Robinson and told him I didn't fancy it. He said I had to go. Cliff Lloyd from the PFA had also heard I wasn't coming and came on the phone saying I had to go. Again, I told him that it wasn't my scene, I didn't like things like that and the only way I was going was if I had actually won the award.

Anyhow, he kept going on and on and in the end said, "Terry, I REALLY think you should come down." I knew then I had won it.

They sent a private plane for myself, Kenny Dalglish, David Johnson and Roy Evans. I didn't even have a drink because I was already dreading having to get up and make an acceptance speech. I knew I couldn't get up there drunk and make a fool of myself.

The award was handed over by the MP Norman St John-Stevas. To be honest, I didn't have a clue who the hell he was. I hadn't enjoyed eating my meal, I hadn't really wanted to be there. The only people who kept me there were Kenny, The Doc and Roy.

I was so nervous as I moved towards the stage, people slapping me on the back. I cuddled the trophy while I muttered something along the lines of 'I couldn't have achieved this without my team-mates'. I couldn't wait to sit down.

Being a footballer and playing in front of 40,000 every week is one thing, having to stand up in a room full of my mates and fellow professionals trying to make a decent speech is quite another.

It all got too much and a few moments after receiving the award, I decided I'd had enough. I told the three of them that we were off. I didn't want to hang around a minute longer.

So, long before the night ended, we were in a car going towards the airport. As soon as we landed back in Liverpool I shot off to Quarry Green.

I walked into the social club at 11.30pm with the trophy and it was still full. They were all cheering and I stayed there until 4am, even though I knew I was training the next morning. That's just who I was; a lad from Kirkby who wanted to be on the ale in Liverpool, not on a stage in London. Quarry Green was my environment, not some posh hotel in the West End.

I felt sorry for the lads running behind me in the warm-up at training the next day. The beer fumes could have knocked them out, although I reckon by then they were used to it.

I look back on it now and think it was a proud moment in my career, but at the time I hadn't really recognised the significance. While that achievement could have turned some people into big time Charlies, that wasn't me because I wouldn't have won that award without the other 10 players in the Liverpool team.

I didn't mean to come over as arrogant with my lack of regard for the awards circus and, if nothing else, at least I turned up for the PFA awards – unlike the Football Writers' Footballer of the Year dinner a few weeks later.

I got a phone call in the players' lounge at Anfield from Norman Wynne of the *Sunday People*. "Terry, you've won the FWA award," he said. "You've played well enough to deserve it all season."

Again, I didn't really get why a rag-bag like me could be the player of the year and, once again, I couldn't really get interested in it all.

The awards were on a Thursday night and just a few days

before I thought, 'I don't want to go'. The day before, I had been to Chester races with my brother Robert and some friends. We had a great day, loved every minute of it and when we stumbled back to Kirkby, of course we ended up in Quarry Green and stayed until around 3am.

There was more racing at Chester the next day but I was due in London and was getting a train from Liverpool at midday. I was dreading it. I had my suit with me and Robert drove me to Lime Street Station. The departures board said my train had been delayed by 45 minutes. That was all the excuse I needed.

"Fuck this," I told Robert. "I'm not waiting here for 45 minutes – we're back off to Chester mate."

I rang Peter Robinson to let him know. "Peter, what would happen if I didn't turn up?" I asked.

"Well, nothing I suppose," he replied. Again, that was all I needed.

"I'm not going then," I said. Next stop Chester.

Peter tried to tell me I was foolish to not accept the award in person but I'd made up my mind. Little did I know that Bob Paisley had agreed to present the award!

On the night when I hadn't turned up, Bob announced to everyone at the dinner: "He's famous for his blind side runs. I can assure you this is the last one like this he will make."

That evidently brought the house down. Later that night when I arrived back at Quarry Green after another day's racing I wondered if I'd done the right thing.

Bob never said a word to me about it. He knew it hadn't been a malicious act, it was just the way I was. He knew I wasn't a nasty fella. You never know, one day I might turn up and accept it – a few years late, I know.

TERRY MAC

I understand that I let the FWA down. To be honest, I hadn't really appreciated the history and significance of the award.

I would now like to apologise for all those people who voted for me because I do regret it now – but you can't turn the clock back, can you?

CHAPTER 11

TIME'S UP

A LOT of people have heard of The Liverpool Way and I certainly wondered what it was in my early days at the club. In a sense, it is as much a state of mind as it is a way of playing. It is about a simplicity and an honesty in everything you do. And that includes bringing in new players to the club.

Bob Paisley seemed to be especially good at that; it was his forte, really. He had good people around him like scouts Geoff Twentyman and Tom Saunders and between them they always did their homework. It wasn't always a case of getting the best players, it was also a question of could they fit in to life at Liverpool?

For that, he would spend hours in discussions with Geoff and Tom and also trust the opinions of Joe Fagan, Ronnie Moran and Roy Evans.

The process would start with the realisation that they needed a player to put pressure on an older established star. They would all give their opinions on who they had seen and those players would then be continually watched and Bob would also venture out to games whenever he could.

There were very few you would call mistakes when it came to actual signings. The only one I can remember in my time was Frank McGarvey. He was a good player, but not what you would call a Liverpool player. He had been signed from St. Mirren but didn't seem to grow at Liverpool and within a year he was on his way to Celtic, where he fitted in straightaway. He just didn't hack it at Liverpool.

Apart from Frank, I can't recall any other top line failures in my era. There was never any need to panic in the transfer market because potential signings were usually targeted around two years in advance and even when some of us signed – and that included me, Ray Kennedy and Ian Rush – there was still plenty of work to do to unleash our potential.

In the dressing room, it's well known that Bob delivered his message in an understated manner. He always said that he refused to scream and bawl at players because he believed that if you talk quietly and considerately, people will listen more intently. To be honest, at times, with his North East drawl, it was hard to pick up on what he was actually saying.

While he was telling you things he would often forget a name and so if he went through the opposition he would say "aye, watch out for him, that Charlie doin's an' that." There was so much respect for him, it was like listening to your favourite grandfather.

Every time he spoke, you listened. We were losing 1-0 to Spurs at half-time in the final of what was then known as the Milk Cup in 1982 and he told us, "You're turning the milk sour." We ended up winning it. Under Paisley, Liverpool won 19 trophies. It was unbelievable. Shanks laid the foundations and took it to a certain height, but Bob went even higher. You were going from Ben Nevis to Everest.

What Bob achieved as a manager will never be repeated anywhere, never mind at Liverpool. I know now we're in an era of high profile managers but Bob was never that, despite what he achieved. He was humble, just a quiet man from a North East mining village.

We had our team meetings on a Friday when he would announce the team. Yet, with Bob, you never knew if you would be in it or not as his mannerisms never gave much away. He'd stand next to the treatment table in the dressing room, which used to have a mini-pitch template laid out on it and he would start going through the side, pushing little magnetic counters here and there. You just had to wait your turn to see if you were in.

With Bob, though, it was never totally clear.

"We'll have Jimmy and that one, and that, here," he'd start. "Then there's Phil here and David and that there." Sometimes we'd be confused as there were two Phils for a start – Phil Neal and Phil Thompson – and two Davids, Johnson and Fairclough! Sometimes, the only confirmation was when you went into the dressing room on matchday and found your boots under the peg where you would normally sit. You knew then you were playing!

Some of the advice was just as patchy. He would tell Jimmy Case, "Keep your high balls low" and he once warned Phil

Thompson that his opposite number was "not quick, but he's nippy." What did that mean? We just knew what he was like and there was the utmost respect for him, despite his quirkiness.

We would have a laugh privately and some of us would take him off, complete with his sayings but we'd give everything for him out on the pitch. He just did things in his own way. His record is there for everyone to see. Six League championships. Three European Cups. One UEFA Cup. Three League Cups. Six Charity Shields.

I never saw Bob lose his temper, although he could swear. One of his favourite sayings if you had done something wrong was "You'll get the fucking game done away with!"

One time, David Johnson and I were going back to our hotel rooms after a night out in London when we decided to have a fruit fight, taking aim at one another along the corridor with the apples, oranges and bananas which had been left in our rooms.

The next minute, one of the doors along the corridor opened and there was Bob in his pyjamas yelling, "What the hell are you playing at man? It's not a party. You'll get us bloody done man." I didn't know whether to laugh at the sight of Bob in his pyjamas or worry about my future. But to be fair to Bob, once he'd let off a bit of steam, that was it.

Another time, I remember we were on a plane going on a trip abroad to the Middle East. We were mixed up with ordinary passengers and to help relieve the boredom, a few drinks were taken.

In front of us was a bloke with a bald head. There's me, Jocky Hansen, Phil Thompson and Alan Kennedy and when our meals came we wondered whether we could put a pea on his head.

We managed to do it. Then next came a carrot. It was Alan Kennedy's turn and he somehow placed a potato on the guy's nut.

By the end, he almost had a full dinner on his head but was still none the wiser. Suddenly, Bob Paisley realised what was going on from further down the plane and he got up from his seat shouting, "Bloody hell man, what are you doing?"

Luckily he couldn't get past Graeme Souness who was next to him. Graeme said he would sort it. All you could hear was Bob yelling, "Bloody hell man, they'll get us thrown off the plane!"

Although Bob was thought of as everyone's favourite grandad, he could be harsh and was prepared to move players on when he thought their time had come. Just before I left, Liverpool got rid of a few established players, including David Johnson. The Doc could have signed a new two-year contract but at the time he wasn't playing regularly, so he asked Bob if he put pen to paper would he be playing in many games. Back came the reply, "I'll just use you when I need you." So he went. You just had to accept that was the way it was.

Liverpool were ruthless when it came to ending players' Anfield careers. It didn't matter what you had done. There were always players waiting to take your place and it was plain for everyone to see that Craig Johnston had been brought in from Middlesbrough to replace me, although I always felt I was a better player than Craig.

I never won the FA Cup while I was at Liverpool and 1980 was tough to take because we lost to Arsenal over four games in the semi-finals. I didn't play in the first game at Hillsborough because I was injured and we ended up drawing 0-0. There were then two more matches at Villa Park, both 1-1 draws, before we eventually lost 1-0 in the third replay at Highfield Road after a goal from Brian Talbot.

The quarter-final had seen me score a goal which is still talked about to this day as one of the competition's greatest strikes. It was against Spurs at White Hart Lane.

When the ball came out to me just outside the area, I flicked it up and thought 'why not, let's have a crack'. I knew as soon as I connected it had a chance because it felt just right and soared high into the net. There was even applause from some of the Tottenham fans. I seemed to enjoy scoring against Spurs but that was all forgotten when we went out of the FA Cup against Arsenal in the fourth match of an exhausting sequence. Can you imagine playing that many matches now? We were having to play games within two days of each other. There would be uproar today.

To be honest, for the team we had in those days, we should have won even more. Not winning the FA Cup in my time was a major disappointment. We had been the favourites to beat Arsenal, even though they had good players like Liam Brady and Frank Stapleton.

We also lost in the European Cup in 1979-80 – going out in the first round to Dinamo Tblisi. We won the first leg 2-1 but got trounced 3-0 away from home and that was the end of that.

At least 1979-80 brought another First Division title – and my big mate David Johnson ended up as our top scorer with 21 goals. He was quick, very good in the air, brave and could always score goals. He was never afraid to get stuck in when needed and he was a great foil for Kenny Dalglish. People go on about the partnership between Dalglish and Ian Rush, who was to come into the picture more and more throughout the '80s, but The Doc and Kenny weren't a bad combination at all and David didn't get the recognition he deserved.

The next season, 1980-81, we somehow only managed to finish fifth in the League which, if I'm honest, was not compensated by winning the European Cup for the third time in five years, plus the League Cup. I also ended up as leading scorer in the League with 13.

Even the fact that I played 60 games for Liverpool that season – the most of my career on Merseyside – didn't alter the fact that I was part of a side that had only finished fifth, not deemed good enough at the time. At Anfield, you were judged on where you finished in the League.

None of us took our starting places for granted. Complacency was something that wasn't tolerated. I never once thought I had arrived as a top Liverpool player.

It prompted Bob to shift some more players out and change things around. Jimmy Case, Ray Kennedy, myself – our days were numbered, or at least drawing to a close. Then Clem decided to go at the end of the season. At Liverpool you have to keep on winning, it's as simple as that.

New lads such as Ronnie Whelan and Ian Rush arrived. I'd been at Anfield a while now and I felt like their grandad.

I would take Rushy and Ronnie to nightclubs in Liverpool. We also used to go to a snooker place. Playing snooker was secondary, the drinking was the priority. We would stay until the early hours of the morning, sometimes as late as 4am. I was supposed to be setting an example to the pair of them – some example! At least they learned how to drink – something which has stayed with them for a considerable amount of years.

Rushy was a quiet lad, coming in from Chester City. It was the same with Ronnie who came from Home Farm in Ireland. It must have been hard for them. I think they appreciated that we took them out. With some of my drinking mates starting to go steady with girls, I had been on the look out for new drinking partners. They didn't take much persuading.

On the field, Ronnie was a quick learner. I had a good season with him. He grasped what was needed to be done and went from good to excellent very quickly while it took Rushy longer. You knew, though, with Rushy it was going to happen for him because he was quick and could score with both feet. At first, he was a bit shy but we soon knocked that out of him with the help of a few pints. Of course, Rushy went on to become the club's record goalscorer and he's one of the best finishers I've seen, without a shadow of a doubt.

The 1980-81 season started well for me. I scored the only goal in the Charity Shield when we beat West Ham at Wembley, but it was in the European Cup that we really started to shine.

We met Oulu Palloseura, a little club from Finland, in the first round and could only draw 1-1 over there with me scoring the goal, but in the second leg at home we thrashed them 10-1 and I helped myself to a hat-trick. Then I scored a wonder goal in the next round at Aberdeen. Kenny found Dave Johnson, who played it first time to me to run on to and from a ridiculous angle, I chipped the goalkeeper with my left foot. Some people say this was better than the goal in the 7-0 win over Spurs. I'm not sure; I'll happily take both!

Aberdeen had a decent side under Alex Ferguson, top players like Gordon Strachan, Willie Miller, Alex McLeish and Mark

Muzzy...is it?: Craig Johnston fakes it with Alan Kennedy, Graeme Souness and me

The big picture: Ray Clemence, Kenny Dalglish and I admire some familiar artwork

Goal buzz: I loved scoring goals and got 81 of them for Liverpool

Low-key farewell: My final Reds appearance came against Dundalk in 1982 in front of only 12,021 fans

International recognition: Wearing a cap received after representing England against Wales

Three Lions laughs: Paul Mariner was good fun on England duty...Kevin doesn't seem so convinced though!

Shady characters: With David Johnson and Mick Mills

Mane man: There was a lot of hair on show when England beat Northern Ireland in May 1979

Arctic blast: I smashed home this goal in Augsburg, West Germany, in a B international in 1978

Making a point: Directing Eric Gates and Bryan Robson

Red and Whites: Liverpool's England contingent in 1977

Aye, aye captain: On tour with England in 1981 in Budapest

The great wall: I don't know if I was more worried about a Brazilian free-kick or getting back up to Kirkby before last orders when England faced the South Americans at Wembley in 1981

Full stretch: In action against Scotland

World Cup walkabout: Me, Kevin, Bryan Robson and Mick Mills head out for a stroll during the 1982 World Cup in Spain

Perfect match: In June 1984 I married my lovely wife Carole. We had two sons, Neale and Greg, and a daughter, Rachel

Great reception: It was nice to have a familiar face with a North East accent as Alan Kennedy accompanied me as I signed for Newcastle again in 1982

Back in the black and white: David McCreery (top) joined me in the pursuit of success for the Newcastle fans

We're going up: A salute for the travelling Geordies as a 2-2 draw at Huddersfield sealed promotion in May 1984

Sheikh them up: After the press reported potential interest in Kevin Keegan from Saudi Arabia, I dressed up as a sheikh and pretended to make an offer to the Newcastle board in 1983

Take that: Kevin is ready to join in the celebrations after I scored at Fulham in 1983

Young pups: With fresh-faced stars Chris Waddle and Peter Beardsley in 1984

Hitting the bar: My shot strikes the woodwork in a 1-1 draw with Blackburn en route to promotion in 1984. When we finally did it one supporter (below right) wanted me to know how happy she was!

Spot the difference: Signing part of a Newcastle United mural at a play area in the city

Looking knackered!: The final stop in my playing career was at APOEL in Cyprus from 1985-87

McGee. It finished 1-0 to us up there and we won 4-0 in the next leg to shut them up because people were talking about them as the next big thing.

I scored again in the next round against CSKA Sofia, a 5-1 win at Anfield, effectively killing the tie. We managed to win 1-0 over there to set up a semi-final against Bayern Munich. We were up against it because we could only draw 0-0 on Mersey-side in the first leg. Not only that, we had been hit by critical injuries which meant that Richard Money was drafted in to play while Colin Irwin also started.

So, going in to the second leg, Bayern were the favourites, especially in front of 77,000 screaming Germans.

We discovered that Bayern had placed pamphlets on each seat in the Olympiastadion with directions of how to get to Paris, where the final was being staged, and where to stay. It was revealed in the press and was quickly seized upon by Bob. "They think they're already going to Paris," he told us. "Let's show these Germans!" It immediately wound us up.

That night in Munich showed the character and camaraderie of the club. I even played with a dislocated thumb. In the first leg, I had gone crashing over their keeper and landed painfully on my thumb and I was in agony. I came off for treatment but Bob kept telling me it was fine. "There's nothing wrong with you, get back on the pitch," he shouted. Turned out it was dislocated. It was still bandaged up for the return leg.

Ironically, it was a similar injury the following season which indicated that my time at Liverpool was coming to an end. Bob would often take us after big games to a hotel in north Wales near Llangollen, the Bryn Howel. It was like a bonding exercise. The players would have a bite to eat and then it was off to a pub at the top of this big hill. It was pitch black, no lights and although we would get a lift there, we would have to make our own way back. This night, I'm the last to leave at around 3am after a few drinks too many. I was all over the place and the next thing I know, I'm falling over a hedge and land in a field. The problem was I had landed on my thumb again and I certainly felt it the next day.

The club bandaged it up and a few days later we were playing West Brom. I wasn't playing too well at the time but I had declared myself fit and, like in the games against Bayern, I was going to play with it bandaged up. This time, though, Bob decided I wasn't able to play. "You can't go running around with that on," he insisted. I felt it was actually an excuse to leave me out.

That West Brom game is one Alan Hansen likes to remind me of. Before kick-off I was sat in the dressing room, frustrated at only being on the bench, and piped up: "Lads, this crossword clue in the programme – *Liverpool striker, four letters?*" There was a moment of silence before I answered the question myself: "None!" I shouted in full earshot of Bob and the staff. Jocky always says only I could get away with something like that, although it possibly didn't improved my chances of staying at Liverpool!

Anyway, I certainly wasn't left out in Munich on what was one of our greatest nights. Already under-strength, we lost Kenny to injury after just nine minutes with young Howard Gayle coming on, but we fought on and with seven minutes to go, Ray Kennedy gives us the lead. Four minutes later it's 1-1 after a goal from Karl-Heinz Rummenigge and they are now just one goal from going through.

Don't forget, we'd achieved a lot in a fairly short time and so belief coursed through the team. We weren't a side to start panicking. If needed, we were capable of seeing games out. In any case it wouldn't have mattered what Bob, Ronnie or anyone had shouted in the final minutes because we couldn't have heard them! There was a great big running track between the dug-outs and us so it was impossible to hear any instructions. You've got to work out things for yourselves on nights like that.

We held on and afterwards, in the showers, Clem was bouncing, singing this victory song, a rousing chorus of *You'll Never Walk Alone*, so we joined in. It was a great return journey with plenty of drink. We were in another European Cup final, this time against Real Madrid. They were a good team with the likes of Vincente Del Bosque and Laurie Cunningham in the side but we were expected to win.

It wasn't the best of games, not helped by the Parc des Princes pitch which was rutted. Before the game we were busily having to place tape over the Umbro logo on our shirts because back then UEFA didn't allow any advertising. So there we were playing in a European Cup final with sticky plasters all over our shirts. Ridiculous.

Whenever Real Madrid threatened, Clem was at his best – in his last game for us. There was nothing in it really but Alan Kennedy was to end up as the hero with a goal not many of us would have seen coming, least of all him.

The most dangerous moment came after we scored. We went rushing over to Alan like a bunch of wild banshees but he had rushed to the edge of this big dry moat. In jumping on to his back to celebrate, some of us almost fell into it which wouldn't have been very clever. Once again our fans had been brilliant, taking over Paris. I was delighted for them. After all, I was one of them. "Well done. Yous lot have deserved it," said good old Bob in the dressing room after his third European Cup triumph.

There were the usual after-match celebrations but, for once, I didn't go out. I stayed in the hotel, doing it by the book – but with a few drinks!

Even when we were winning the European Cup, I always thought I was just one game away from being left out of the side and as we went into the 1981-82 season, the writing did appear to be on the wall for some of us, including me.

As happens at all clubs, there were more new faces like Mark Lawrenson and Craig Johnston while Ian Rush and Ronnie Whelan continued to make names for themselves. I found out I was being substituted on more occasions than I would have liked and that included in the League Cup final against Spurs, which we ended up winning 3-1 after extra time.

We were losing 1-0 and during the second half Bob decided to bring me off. I had been crap, but I wasn't the only one. We had all been rubbish. Sometimes you just can't get involved in the game but before I came off I felt I had been getting more on the ball and I had hit the top of the bar. I felt I was growing into the game.

Suddenly I looked over to the touchline to see my number go up. I was fuming and as I came towards the bench I shouted: "Fucking typical, it's me again." Joe Fagan told me to shut up. I booted the water bucket. "The same fucking numbers come up all the time – eight and 10," I bellowed. They were mine and Jimmy Case's. It didn't spoil the victory for me, but I knew the end of my time was getting closer and closer.

Continually bringing in new players was one of the secrets of Liverpool's success. Ray Kennedy had left in January to join up with John Toshack at Swansea and we now had Bruce Grobbelaar in goal after Clem had left for Spurs. He would keep us amused by telling us stories about when he was in the Rhodesian, now Zimbabwean, army. A great character. He wasn't as good as Clem but who could be? All goalkeepers make mistakes, it just seems that Bruce's were always highlighted because he was so high profile.

We clinched another title against Tottenham with a 3-1 victory at Anfield. I was sitting in the stand rather than being on the pitch. I'd been dropped for the Manchester United game at Old Trafford in April – Craig Johnston came in and scored the winner – and hadn't been selected to play since. I knew then that the end of my Liverpool career was looming even though it had been my best ever season for goals, hitting 20 in all competitions.

In fact, I'd already had the opportunity to leave Liverpool for a lot more money.

I was sitting at the back of the coach going to an away match when Bob motioned to me to come and sit next to him. "They've been on. The Froggies. Them who make the wine," he said.

I didn't have a clue who he was talking about. He then remembered. "You know them wine makers, Bordeaux."

"Do you want me to go Bob?" I asked, straight out.

He just looked at me without uttering a word and that told me no-one was going to stand in my way. But even though there was more money on offer than I was earning at Liverpool, I believed I was still better than Craig Johnston, the player brought in to eventually replace me. I thought 'I'll show them'.

Of course, money is important, but I still wanted to win things with Liverpool.

I stayed that season and collected another First Division title winning medal but in September, 1982, just a month into the following season, I was off. It wasn't exactly a triumphant farewell to the club I had served for eight years.

When your time is up, it's up, there is no sentiment.

I could have stayed and possibly have been awarded a testimonial. I still had two years left on my contract. But once it's in your mind that they don't really want you anymore, it's time to move on.

I told Thommo and Jocky Hansen that it looked like I was on my way. Obviously they didn't want me to go but in football you get used to players leaving – it's just part of being a footballer. It's a harsh business at times.

There was no bitterness. I knew Craig was going to eventually replace me but I got on fine with him. He was a great lad, probably as mad as me, always prepared to act as the joker. Playing for Liverpool was something I could only have dreamed of, representing the club I had watched as a lad, hemmed into the boys' pen on the Kop. I enjoyed every minute.

And if it hadn't have been for Newcastle coming in for me with Kevin Keegan already there, then I probably wouldn't have gone when I did.

Kevin had signed at the beginning of the 1982/83 season. I had received a call from my old Newcastle manager Joe Harvey asking me if I would be interested in returning to Tyneside. Arthur Cox was now the manager.

I'd actually watched the highlights of Kevin's debut at St. James' Park on TV. The ground was full, Kevin scored the only goal in a 1-0 win over QPR and I thought to myself 'Kevin is going to get that place going'. I never really thought at that time that I would be involved. But watching the game on telly certainly gave me a tingle down the spine and two or three weeks later, I was getting the call from Joe.

I said I would have a chat with Arthur, no problem, so I drove up to the North East with permission from Liverpool. I met Arthur and Joe in a hotel. They were desperate for me to join up again with Kevin.

I didn't sign straight away because I needed to sort out a few things with Liverpool. I went to see Peter Robinson and told him I didn't want to hang on and play in the reserves, I wanted to play first team football but knew I was due some financial reward and they offered me a loyalty bonus, which I accepted.

There's no great emotion involved when it comes to settling the financial side of things. You are just a commodity. One day you might be an idol, the next they want you off the books. It's life and it's not just related to football. I wanted the best deal I could get and then it would be time to move on.

Before leaving I played one more game, a European Cup tie against an Irish side, Dundalk, at Anfield. There were just 12,000 there and none of them would have had a clue that this was going to be my last ever Liverpool appearance.

I wish now I had done a John Aldridge and said farewell by throwing my shirt and boots into the crowd – well, if you could call it a crowd! I saw a photograph recently of that game and there's me in action in front of the Kemlyn Road stand with just one person sat in the middle!

I just walked off the pitch as normal and that's when it really hit me.

TERRY MAC

My heart was pumping knowing that Liverpool were prepared to let me go. If it hadn't have been Newcastle with Kevin up there I would have probably stayed. I went back up to the North East feeling really hurt. My family were devastated that I was going. It was horrible.

I've never really had the opportunity to thank the Liverpool supporters who had been great to me. I'd also loved every single minute of going in for training at Liverpool. The banter in the dressing room had been great, you never stopped laughing. The camaraderie was incredible but now the stark realisation set in that I would no longer be part of it.

I remember getting changed for that last game thinking that I didn't really want to play against Dundalk at a ghostly Anfield. Bob didn't really say anything. There's no sentiment. Your time is up and that is that.

CHAPTER 12

ENGLAND

MY first call up for England came in September, 1977, shortly after we had won the European Cup when I was 25 years old. The friendly against Switzerland at Wembley involved new Three Lions boss Ron Greenwood calling up seven Liverpool players: Ray Clemence, Phil Neal, Emlyn Hughes, Phil Thompson, Ian Callaghan, Ray Kennedy and myself. Cally's last England cap had been 11 years before. He was different class, Cally.

I'd played in the Under 23s under Don Revie, but this was my senior breakthrough. It had been a fair wait but I was absolutely delighted.

For the Swiss game, our starting XI may have included six Liverpool players plus Kevin Keegan – who had only just left for Hamburg – but it didn't matter because we were crap. It was a goalless draw and nothing really sparked.

I don't know what it is but I'm sure I never really played as well for England as I did for Liverpool. I know I'm not alone in feeling that way.

As usual, my family made another trip to Wembley for my debut. My mum had died around three months earlier so this was a bit of a pick-me-up, although nothing of course could compensate for losing her. I wasn't anxious before kick-off – I was never really nervous, even before big games. Some players were so full of tension that they would be physically sick.

I ended up playing 25 games for England, not a great amount but 25 more than I ever thought I would manage.

Ron Greenwood was one of the nicest men you could ever wish to meet. He was good to me, a father-like figure, very knowledgeable. Everyone loved him. He took me to the 1982 World Cup finals when really he shouldn't have.

I made it into the squad for the 1980 European Championship finals but we ended up finishing third in the group behind Belgium and Italy. In the first game, against Belgium, I came on as a substitute in Turin and it ended up 1-1. I didn't play against the hosts Italy who won 1-0 to make our final game against Spain irrelevant because we couldn't qualify for the next stage. That was my best game. We won 2-1 in Naples – Ray Clemence saved a penalty – but it was a disappointing tournament, one which was also plagued by crowd problems.

We were lucky to get to Spain for the 1982 World Cup finals. The qualifying group saw us lose 2-1 in Switzerland in May '81. We were losing 2-0 when I was brought on. I scored about ten minutes into the second half, Steve Coppell playing me in.

Once we got back to 2-1 we expected to get an equaliser and maybe go on and win the game, but we lost.

And it was by the same score that we were beaten in a famous game in Norway in September '81. I started the game and Bryan Robson gave us the lead in the 15th minute, but Norway scored twice before half-time to record a shock victory.

None of us will ever forget that Norwegian commentator Bjorge Lillelien mocking us. He was shouting 'Maggie Thatcher, can you hear me? Maggie Thatcher…your boys took a hell of a beating!'

It was a tough old campaign – we also lost to Romania – and if you lose three times you wouldn't normally go through, but we qualified, sneaking into second place by beating group winners Hungary at Wembley in our final game.

When you think that England hadn't qualified for a World Cup since 1970 it was important that we got there, but to be honest, after losing my regular place in the Liverpool side, I wasn't expecting to go to Spain. Normally that would be the end of your international ambitions. Mind, a trip abroad with Liverpool almost put paid to my World Cup place anyway.

It was an end-of-season break and we were sat on the beach but having no suncream, I got burnt to a cinder. Drinking copious amounts of beer didn't help my capacity to look after myself in the blazing sun. The next day I could hardly move and to make matters worse, once we arrived back in England I was due to travel down to London with the squad to get measured up for our World Cup suits.

It was agony trying to get my jumper off before easing into the suit. Emlyn Hughes, who had witnessed at first hand my stupidity in the sun, didn't help by smacking me on the back at every opportunity. I was calling him every name imaginable peppered with plenty of expletives. He was laughing his head off.

Even though I had been measured up for a suit, I still didn't think there was any chance of me going to Spain. But Ron came up and told me I was definitely on board the plane. That was brilliant news. He told me I was great around the dressing room. He knew I wouldn't be a problem if I wasn't in the side. I couldn't thank him enough and true to his word, I went. I loved being with England because, like Liverpool, the lads loved a drink – well, half of the team was from Anfield.

The Liverpool lads would usually pile into a mini-bus to take us down to London when we were meeting up with the rest of the England squad on the Sunday. I would have had four or five pints in a social club before making the trip down south. Then it was a case of taking a couple of crates of beer and lager with us in the people carrier. We'd put them down the middle and help ourselves on the journey. You just hoped Ron or coach Don Howe wouldn't be in the hotel lobby waiting to greet you. We'd all had a big drink so it was a case of trying to appear sober.

We would have some food and be told to meet up for breakfast and training the next morning at 9am. 'Yeah, fine boss, see you then' we would reply before pretending to go up to our rooms, only to slip out to the pub.

Most of the players would end up there, not just the Liverpool contingent. Strangely, though, we would never see Glenn Hoddle or Kenny Sansom. We wondered what they were up to. Somebody told us they would sneak off to a nightclub around the Seven Sisters area, as both of them knew the territory. One day we decided to track them down. And, sure enough, there they were!

Few of us would be back at 2am, even though we were due to report for training at 9am.

I couldn't believe it one night. I was sneaking in at around 3am when who's sitting in the lobby? Ron and Don.

Ron asked me "What time do you call this?"

I could barely get any words out before he calmly added: "Speak to you tomorrow, get to bed."

I was thinking to myself 'there's still others out there in a far worse state than me!'

They didn't really want you drinking, but they knew it went on. That was the way we were and, to be fair to Ron, he knew we were bonding. We all got on.

There were no cliques. As Liverpool players we got on well with the Manchester United lads, for example. Bryan Robson had become a big mate of mine. He would drive over to Quarry Green in Kirkby and would often bring Paul McGrath and Ashley Grimes. The friendship with Robbo had developed through England get-togethers. The locals loved it, even though they played for Manchester United. Robbo was an ordinary guy just like us. We would have games of snooker together.

Some people might be surprised because of our different upbringing, but I also became big mates with Trevor Brooking who we used to call Hadleigh, after the posh character from the popular TV series of the day.

Trevor was so well spoken compared to the rest of the England boys, but we got on really well. A group of us, including Hadleigh, would often go to watch greyhound racing at Wembley Stadium on a night off. It was really enjoyable.

One evening there was myself, Kevin Keegan, Phil Thompson and Trevor and as we were coming down the steps of the stadium we noticed some spivs trying to entice you into a card game of 'chase the ace'. You were supposed to bet money on where you thought the ace would end up as one of them feverishly swapped three cards, including the ace, around. They would also employ some ringers who would 'win' substantial amounts of money for guessing correctly.

It was to lure you in and make you believe it was so easy to guess where the ace ended up. Of course, when we came to play it was completely different and we must have had mug written on our foreheads as they cleaned up. Whatever money we'd won on the dogs we'd lose on the cards, Hadleigh suffering with the rest of us.

Trevor never went drinking with us but we all liked him because he was a genuinely lovely, warm man. He got on very well with Kevin and that shows that although sport means different characters brought up in contrasting environments, you can still strike up a close friendship.

One time, Ron allowed a group of us to go to the Derby at Epsom. It was then staged on a Wednesday and Ron gave his permission providing we were back at the hotel by 6pm. We got a helicopter from the grounds of our hotel on the outskirts of London to the racecourse.

After landing, we were walking towards one of the stands when we bumped into Willie Carson, the top flat jockey who was in the race. He knew Mick Mills and told him to have a few quid on his mount Henbit. The horse won and so we all did very well and even managed to get back to the hotel before the deadline.

On another occasion, a group of us were invited to a day out at the races to go and see a horse called, wait for it…Kevin Keegan! There was myself, Bryan Robson, Phil Thompson and Joe Corrigan amongst the group. A few drinks were, of course, part of the occasion. We entered the ring and had a chat with the owner, trainer and jockey. We were then asked to carry out the tradition of helping the jockey into his saddle.

It fell to me to supply the assistance. I ended up applying too much pressure and the poor jockey was hurtled over the horse and ended up in a crumpled heap on the other side of the startled animal. We quickly made our excuses and left.

We'd also noticed that, in the meantime, Joe Corrigan had disappeared. We couldn't find him anywhere. Eventually, while walking on a field near the main grandstand, we spotted him fast asleep on the lawn.

People were having to clamber over him because, as everyone knows, Joe wasn't exactly a small figure.

Mostly, with England, I would room with my big Liverpool mate Phil Thompson, but for one game he was injured and so I travelled down to London knowing that Terry Butcher would be my unfortunate 'guest'. Big Butch also made the mistake on this occasion of coming out for a drink with a group of us. It was a typical boozy night and safe to say Butch was a bit worse for wear by the time we returned to the hotel.

There were two single beds in the room. I'm in the one by the window and in the middle of the night it's pitch dark and I can hear a rustling noise.

All I could see was a huge shadow, so I dived up and put on the light to see poor Butch being sick. He hadn't been able to find the bathroom. Sadly, the demon drink had struck to leave a mess, not to mention a stink, all over a wardrobe mirror.

Butch was a warrior on the pitch, someone you would always have by your side, but it appeared he had been no match for the drinkers in the England squad. After that night I bet he couldn't wait for Phil Thompson to get back to full fitness!

Poor Garry Birtles met the same fate when he was asked to room with me on another occasion when Thommo was out injured. I met up with Garry a few months ago and one of the first things he did was recall the night when he confessed he had never been so ill.

Again, it was another heavy drinking session with the usual suspects and the following morning in training while I was out in front as usual, breathing beer fumes over everyone during a running session, Garry was struggling in the slipstream trying desperately not to be sick.

After another England game, myself and Tony Currie found ourselves in the headlines for the wrong reasons. Neither of us even made the substitutes' bench so we took ourselves off for a drink in one of the bars. We had a right few before the kick-off, including a round or two from a journalist who was warming up for the game.

To our horror, a few days later he reported in his newspaper that we'd been drinking before and during the game. We were expecting a right rollicking but luckily nothing was said. It was a dirty trick to play on us and was disappointing because usually during that era you could strike up good relationships with football reporters.

I got on well with the regular national newspaper lads who covered Merseyside when I was a player; reporters like John Keith, Colin Wood, Matt D'Arcy, Mike Ellis. There was also Chris James who worked for the *Daily Mirror*. I don't know whether it was because Chris was under extra pressure from his office, but he would often annoy the players. Every time we had a poor result at Liverpool – and there weren't too many of them – you would wake up the next day to Chris writing in his paper about how the mighty have fallen, that the empire was crumbling. Usually, at the end of the season, we would still end up by winning the League or the European Cup. Then we would slaughter him.

Generally, though, we had a good relationship with the reporters. Now there seems a lack of trust between players and the media. With the advent of smartphones with cameras, players can't do a thing without it seemingly being reported. I would have been in the papers every day and all over Twitter!

For the 1982 World Cup, our base was in Bilbao, which was like a fortress. If we were going out for a walk we had to have armed guards, so we couldn't really get up to anything even if we had wanted to. I think we spent most of our time there playing bingo!

Although I was part of the squad I didn't make an appearance in the tournament, but I did play in a warm-up game against Iceland in Reyjkavik. I didn't know it at the time, but that was to be my 25th and final cap in an England shirt at the age of 31. Even so, I'm proud to say I was part of an England World Cup squad and I've still got the security pass with my photo and Espana '82 on it.

Unfortunately the squad Ron took to Spain wasn't in the rudest of health. Kevin had continual problems with his back and was given permission to travel to Germany to try and get it sorted. Trevor Brooking also had an injury.

We won our three games to top the group but needed to beat Spain in the second round after drawing with Germany to progress further. It was goalless and Ron Greenwood needed to gamble. He did by sending on Kevin and Trevor for the final 20 minutes – neither of them had been involved until then. Kevin had a great chance, but it passed him by and we went out.

I had become closer to Kevin through the England experience. We would play tennis and golf together and I'd always liked his patter. We also loved playing cards. He was happily married to Jean, so he wasn't part of our drinking group but I still got on great with him. He's just an unbelievably nice fella, always bubbly. We became really close when I joined him at Newcastle in 1982. With Jean back at their home in Southampton and Kevin in the North East, we would be together going to the greyhounds and horse racing. We would also play pool and snooker, just me and him.

Realistically, I knew the World Cup would be my last international involvement, although if Ron had stayed, who knows? Bobby Robson came in and immediately called time on Kevin's career – but the way it happened wasn't right and I know Bobby regretted the way it was done. The first Kevin knew that he wasn't in Bobby's squad for his first game was through the media. All it needed was a phone call from Bobby to explain that he was going in a different direction. Kevin would have understood that – but to not even get a call? Kevin was really upset about it. I never got a phone call, not that I expected one. Kevin had done a lot for his country. He had been the captain after all.

I know I've gone on about some of the drinking binges but at the same time playing for England was a serious matter. No-one wanted to miss out, even for friendlies. There was a terrific pride – it was the pinnacle of your career. I don't know if it's quite the same these days. In my first few years at Liverpool, it was a sad place to be when the likes of Ray Clemence, Phil Neal and Thommo disappeared with England. You were left behind wishing that one day you would be making the same trip, reporting for international duty. Training with just a few of the 'left-behinds' really hurt you. It certainly gave me an extra incentive to try to win a call-up for England.

After that first experience against Switzerland in 1977, I just wanted more and more of the same.

The games against Scotland were always a highlight because, of course, at Liverpool we had some big name Scots like Kenny Dalglish, Graeme Souness and Alan Hansen. The banter in the Anfield dressing room before these battles was fantastic. It was a game you didn't want to lose because the ribbing would go on for ages.

One of the best matches I played in against the Auld Enemy was at Hampden Park in 1980 when England won 2-0. You can imagine the bragging rights for the England boys as soon as we got back to Melwood. We knew we would have been battered by the Scottish lads if we had lost. The talk would start long before the game. What we were going to do, what they were going to do to us and so on. There was no bitterness but there was no way you wanted to be on the wrong side of the result.

When we won I couldn't wait to get to the training ground. In fact, I would be there especially early waiting for our Scottish friends to make their appearance. As soon as Jocky, Graeme or Kenny arrived I would call out: "Everything okay? Did you have a nice weekend?! What happened on Saturday? I can't remember!"

It was good humoured but that wasn't always the case on the

pitch. I only played against him once, but I kept away from Souey. I knew that he would have broken me in two if he got anywhere near me!

A fantastic reminder of that 2-0 victory at Hampden is Kenny Dalglish's shirt. I asked him whether I could have it, even before the final whistle. Maybe with the way it was going for Scotland it wasn't exactly the best timing, but Kenny said yes.

To win in Glasgow was a fantastic achievement considering the quality of the Scotland team in those days. As well as the Liverpool trio I have mentioned, the Scots also had top players like Gordon Strachan, Alex McLeish, Joe Jordan, Danny McGrain – fantastic footballers.

All the First Division sides would have some influential Scots. For Liverpool, Jocky Hansen was one of the best central defenders anyone has seen. You have to ask yourself these days, where are the good Scottish players? There aren't many. To be fair, you could say the same about English-born players. I'm afraid the Premier League is now swamped by foreign players and it's more difficult for decent young Brits to break through. Look at Chelsea – they often have around 40 players out on loan – what's the sense in that? This is stifling the opportunities for kids of 18, 19, trying to break into first teams.

You also now have the situation where it's all about instant success, so instead of trying out a promising talent, the big clubs spend £30 or £40 million on an established player. In doing that they believe they are reducing the risk factor.

The other big issue, of course, is that you don't see young lads outside in the streets kicking a football. We'd play with anything we could find.

As I've already said, in my case with a doll's head!

CHAPTER 13

THE ROAD BACK

NOTHING much had changed in the eight years I'd been away from Newcastle. The club had, if anything, gone backwards. St. James' Park was in decay, the Leazes End had been demolished and the whole ground was badly in need of redevelopment. The crowds had dropped to around 17,000 before Kevin's revival. They were in the Second Division and, all in all, the club was in desperate need of a lift.

Yet Kevin changed all that. 36,000 squeezed in to see his debut and I knew this could be take-off time.

I was 30 and Newcastle bought me for £50,000. Liverpool had originally told me the fee was £100,000 but Arthur put me right about that. Liverpool couldn't have thought that much of me in the end! Three months earlier I'd been in a World Cup squad.

I also took a big pay cut to join up with Kevin. I made my debut at Rotherham, a game in which we won 5-1 and I played Kevin through for the first goal in a match where he scored four.

You can't get a better welcome than knowing one of the best players Europe has ever seen wanted you alongside him. Kevin knew what I felt for Newcastle. "This is made for us now," he told me. "But there's going to be a lot of hard work. One thing's for certain, you will love working under Arthur."

I imagine Arthur had run it past Kevin about bringing me to Tyneside. I've no doubts Kevin would have backed him up because there was nothing wrong with my fitness. He knew I liked a drink and a good time, but he also knew I would never let a club down on matchday. Me and Kevin were never short of conversation, most of it surrounding what should happen at Newcastle and, of course, sharing a few horse racing tips. Kevin was still very keen on the horses.

The hammering of Rotherham might have been a great start but it didn't last. A week later, I got myself sent off at Oldham for swearing. I'd called the referee 'a wanker' which cost me a suspension and I didn't learn the lesson because I got dismissed again three months later against Bolton. I'd used the same terminology to describe a linesman, who immediately flagged to bring the referee over. He warned me that if I repeated it I would be off. Instead of giving him another verbal blast I just aimed a hand gesture in the linesman's direction, which was enough to see me heading down the tunnel. Arthur wasn't very pleased to say the least.

I'd already been in to see him because I felt I was struggling playing-wise. I had been used to playing with some of the best players in Europe at Liverpool. Here at Newcastle, I was making the same runs but while at Liverpool Ray Kennedy or Graeme Souness would find me, here nothing was happening. The ball was never finding me. "Behave yourself," was Arthur's retort. "You know what you're playing with here, just get on with it." So I went out of his office with my tail between my legs.

We had the nucleus of a decent team with players like Jeff Clarke, John Anderson, Imre Varadi, a young Chris Waddle and Kevin, but it was frustrating for me early on. Kevin was okay because he could dictate the play, go past people and make things happen. I was a different kind of player and it wasn't clicking so I took a leaf out of Kevin's book and just got on with it. It was up to me to adapt. I just had to change my game.

Even though Bobby Robson had cut short his England career, Kevin was still one of the best players in the country. He had nothing to prove.

Over the years we have often mentioned that both of us would have loved to have played for Newcastle at the peak of our powers because we both loved the club, yet our best football came while we were at other clubs.

Kevin was still excellent in what he did for Newcastle. He gave everything. He also doubled up as my driver when he was in the North East because I had been banned from holding the wheel. In fact, I was banned twice for drink driving while I was a player, something I'm not proud of. It was a completely different era when people wrongly tried to get away with it. I've had some mad moments in cars and I'm lucky I never ended up dead. Now I'm a believer that there should be zero tolerance when it comes to drinking and driving. You shouldn't even be legally allowed to have one pint – although I certainly didn't use to follow that doctrine in my bad days. What a lunatic.

Coming home from Bury one night when I was playing for Liverpool I was full of drink on the M62, close to some services, when I fell asleep at the wheel. The next thing I know, the car has hit the central reservation, it's spun around, hit the barrier on the hard shoulder and I've come to see the road sign to Liverpool again. By some miracle, I'm still facing the right way. I kept on driving to my dad's place in Kirkby and climbed into bed. I got up the next morning, having completely forgotten about the incident and couldn't believe it when I saw the state of the car. It was a wreck. Everything was hanging off, bumpers, the lot. I was running late and didn't have time to call a taxi, so I jumped into the car and drove to Anfield.

We would park the cars there, get changed and then hop on the coach to Melwood for training. I didn't want anyone to see the state of my car so I tried to hide it between two cars at the far end of the car park but as we're driving out in the coach, someone shouted for us to look at the mess a car was in. It was Tommy Smith. "Whose car is that? It's a right wreck," he said, as subtle as ever. All I could hear in unison was: "It's Terry's!"

"What's happened?" Bob asked, and I just had to tell him I'd been in an accident.

I'd had a lucky escape.

Another time I was going home to Kirkby after having a right bender in Liverpool and I suddenly noticed a torch in the middle of the road shining in the direction of my car. It was a policeman.

There was no way I was going to stop because of the state I was in, so I went around him and dashed off home. I got into the house and the next minute there's a knock at the door. I wondered whether I should open the door because I was pissed.

I did and he came in and immediately recognised me. "Is that you Terry? Was that you in the car that has just gone past me?" I admitted it was. "In future be very careful because you almost knocked a policeman over!" he replied.

Another night, a group of us including Jimmy Case had enjoyed watching The Hollies play in Southport and we're driving back towards Liverpool. I've got a girl with me in my car and we're now on the Formby bypass. I felt tired and the next thing my eyes are shut and we've gone straight through this roundabout. By a stroke of luck we had missed a load of bushes and ended up slap-bang in the middle of the roundabout. You couldn't see the car from the road.

Jimmy and his missus had been following us and had witnessed everything. He got out of his car and told the two of us to get into his car so we could clear off before the police came on the scene with the obvious consequences. We just left my car on the roundabout, hidden by the bushes.

I later phoned a big mate of Bob Paisley's, Bob Rawcliffe, who was a car dealer. I told him what had happened and where he could find my car. I went with him the next morning in his recovery wagon and he managed to drag it out without the police knowing a thing about what had gone on. Mind, the car wasn't in the best of conditions – again!

I cringe now about some of the things I got up to, but that was the way I was. I was just completely daft.

It was inevitable I was going to get caught one day – or should I say one night. It happened when I was coming back from a night out in Bury again after borrowing a car off Bob Rawcliffe as mine was getting repaired, just for a change.

I got my brother Robert to drive me over to Bury on the

TERRY MAC

Thursday night. We'd been to a nightclub called Benny's, owned by a mate. Lots of footballers would go there including Bryan Robson. In fact, Robbo went there so often we dubbed it the *Robson Piano Bar*. Peter Reid was also a regular.

Anyway, at the end of the night, in my wisdom, I decided to drive instead of my brother. It was a crappy old car but I still wanted to drive it. We're in the Whitefield area, just before you get on the M62. We're just passing a row of shops and restaurants – Colin Bell owned one of them – when I could see a blue light flashing in the rear view mirror. I was pulled over by the copper. He asked me if I had been drinking and I admitted I'd had a couple – which was a complete lie because I'd started at 7pm. It's now 3am. He told me to step outside my car and blow into the breathalyser. I was panicking because it's now the early hours of Friday morning and I've got a game for Liverpool against Arsenal on the Saturday. I thought 'if this gets out in the press I'm for it, big time'.

I pleaded with the policeman, insisting I was fine to drive. He just said there was no way because I was well over the limit. I think the breathalyser had virtually melted. I had to go into the police station and although they did me, I wasn't thrown into a police cell. They booked me, told me I would be appearing in court and let me go. So I said goodnight and went to pick up my car keys! They couldn't believe it. They quickly told me I would still be over the limit. "Fair enough, " I said "but could you drop me off at home?" I was quickly reminded they weren't a taxi firm and I would have to get one of my own to take me and Robert back to Kirkby.

I'm now praying in the taxi that this news of my arrest doesn't hit the papers.

At training, on the Friday morning, I told all the other players, but there was no way I was going to tell Bob or any of the coaching staff.

I didn't have to. On the Saturday morning we're in a local hotel, the Lord Daresbury, preparing for the Arsenal game. The papers had dropped and there I was all over them revealing I had been breathalysed. I immediately thought Bob would pull me out of the team, but he didn't. I did play and played well – and it was never mentioned. All they really cared about at Liverpool was winning things.

It didn't prevent me getting a 12-month ban from driving which was still in operation when I joined Newcastle. It wasn't long after my ban finished that I ended up being done again because I obviously hadn't learned my lesson.

I'd now moved up in the world regarding cars and had a BMW. Kevin would usually go home to Southampton every weekend following the game, leaving me to my own devices. I had a house near Ponteland Golf Course on the outskirts of Newcastle and I had by this time met my wife-to-be Carole, but she would go back to her home in Liverpool on the Sunday night, so I'd be left twiddling my thumbs.

One Monday I went into training, finished off what I had to do and was a bit bored because Kevin still wasn't around. Arthur Cox had given him an extra day off, which he often did.

Around the corner from the Benwell training ground was a working men's club where I used to go quite a bit. I became friendly with the steward there, Alan Robson. He was into his horses and greyhounds, so I'd always enjoy a chat.

He was the perfect host, knew what was going on, loved the gossip and would make sure I wasn't pestered. I always looked forward to a catch-up with Alan. I went in this day just for a bit of company really. "Just give me a shandy," I told Alan. He couldn't believe it.

Later he asked if I wanted another drink and I requested another shandy. He wanted to know what was wrong with me. I told him I had my car but I then decided to have a half of beer, another half of beer and so on. "Give me your car keys," Alan said, as I got into my stride. I must have had around 10 pints in the end. It wasn't a problem because I wasn't driving. Until it was time to go, that is.

It was about 9.30pm and I went looking for Alan to order me a taxi but he'd gone off to bed, absolutely pissed. I didn't know what to do. Then I noticed my keys on a table behind the bar, so I got into the car and went along the back route towards my home.

I'm not far from home and just in front of me is a big recovery lorry, parked up. I'm so blitzed that I momentarily nodded off. That was enough for me to hurtle into the back of the lorry. I'm nearly half way up it and I've smacked my head against my windscreen and cracked it. I'm completely dazed and I decided for some strange reason to manoeuvre myself into the passenger seat.

Eventually the police arrived on the scene, alerted by the owner of the recovery vehicle who couldn't believed what had happened. I actually knew the copper who took me to Morpeth Police Station.

They took a blood sample to confirm I was over the limit, but my head was so dazed that when they gave me my tube I just grabbed it, threw it on the floor and smashed it with my foot, believing they wouldn't be able to charge me.

I didn't realise they already had a sample – and this was mine. Anyway I was done and once again I had to get a taxi home.

I phoned Arthur Cox and told him what had happened, that I'd let him down and I apologised. Arthur just told me to get myself into training the next day and we would have a chat. I was embarrassed about what I had done. I'd also banged my knee and cut myself. Arthur looked me up and down in his office and gave me some great advice. "Your lovely girlfriend, get her up here to the North East and marry her," he said. "As quick as you can. You need someone to look after you."

I told Carole. She came up and we've been together ever since, having been married in the summer of 1984.

When I met her she was working in a bar in Ainsdale, Southport, one of my regular watering holes, Toad Hall. It was quite upmarket compared to some of the Liverpool and Kirkby bars. It was quite rural – in fact, they couldn't build a road through part of the area around Marine Drive because, I believe, the local wildlife needed protecting.

As far as Carole was concerned, it was a means of earning extra money because she had a full time job. Her friends Jane and Sharron would always be there – they are still close friends now. I would say hello to her but at the beginning she thought I was a little uncouth. She often reminds me that one of my first bits of conversation was asking her if she was on the pill! I'd be out with Phil Thompson, Alan Kennedy, Ray Kennedy and Alan Hansen, so you can imagine the chat with girls. I really fancied her, she was really fit – and still is.

When I first really got to know her was on holiday in Ibiza. I was there with Peter Reid and Paul Bradshaw, the Wolves keeper, and the owner of Benny's nightclub, Paul Ingham. We were sitting around the hotel just a couple of days into the holiday when I heard this voice, "Terry!" It was Carole with her friend Sharron. There was a fella with them. So we asked them to join us. After that they came over to our hotel, would enjoy a few drinks, use the swimming pool and that's how I got to know her.

Later, when we got back to Merseyside, Tommy Smith had a big do at one of the clubs we'd go to called the Castle Court club in a backstreet near Liverpool Town Hall. I've heard since that Carole would go around different bars to try and bump into us – although she may tell a different story. She found out this night that I was going to Tommy's get-together.

The usual – me, Jocky Hansen, Phil Thompson and Alan Kennedy – had been out all afternoon and evening. As we're going downstairs to the club, Carole spotted me and we had a chat and exchanged phone numbers and eventually started going out. At first, the problem for Carole on our dates was that I wouldn't be alone. I was very family-orientated and I was still living with my dad. When I started courting her she would pick me up because I was banned. Carole would be dead excited but then out would come my dad, my brother Robert and off we would go to Quarry Green social club. Every Sunday.

In the end she put her foot down and said she would only go out if it was just me. So then sometimes we would go to a Chinese restaurant, I'd get some food down her neck…and then we'd rush off to Quarry Green! I knew, though, that if the relationship was to go anywhere I had to change.

Anyway, when Arthur made the call to bring her up to the North East that started to calm me down. If it hadn't have been for her, I don't know where I would have ended up.

CHAPTER 14

FUN ON THE TYNE

THE disappointing thing was that although Kevin had helped revitalise Newcastle, we didn't manage to gain promotion during that 1982/83 season. It didn't stop us having plenty of fun, though.

Before the start of the next season we went on a tour which included games in Japan, for the Kirin Cup, and Thailand. We were big now because of Kevin and so the club was determined to cash in with some prestige and lucrative friendlies.

When we were in Bangkok we had to move from the plush hotel we were staying in to another one further up the country just for a kip before the game that night. Little did we know we had been booked into a brothel.

The name was the first giveaway, 'The Happy Hotel', although initially we just supposed it was some kind of Holiday Inn. The strange thing was there were mirrors everywhere.

Arthur Cox – which sounds like a service on offer there! – wasn't exactly up to the mark with these sort of things and just said it was a nice hotel and we were to get up to our rooms. The walls were a psychedelic red. "Arthur it's a bloody knocking shop," we said.

The players were sharing and, as usual, Kevin and I were rooming together. We got up to the room, opened the door and saw a round bed in the middle of the room surrounded by mirrors. There were even mirrors on the ceiling. We needed a sleep, so we both got into the bed. Kevin looked up at the ceiling mirror and said: "I don't fancy you!"

Arthur just sat up in the lobby. There was no way he would have gone into one of those rooms. Arthur was prim and proper, but what a manager and coach. People say Bob Paisley must have been my all-time favourite manager. I wouldn't say that. I would say Arthur Cox. He was hard, tough. He loved football and was just desperate to do well. He wasn't afraid to tell you off in front of everyone, no matter who you were. He was a really good guy and I keep in touch with him. Kevin speaks to him all the time.

For pre-season training, Arthur took us to the Gateshead International Athletics Stadium – not inside it but outside – where we ran up some great big hills. It was exhausting and we used to think, 'What the hell are we doing this for? We want to play football, not climb bloody great big hills.' Arthur would have none of it. We had to do it. "Get up there," he would shout like some sergeant major. He looked like Oliver North, that no-nonsense American colonel.

We were due to run up the hills one afternoon and in the

morning Kevin said to me that we were going to a place next to the theatre in Newcastle where you could hire all sorts of costumes.

We got dressed up as two commandoes, complete with camouflage and back packs and turned up at Gateshead. The lads loved it and, to be fair to Arthur, he fell about laughing – but we still had to run up the hills with our war equipment on.

Kevin and I were at it again when there was talk of a Middle East club wanting to sign him. The speculation was huge in all the press, so Kevin and I decided to play a trick on Arthur and the club.

Kevin went to Arthur and told him there was going to be some representatives from the Middle East arriving later that day to talk about the possible transfer. He would have to notify the chairman Stan Seymour to come to the ground, plus the secretary Russell Cushing. He told him they were due at 2pm. Kevin knew I had the whole Arab regalia from a trip we had made in the past to the Middle East when all the Liverpool players were handed the garments as a present.

Kevin went into the office to join Arthur, the chairman and secretary to await the visitors. Kevin had also told them that they had to take their shoes off because it was good manners in the presence of people from The Gulf states. That wasn't too easy for Stan because he was a big, big man.

Little did they know, it was me knocking on the door. I came in all robed up.

Kevin told them they had to stand, which saw Stan struggle to release himself from his seat. When he did, his trousers started to fall down like in some Brian Rix farce.

Stan was a larger than life character. He loved being involved in the Newcastle boardroom, although at times it must have been an uncomfortable ride due to the club's constant struggles.

I watched them looking anxiously out of the window making sure they took their shoes off so as not to offend their 'illustrious' visitor.

Eventually they realised what was going on. "I can't believe you've set us up," Stan chortled. Kevin was beside himself, hardly believing that Stan could have got himself in such a state. "Maybe a new pair of trousers would be a good idea," he told him.

But we hadn't finished there. Now everyone was in on what was happening, we decided to continue the plot and try and play a trick on Alec Mutch, who was the physio. He was a very serious guy.

Kevin told Alec there were some important people from the Middle East at the ground and tradition insisted that everyone else had to remove their shoes in their presence. At first Alec refused, but eventually agreed and he had to walk around in his socks.

To put him out of his misery I went up to him and started taking off my robe. You could have knocked him over with a feather. "Terry! Bloody hell, you so and so," he shouted.

After missing out on promotion in 1982/83, we felt we needed some more players to give it a real go in the new campaign.

Arthur assured Kevin and I that he would get them. We felt we were short of quality and Kevin wanted experienced, ready-made players. The next thing we know, Arthur is signing someone called Peter Beardsley. Kevin couldn't believe it because we didn't know too much about Peter, who had arrived from Vancouver Whitecaps for £150,000. Arthur just said to wait until we had seen him in training.

Well, it only took a couple of sessions to realise what a good player he was.

Peter could go past people for fun. He could do anything really. If he lost the ball he was like a little terrier snapping to get it back. As soon as he lost it you knew he would retrieve it. Some of the goals he scored were incredible. I remember one he stuck in at Portsmouth after beating five players, including the goalkeeper.

Arthur actually missed that goal because it happened on the stroke of half-time and he had gone into the dressing room to deliver a rollicking because he thought we weren't winning. He launched into this verbal tirade, saying our performance hadn't been good enough before we interrupted him and told him about Peter's goal. "Okay, well played boys," he continued.

Chris Waddle had also come into the team – and what a player he was. Like Peter, The Waddler had been a surprise to Kevin and I. Here we are looking for experienced players and Chris had arrived from non-league having been playing for Tow Law Town in the Northern League.

Arthur used to batter him. The Waddler had been working in a sausage factory and Arthur would threaten him, saying he could be back working with sausages if he didn't improve. But really, Arthur made him. Chris's big mate at the club was another player plucked from non-league – Steve Carney. Steve had worked at the airport as a baggage handler and Arthur would also have a go at him saying he would be back on the conveyer belts if Steve wasn't performing.

We now had a decent team, Glenn Roeder being another good

addition to the squad. Imre Varadi had been another option up front with Kevin – and he even managed to survive landing a punch on Arthur during training.

When the weather was bad, we would go into the gym. It was narrow and surrounded by brick walls. We would have football games in there. If you were pushed into the wall you certainly knew about it and the matches were quite often feisty.

One day, Imre was pinned against the wall as he was trying to protect the ball. What he didn't realise was that it was Arthur behind him. Arthur would often join in the games. Imre lost his rag at being kicked against the wall and swung around and landed a punch on his assailant. He had just smacked the manager in the mouth. Arthur landed on the floor, picked himself up and, still stunned, wailed: "Play on, play on." Perhaps it was a co-incidence, but Imre was then sold to Sheffield Wednesday in the summer of 1983!

One of the best goals I scored in the 1983/84 season was in a 3-1 win over Middlesbrough at St. James' Park. It was a chip after a Chris Waddle shot had come back out. I bent it into the top corner.

Because I had scored goals at Liverpool I think most people expected me to keep that going at Newcastle, but I was older and, with respect, not playing with the same calibre of players.

I had built my reputation at Anfield on the blind side runs which often ended with a goal. It took time at St. James' Park to work out that same understanding with the players – that they knew when to release the ball.

There was also extra responsibility resting on mine and Kevin's shoulders, because we had the experience. We needed to use that to help the other players. The fact that we won promotion and I scored some crucial goals, like an equaliser at Chelsea, proved that we had done our jobs.

We didn't spend much money but the momentum built throughout the season and there was now an expectation that we would go up, which we did, winning our last home game against Brighton in front of a full house of 35,000 at St. James' Park. Kevin, Peter Beardsley and Chris Waddle scored as we beat them 3-1.

A few weeks earlier, Kevin had been involved in a real scare when he damaged a retina during a testimonial game at Middlesbrough for John Craggs. Someone accidentally poked him in the eye. I went to the hospital with him where he had to have laser treatment. He missed a few games, but was back for the promotion push.

He had already announced that this would be his last season as a player. He decided his time was up during an FA Cup game at Liverpool in January, 1984 when Mark Lawrenson caught him up and made a great tackle. Kevin had been yards ahead of him. No-one used to be able to get back at Kevin like that in his pomp, so Lawro made the decision for him. I also think it hurt more because it was at Anfield against his former club.

I remember listening to the FA Cup draw a few weeks earlier. Liverpool were out first and at home and just before our number came up, Kevin had whispered to me: "No, please not Newcastle." Of course, fate decreed that it was. "We haven't got a team yet to take them on," he told me.

Don't forget, he had already suffered one humiliation going back to Anfield with Hamburg in the Super Cup when his new side were pummelled 6-0. I think he sensed it wasn't going to be a good night for Newcastle, although even he couldn't have predicted this was the game which would hasten his retirement as a player. This time he ended up on the wrong end of a 4-0 scoreline.

Before the game, held on a Friday night, there were knocks on our dressing room door and a few of the Liverpool lads like Graeme Souness were urging me to step outside into the corridor. I didn't want to know because I knew they would be up to something. I wanted the door locked. In the end, I had to go outside just to shut them up. There they all were, my former team-mates complete with fake blisters on their lips, taking the mickey out of me because I would often suffer from cold sores.

It was the only time that night that I did laugh because we got absolutely hammered. We didn't, as Kevin predicted, have a team to take on Liverpool. It was a struggle to get out of the Second Division and it had taken a lot out of Kevin.

He hadn't told me what was going on in his head that night. But I know he informed Arthur that, come the end of the season, that would be it. Once Kevin's mind is made up, nothing can change it. This was January so, just like at Liverpool in 1977, he had given them plenty of notice.

At least it was a fairytale ending to his careers with both clubs. Winning the European Cup with Liverpool and promotion with Newcastle.

A few days after promotion, we played Liverpool at St. James' Park in a testimonial for Kevin with the money going to charity. At the final whistle, Kevin was whisked away off the pitch in a helicopter. It was only taking him to the Gosforth Park Hotel for the reception, but it was a spectacular farewell. We were left to walk to the hotel – no, only joking, we got taxis. I had scored one of my best goals against Liverpool in the 2-2 draw.

The noise that night was incredible and to see him disappear into the night sky with the help of a helicopter was straight out of a fantasy novel, even if it was only taking him less than a mile down the road! Everyone in the ground thought he was being taken to his home in Southampton.

Liverpool were playing in the European Cup final just a few weeks later, but you wouldn't have known because they were really up for the game especially because of the atmosphere within St. James' Park. They weren't able to participate in too many drinks afterwards because of what lay ahead.

The pair of us helping Newcastle win promotion was a wonderful last act as players together.

Kevin and I had won a lot of trophies. We also had a lot of respect for Arthur, but really what made it was seeing the fans so happy after everything they had gone through. I'd been there between 1972 and 1974 so I already knew how loyal they were and it didn't take Kevin long to feel the same. What we achieved that season was one of the highlights of our careers.

As usual, Kevin took everything in his stride, there was no going back on his decision to finish playing. Little did we know that Arthur was on the verge of making a big decision for himself...

I was due to get married after the season and because I'd taken a pay cut to come to Newcastle and we were now in the First Division, I thought it was fair the club reviewed my deal. Arthur was also in talks over a new contract.

I went into the office to talk about mine and Arthur was in there with the chairman Stan Seymour and the secretary Russell Cushing.

Arthur was behind Seymour and was secretly gesturing to me to knock it back. He's waving his arm and shaking his head so I got the message and told them I would like to delay any decision. To be honest, I didn't know what the hell was happening.

When we got out of the office, Arthur revealed that he had been having trouble with his contract. There was a chance that he might not be staying – and didn't want me to commit until the future was clearer.

A few days later, I'm at Ascot Races with Alan Hansen and Alan Kennedy when the news came out that Arthur had left Newcastle United.

"What's going to happen to me now? Who's going to come in as Arthur's replacement?" I blurted out to Jocky.

"Aye, you might be retiring and joining Kevin in Spain," Jocky quipped.

Before I knew it, they had appointed Jack Charlton. I got a call from Joe Harvey who told me Jack wanted to speak to me. I was down at Ascot and due to get married in Liverpool just a few days later. He was persistent, saying I needed to come up to see Jack to get things sorted.

So I drove up from Ascot and was shown into the manager's office by Joe who then left me, saying Jack would be in shortly. I'm still sitting in there 10 minutes later and there's no sign of Jack and I've driven non-stop from Ascot Races for this. Finally, he came in. I'd never met him before. He shoved the new contract in front of me to read. I quickly discovered it was the same money. He told me it was good money. I disagreed. He asked me what was I going to do? I replied that I was going, I was finished with Newcastle.

"You'll be back," he shouted. "You fucking watch," I retorted. I never spoke to him again.

He then tried to stitch me up in the local paper saying I was being greedy. I also had my say in the press and it became a war of words.

By the time pre-season training came around, I didn't have a contract but they still held my registration so I couldn't sign for anyone else.

I needed to keep fit so I decided to run around the local golf course. The club had to keep paying my wages because the moment they stopped I would be liable for a free transfer. I was desperate to play. Now I was running along the roads, around the golf course, everywhere to keep up my stamina. I got a couple of calls, one came from Carlisle, but I didn't fancy that after Liverpool and Newcastle to be honest. Then they stopped paying me my wages.

In one respect that was good because I was now legally free to go anywhere I wanted. The problem was most clubs now had sorted out their squads for the season which was well underway. Not exactly perfect timing and maybe not the way I really wanted to call time on my Newcastle career the second time around. I was 33 and also needed to earn some money.

On a personal level, I also received some bad news around this time when I was told that my brother Charles had died. In some ways, it was a relief because he never had a life. I have to confess that a part of me was glad to see him pass away. It just felt that there was nothing for him to live for.

My brother Peter was told first about Charles' death because my dad was staying with me in Newcastle. By then, of course, my mum had sadly passed away. Communication wasn't great in those days. Pete was told that Charles had died during the night. Pete waited for Dad to return to Kirkby and then he told me on the phone.

It had been horrible for Charles and for everyone who had seen him suffer over the years. Sadly, in life, tragedies like this happen. I think at times I was badly affected by his plight. But it wasn't something I discussed with my team-mates or anyone in football. It was something I largely kept to myself.

Eventually I got a telephone call from Cork City who said they would look after me and help me get fit. They would pay me a decent amount and playing in the League of Ireland would place me in the shop window, plus I didn't even have to move to Ireland.

It was great, really enjoyable. They picked me up from the airport on the Friday and would take me around the city, stopping off at all different bars. I was with the manager and the chairman and they insisted I should have a drink, even though I would be playing the next day. By 6pm I was pissed.

The next afternoon I'm playing and after the game they would take me to the airport to return home until I was due back in Ireland for the next game. I would leave with a big brown envelope.

After around six weeks doing this, Tommy Cassidy, a former Newcastle team-mate from the Seventies, rang me. He was manager of a big Cypriot team Apoel Nicosia. He asked me if I fancied playing for him. We'd just had our first child, Neale.

"Terry you'll love it out here. It will be a great life on and off the pitch," he said in that unmistakable Irish brogue.

"There's no harm in me coming over for a chat I suppose," I

replied. I talked it over with Carole and she was up for it. There was no harm in giving it a go.

Tommy again insisted I wouldn't have a problem with the football but, to my horror, I struggled for the first few months. It was a lot hotter than Newcastle for a start, not that that really bothered me. I was also trying to make my normal runs off the ball – ones that had been my trademark at Liverpool – but the ball never used to end up coming anywhere near me. It wasn't a lack of effort, but it just wasn't happening.

During the 1985/86 campaign Tommy pulled me in and asked what was wrong with me. "I'll turn this around," I told him. "Promise."

A week later, I scored two against our local rivals and everything took off from then. We ended up winning the league for the first time in six years. The local rivals, Omonia Nicosia, had won it every other season so we were now heroes.

The Cypriots were fanatical. You had to win games. If we lost, some of the fans would follow Tommy home in their cars and give him real grief. If you won, they couldn't do enough for you. When Carole and I wheeled Neale down this main street in his pram we would be showered with gifts from the baby shops. There would be new shoes, new outfits, the lot. But it would only happen if the team had won.

I was there for two seasons. Towards the end of it, Carole went back to England to have our daughter Rachel because I knew I wasn't going to renew my contract. We got to the Cup final in the second season against Apollon Limassol, but lost 2-0 when we were expected to win. I found out later that four of our players had allegedly taken bribes, three of them were brothers. That cost me a Cup winner's medal.

TERRY MAC

Another incident over there almost cost me my life.

After having a few too many drinks in Nicosia one night, I got in the car and in trying to get home I ended up in the pitch black going up this dirt track after first crashing through a barrier. Suddenly out of nowhere this figure appeared with a great big rifle. He was a military policeman guarding the border between the Cypriot side and the Turkish sector, which you weren't allowed to enter. He told me in no uncertain terms to turn back and that I had been lucky not to have been shot.

Many over the years hadn't been so lucky. Normally it was shoot first and ask questions second because of the growing tension between the two countries.

On that night I could easily have been mistaken for a terrorist instead of someone who had been intent on having a good time.

CHAPTER 15

SAVE
THIS CLUB

I COULD have stayed in Cyprus for another year but with Carole expecting again we decided to come home. While we were away, the place we had in Newcastle had been flooded when a pipe burst. Luckily, we came back to a house which had been dried out thanks to my ex-Newcastle team-mate David McCreery and his wife Julie, who had been keeping an eye on it for us. The next door neighbours had alerted the McCreerys who came to the rescue.

I knew once I arrived back in England that it was the end of my career. I was 36 that December, but I was still as fit as when I was in my prime. We had always trained really hard in Cyprus. It hadn't been a problem to me and I loved the sunshine. A lot of my team-mates didn't like playing when it was too hot but I thrived on it because of my stamina. I knew some players would wilt in it but I wouldn't. Kenny Dalglish has often referred to my stamina and claimed I have four lungs. Three of them were probably for drinking!

I'll let you into a little secret. When I was a frail youngster at Bury they decided to try and build me up with a magic potion. They must have been trying to turn me into Popeye The Sailor Man! They came up with this special diet which I passed on to my mum. I had to take a ruddy great spoonful of pure malt every day and make sure I had a big steak twice a week. Bury contributed to the cost because we couldn't afford to buy two pieces of steak every week. No-one in Kirkby could afford steaks. Luckily it appears that copious amounts of lager didn't affect the success of the process.

There were no options when I came back to England. The phone didn't ring, so really I had no choice but to call it a day. Being in Cyprus I was obviously out of people's thoughts, but I wasn't bitter because I had played until I was 35 while a lot of players are finished at 32, 33.

Some people can never let go. I know, for instance, Alan Kennedy was desperate to play on as long as he could and there's nothing wrong with that but I didn't want to go down the leagues, ending up in non-league football. I wanted to finish at the top. I think I did. With Liverpool I finished on a high, with Newcastle we won promotion and in Cyprus I helped them win the League for the first time in six years and got to a cup final.

So when I returned to our home in the North East and the phone didn't go, it honestly didn't bother me.

Instead, I joined forces with a mate – or ex-mate as he is today – an old drinking chum from Salford, who had a catering company. You would see his chip vans, burger vans, hot dog stalls outside many of the football clubs he had contracts with. He would be at fetes, shows, all over the place.

You wouldn't have seen me with an apron on dishing out fish and chips or burgers or serving up the onions, instead I was making sure all the vans had enough stock. I went around the country and you would have seen us at the Yorkshire Show, Aintree and other race tracks. Manchester United was his big earner, but I never used to go there due to our old football rivalry when I was with Liverpool.

I had put £10,000 into the business and at first I was being repaid but after one event there was no payment. "Don't worry Terry, we'll sort it," my mate insisted.

I believed he would be true to his word but as time went on and I carried on selling his burgers, it became clear that I wouldn't see a penny of it. I think I was owed around £7,000 – the most expensive burgers I've ever known!

Around this time we also sold our property in Newcastle and moved back to Liverpool because Carole was homesick, so we had a house built near Ormskirk that Carole loved.

I was starting to settle into football retirement and, fortunately, we had enough money to look after ourselves. Everyone seemed to think that I would be daft where money was concerned because of my past.

At Bury, we would receive our wages in a brown envelope. I couldn't wait to open it. Christmas had come early as I quickly made my way to the bookies. There were never massive bets, the odd quid here and there, but I couldn't stop and the losses started mounting up, meaning I would be struggling to pay the rent.

But I wasn't completely stupid. I was able to rein myself in knowing that some players have wrecked their careers through excessive gambling. I still liked a bet in the later years, but I was sensible, so we didn't have any money worries when I finished, which wasn't always the case in those days with players.

Liverpool had also been the pioneers of an excellent pension scheme through Standard Life. When we won League Championships and European Cups – which might mean a bonus of, say, £7,000 – we were advised by the club to put in to the pension pot. Many of the players did it and they are now reaping the rewards of that advice. Liverpool were one of the first clubs to do this – making sure their players were well looked after in retirement and, to this day, I still enjoy a salary from that.

Saying all that, I would have swapped the tax I paid for my actual salary any day of the week. It was crazy the percentage of tax we had to pay. It was more than 80 per cent but we couldn't do anything about it. It wasn't just footballers, it affected show-business personalities and anyone earning really decent money. No wonder so many people left the country to try to save more of their earnings.

Even though my playing career had come to an end I was anxious to try to retain my fitness, so my old mate David Johnson and I had a chat and suggested that we ask whether we could go training at Liverpool. He had a word with Graeme Souness, who had been appointed as Liverpool manager in 1991, and he agreed that we could use Melwood.

We would go early in the morning and be out of there by 10.30am before the players were due to start. We'd do a few runs and then leave. We didn't want to be seen by the players because it would only make them wonder what we were doing there.

The only player I was in touch with was Micky Quinn, a Scouser who was Newcastle United's star striker. Micky was into his horses and I rang him up virtually every day for tips and racing news. That would usually mean ringing the training ground because the phone was in the treatment room.

One morning, in February 1992, I read that Kevin Keegan had just been appointed as Newcastle manager. I couldn't believe it. As usual, I went to Melwood to do my training with The Doc and rang Newcastle's training ground to talk to Quinny. The Newcastle physio, Derek Wright, answered the phone this day. "Quinny's not around," he told me. "But someone else wants a word."

"Terry, it's me, Kev," the voice went. "What are you up to at the moment?" It was Keegan. "I'll give you a ring later on tonight."

That night, the call didn't come. I was anxious, asking people like David Johnson what would Kevin be doing trying to get hold of me. He told me Kevin must be ready to offer me a job. "What could I possibly do?" I replied. I was about to find out.

The next day I was later than usual leaving Melwood and bumped into Graeme Souness, Roy Evans and Ronnie Moran, who were all coming in to get training started for the day.

"What do you think to Kevin at Newcastle?" Graeme asked. I told him he'd wanted to chat with me and Graeme agreed with David Johnson that a job was on the cards.

"Doing what?" I said. "Driving the coach?!"

Ronnie and Roy both agreed with Graeme though and said exactly the same thing. "They're going to offer you a job," Ronnie said. This was all happening very quickly and then, all of a sudden, Graeme asked me and The Doc whether we fancied another run around Melwood with him.

That was no problem for us and off we went. As we got going, Graeme laid it out straight. "It looks like Ronnie might be retiring at the end of the season," he said, barely out of breath. "The way Ronnie is talking means it looks like he's packing it in. Do you want to come in and take the reserves?"

That left me pretty speechless, for once I didn't really know what to say. Of course there would have only been one answer if the call had come – a resounding yes.

When I got home I told Carole about it and she could see how excited I was at the prospect of a job at that level. But at the same time I thought I'd never done any coaching in my life. Anyway, we would see how things panned out.

Life has a funny way at times and what happened next proved it. While I was still digesting the possibility of an offer from Graeme I got the call from Kevin as I was on my way to Bangor Races.

"Terry, I want you up here with me," he said. "It's only going to be until the end of the season. When can you come up?"

I still didn't really know what I could or couldn't offer coaching-wise but my mind was instantly made up.

"I'll be there, first thing tomorrow," I said. I stopped the car, turned back and went up to Newcastle.

I set off for my new job early in the morning and got to the Benwell training ground just before the players were about to start their sessions. I was told to get my kit and we'd have a proper chat later.

It was February, 1992, and despite Kevin telling me that we would only be with the club until the end of the season, life at Newcastle has a way of getting under your skin.

I couldn't wait to join in the training. Kevin told me there were good young players there. I knew Lee Clark because everyone had been trying to sign him. He was being heralded as the new Paul Gascoigne. As I got to know him, I used to tell Lee that different managers had been on asking about him. Clarky would also read stories about himself in the papers and so he couldn't wait to get out on the pitch and show he could be as good as Gazza. In truth, there has only been one Gazza. But it kept him fired up and proved to me that maybe I did have something to offer on the coaching side, that I could influence players, maybe on the psychological side as well.

Then there was Steve Watson, Alan Thompson, Robbie Elliott. The club had great expectations of them especially after the previous manager, Ossie Ardiles, had given them opportunities in the first team.

However, despite the flourish of youth, the club was in dire straits and heading for the old Third Division – and in all probability, oblivion. That's the reason why Kevin had taken a desperate call from the new owner of the club, Sir John Hall. Sir John told him there were only two people who could save Newcastle United and they were now talking to each other.

There was no money. There had been fighting in the boardroom with Sir John trying to take over. "Kevin, if Newcastle end up in the Third Division, it's over," Sir John had told him. "It's the end of Newcastle United Football Club."

If it had been any other club, Kevin wouldn't have taken the task on. He loved Newcastle and with his father coming from Hetton-le-Hole, he had an affinity with the Geordies which had shone through in his two years as a player there.

The fans loved him and they still do to this day. I had the same affinity.

The club was in a terrible state. The first thing Kevin did when he arrived was to have the training ground fumigated and repainted. You want players looking forward to coming into training, not suffering a stinking ramshackle hut in which they have to change.

Despite the club's precarious position, Kevin wanted the best. "You will stay in the best hotels and eat the best food," he told them. "The price for that is simple," he went on. "We have to win games."

The first few weeks together weren't the best. In our first game, we beat Bristol City 3-0 but we were still in a right mess and everyone thought we were going to be relegated. Promises weren't being kept and Kevin was quickly becoming very frustrated. He wanted to bring players in on loan, but kept on being blocked. Nothing was happening, so much so that Kevin famously said: "It's not what it said in the brochure."

It was very true. The things the club said they would do weren't forthcoming. Kevin spoke to the chief executive Freddie Fletcher and also had words with Sir John, but they couldn't placate him.

One Friday in March, Kevin snapped. "Terry, get in the car – and drive," he told me. We headed along the A69 towards Carlisle. "We're going to the Lake District," Kevin announced. "Let's get away from it all."

"Hang on," I said. "We've got a home game against Swindon tomorrow. Are we doing the right thing here?"

"They shouldn't be allowed to get away with this," Kevin said, meaning the board. "They're not giving us what they promised."

I agreed wholeheartedly with him but this wasn't the way to go.

"Let's turn back," I said. "Let's win the game against Swindon and then we can decide if that's the end."

He agreed and I quickly did a U-turn. We were on the road back to Newcastle and soon back at the Gosforth Park Hotel, where we were both staying. The next day we beat Swindon 3-1.

After the match we both got into our cars and headed back to our respective homes thinking that was it – the end of a short spell back at Newcastle. We didn't tell the players, although they soon found out and couldn't believe that Kevin wasn't coming back. Then all hell broke loose, it was all over the newspapers and other media outlets.

The phone calls started arriving from the Newcastle hierarchy to Kevin, pleading for him to come back, and they insisted that things would change. My phone rang.

"One more chance," Kevin said. "We're going back."

To be honest, I was absolutely delighted.

It was still hard and we had a hell of a job on our hands to try to avoid relegation which would have been curtains for this famous football club.

Kevin always wore his heart on his sleeve. We had a great rapport. His team talks were just fantastic. The hairs on the back of your neck would stand up. Most of them would tell the players it was the best time of their careers. He was honest with them and if hard decisions had to be made, he made them, but explained why he was doing it.

At the Gosforth Park Hotel, we had connecting rooms and most evenings we would be poring over the remaining fixtures, staring at the league table trying to picture us getting out of the relegation zone. How many points did we need? Were we going to stay up on goal difference?

We lost a few games but were still in there fighting and we knew we had to win our last home game against Portsmouth if we were to have any chance of staying up.

Going into the match, we were in the relegation zone, 22nd in the Division Two table.

It was nerve-wracking, but we managed a victory thanks to a goal from David Kelly five minutes from time. St. James' Park just exploded. We then knew that a win at Leicester away in the last game would guarantee our survival.

The pressure had been immense with Sir John telling everyone there wouldn't be a club if we were relegated and that was some burden for Kevin to have to carry. People's livelihoods were at stake at the football club. Then there were the fans who lived and breathed Newcastle United. It was their escape at the end of a hard working week and it was frightening but Kevin, despite all this, was so positive. He convinced everyone we were going to stay up.

As it happens we didn't have to win at Leicester because other results went for us. But that didn't stop us pulling off a 2-1 victory with a last minute own goal to finish 20th, four points above the dreaded drop zone.

The journey back was amazing. I've never seen fans so animated. It was as if we had won the League, FA Cup and European Cup in one day. The noise was incredible.

That was the end of the Newcastle journey as far as Kevin and I were concerned, though. He had promised me a job until the end of the season and now that was here. There had been no discussions about the future. "That's it mate," he said, and I told him it had been the best three months of my life. It had been a roller-coaster, but we had achieved what no-one had predicted.

We were still in the Second Division and the club was still in existence. We'd saved the club.

Kevin went his way and I went mine, back to near Ormskirk where I was still living.

I got home and went out with a mate who had been at the game. He was an Evertonian and admitted he had never seen anything like the celebration scenes amongst the Newcastle supporters.

I know what it had meant to Kevin to keep the club up and thought there was still a door open for him to continue if he could be convinced about the future under Sir John Hall.

As the summer went on, there were discussions between the club and Kevin and for me that meant there was a chance of the partnership continuing.

One day, the news I'd been longing for came through. I was enjoying the warm summer weather in the garden when the phone went.

"We're going back," were Kevin's first words. No introduction. I knew exactly who it was and exactly where we were going. "And we're going to really save this club."

I couldn't believe it. We were back in business at Newcastle United.

CHAPTER 16

ON THE UP

S IR John Hall and Freddy Shepherd – who bleeds black and white and had also been involved in buying the club together with Sir John's son, Douglas Hall – kept their promise to invest both in the team and in the decaying stadium.

Kevin is very shrewd and knew what could be achieved at Newcastle with the right backing. He brought in some really good players like John Beresford, Paul Bracewell, Barry Venison and Robert Lee.

The previous season Kevin had also brought in Brian Kilcline and appointed him as captain. 'Killer' had helped save us from going down and Kevin often refers to the big centre half as his best-ever signing. He was a real character, although you wouldn't want to mess with him.

'Killer' suffered the ignominy of having his famous moustache shaved off on one boozy trip somewhere. Kevin would give the players permission to let off steam at times, always providing there wasn't any trouble – any antics which would see them on the front pages.

Anyway, one night 'Killer' had fallen asleep after a good few drinks and he woke up minus half his 'tache. Not surprisingly, he wasn't too happy and began the search for the guilty men. No-one owned up. If they had, I would hate to think what the repercussions would have been.

Killer was magnificent as a player and was great for the dressing room. He had great presence on and off the pitch and everyone looked up to him, but he was a little eccentric. He lived on a barge – I think he still does. The fans loved him because he was different with his long, flowing locks and Merv Hughes-type moustache.

Micky Quinn – my horse racing tipster – was still there too. In the summer, his contract had expired and the club had made him a new offer. He asked me what I thought and I told him he was the main man and should ask for more money.

"You're the leading scorer, try to get some extra bonuses written in too, mate," I advised him. He went back to them and they agreed everything. It was a fortune in those days and he couldn't thank me enough.

Anyhow, one day Kevin wanted to see what salaries all the players were on so he could plan for the future. Who to keep, who to let go. He started looking through all the contracts and when he came to Quinny's he was shocked. "Hell, you want to see what he is on," Kevin told me. I replied that I knew exactly what he was on because I'd told him how to negotiate the deal! I had to confess.

Most of the time the board came up with what Kevin wanted

and some of the signings were beyond belief for a club that had only just stayed in the Second Division. Barry Venison, for instance, was outstanding. He could play centre half and central midfield as well as right back and he was a really bright player. At that level, he was the best around. He had played for Sunderland and so even though we brought him from Liverpool, he still had to win the Newcastle fans over. He did that in no time at all. They adored him. He was brilliant, amongst the best two or three players we signed for the money. He only cost £250,000.

Barry had always been mature for his age, he was old school in many ways. He believed in working hard on the training ground and would always have an opinion if he felt it helped. The younger players looked up to him. He was also a dedicated follower of fashion which gave him street cred with the youngsters, although the older ones would rib him for his dress sense.

Some of his jackets were a bit outlandish to say the least but at least it gave us something to take the mickey out of. He liked a few drinks and was a bit of a Jack the Lad around town. Now he is happily living in California and I believe doesn't drink!

Kevin knew he had to make changes if we had any chance of getting into the Premier League. Quinny was sold to Coventry City in November, 1992 and in the February of 1993 we spent £1.75 million on Andy Cole. It was me who had to go and give him the once-over.

"Go and watch him for us," Kevin said. "Bristol City are at home tonight." To be honest, I didn't fancy going all that way by car so Kevin asked Douglas Hall, the vice-chairman, if we could use his private plane. Douglas said there would be no problem.

We flew down to Bristol and went to the game, but Andy only

lasted around 30 minutes before he went off with a hamstring injury. We couldn't believe it. We'd gone all this way and there was Coley limping off.

What happened next impressed me.

Suddenly he came back on with a big strapping on his leg. I don't think he stayed on too long, but that was enough for Kevin. In his view, anyone determined to carry on with a hamstring injury really wants to be a player. He was a magnificent signing. I've got a lot of time for him. He was a great lad.

Coley first knew about our interest after he came out of a launderette not far from where he was living and found a note on his car windscreen asking him to ring Bristol City as soon as he could. I hadn't seen anything like him for a long time when it came to finishing. He was so quick, rapid. You would go a long, long way to see finishing as clinical as Andy's. He scored goals for fun for us.

Coley was not outgoing compared to some of his team-mates and could be a bit of a loner, but that didn't stop him being liked. It takes all sorts to make up a dressing room. I seemed to be able to tune into his wavelength easier than some others. Players would have to pass the room where Kevin and I were based to go to the medical room. It depended on Coley's mood as to whether he would look into our room and say good morning or just turn his head the other way towards the toilets and not say anything.

But on the pitch he always delivered. He'd had a good upbringing with Arsenal before going to Bristol City and him and Peter Beardsley, who signed the next season, were incredible up front. We had a good team, but Cole's goals were the icing on the cake. He was a brave player as well. He didn't pull out of anything.

Far from being put off by the challenge of trying to lead Newcastle to promotion, Kevin was inspired. We had some start to the season. We won the first 11 games, which almost smashed a Football League record. Win number 11 came away at Sunderland 2-1.

"We could win every match this season," I told him.

"Don't be so bloody soft," was his reply.

The next week at home to Grimsby Town we lost 1-0. He quickly reminded me of what I'd said. It was a reality check.

There weren't many more blips and with Andy on fire up front-during the run-in – he scored 12 goals in 12 games including a hat-trick in a 6-0 win against Barnsley – we ended up winning promotion at Grimsby, of all places, with two games to spare. We won 2-0, Coley and David Kelly getting the goals. Let the celebrations begin!

Alan Oliver, the *Newcastle Evening Chronicle* reporter who covered all our games, would often see me after an away game and ask me if I wanted a beer. I always refused because I had promised Kevin that I would never drink when I was officially on duty with the players.

People would think there must be something wrong with me turning down the offer of a drink, but I wasn't going to let Kevin down. There was no way I was going to get blitzed after games. This time I made an exception. We had just won promotion so why not have a drink?

It was a great journey back to the North East. Fans were leaning out of the car windows waving flags and it still gives me a tingle now.

To go from the relegation precipice to the Premier League in less than 18 months was absolutely incredible.

It gave me as much pleasure as lifting the League Championship or European Cup with Liverpool. We had achieved so much in such a short time and completely against the odds.

The celebrations continued right through to the last game of the season when we played Leicester at home. We ended up thrashing them 7-1. It could have been 20-1. A new stand was being built at the Leazes End and the club had Lindisfarne playing there to make it a real party atmosphere. What a day.

When Kevin Keegan goes to a club you know something is going to happen. He has tremendous drive, but he's also a realist. He won't make promises he can't keep. His influence on people is unique. The fans are his lifeblood and he treats everyone as an equal. I've never ever seen him turn down a request for an autograph. Quite often, after Newcastle games all over the country, he would keep the coach waiting 45 minutes while he sat on the front seat signing every autograph, maintaining to the queue of eager fans that no-one would leave disappointed. It would be no different, no matter if we had lost. There would be no moans from the players because they knew what it meant to Kevin. They were also encouraged to do their bit by their manager. They knew there was nothing that Kevin couldn't achieve through his personality and drive.

In fact, the only ambition Kevin wasn't able to fulfil was riding in the Grand National!

That was something he has always wanted to do. He loves his horses and he kept on telling me that one day I would see him at Aintree in the famous race on board a horse. It wouldn't have shocked me if that had happened, but it wasn't to be.

Maybe if he had stayed out of football longer Kevin would have got there!

Once the summer had finished, we had to wake up to the reality that we were now in the promised land of the Premier League – and the fans were really up for it, as we were to quickly discover.

For training, we had to move from Benwell after half of it was transformed into housing. We knew to progress we had to move, but the club couldn't secure anything in the Newcastle area. It meant sharing Durham University's facilities which wasn't ideal, but we had no choice – there was nowhere else.

It was a real eye opener for some of the students. There was many a time when you would see David Ginola, Les Ferdinand and Peter Beardsley getting changed next to someone who had come in to play squash. You would have our players getting showered the same time as lads who had just finished playing five-a-side. I bet some of the kids couldn't believe who they were next to. They would wipe the soap out of their eyes and Andy Cole was there right in front of them.

Outside, there would be two or three thousand fans wanting to watch training. It was great business for the burger vans who would pitch up, none belonging to me by the way – those days had long gone!

Kevin embraced all this. He wanted the players to see for themselves what the football club meant to the supporters. Far from keeping the players away from them, he insisted that they mixed and be part of it.

Coley got it right in the neck one lunch-time when he tried to make a quick getaway. "Where are you going?" Kevin shouted when he noticed. "Go and spend time with them. These are the people who pay your wages." To be fair to Coley, it didn't happen again and he was very popular with the supporters.

One morning, Kevin and I were watching training – and it was an absolute pleasure seeing these players – when he asked me if I fancied a burger from one of the vans. "Yeah, why not?" So there we were – me and him eating burgers and, in between bites, shouting commands to the players who could hardly believe what they were seeing.

It was just invigorating. The whole place was taking off and we were part of it. There was a great camaraderie between the players and the fans – a complete contrast to what normally goes on now with players mollycoddled and kept away from the people who pay decent money to watch them.

We signed more players during the season, Ruel Fox and Darren Peacock among them, and managed to finish third which was incredible. We had some great results along the way. Coley scored a 26-minute hat-trick in a 3-0 win against Souey's Liverpool at St. James' Park, and we won 2-0 up at Anfield.

We also won at Everton and Tottenham, held champions Manchester United twice, put five past Aston Villa and beat Arsenal 2-0 on the final day of the season to finish above them and qualify for the UEFA Cup.

You don't see that happen now, a newly promoted side finishing in the top four, and under the current rules that would have meant Champions League football at St. James' Park.

The club was prepared to spend big money and once Kevin had the chance of speaking to a player that was usually it, he would be on his way – even if at times he would bend the truth a little.

We were after Robert Lee, who was with Charlton, but so were Middlesbrough. "You should sign for us," Kevin told him, before adding, "Newcastle is a lot easier to get to than Middlesbrough."

Kevin had worked out that Robert wasn't too sharp on his geography! Of course, Newcastle is further north but he finally swung the deal by insisting it was quicker to get to Newcastle from London. Well, it was if you went by plane to Newcastle Airport!

Robert was a top player, as was Paul Bracewell who had joined us from Sunderland – a brave move.

One day the two of them, after a game, decided to go out in Byker, not the most salubrious area of Newcastle. Barry Venison, who was also out, said the wrong thing to one girl in a rough old pub and Brace ended up being punched in the face by one of the other girls, leaving him with a black eye. It taught them not to mess around with the ladies in that area. You can imagine the lads in the dressing room when they got to hear all about it – attacked by a girl!

It was a great dressing room led by Kevin who was so passionate. Kevin wanted to be the best at anything he did. He wouldn't tolerate any bad apples in the dressing room but loved characters, even if they took a bit of handling.

Warren Barton was bubbly, a typical cockney with plenty to say, but a good fella. You would have John Beresford chirping away. It was a good mix because as well as the senior players we had good youngsters like Lee Clark and Steve Watson. They all stuck together and went out together every week. They loved each other's company.

We quickly discovered that David Ginola was a smoker – I think a lot of the French players smoked. They thought it was a natural thing to do. Kevin quickly put a stop to it especially when David began to light up on the coach. At first we thought the coach was on fire when the smell wafted over.

A quick glance backwards showed that the smoke was coming from our Frenchman. He was told that the days of smoking on football coaches had long gone! Reluctantly, he stopped, but I know whenever he could, he would light up – as long as Kevin wasn't anywhere near.

Our first year in the Premier League had been a huge thrill and success. We were the up-coming team in the division. We'd been the first promoted side in a long time to make the rest of the league sit up and take notice.

Good times – great times, in fact – were looming.

But not before Kevin's skills with the public were put to a huge test following a phone call from Manchester United…

CHAPTER 17

THE ENTERTAINERS

PICTURE the scene. It's January, 1995, and halfway through the season, Kevin and I are stood on the steps of St. James' Park having to speak to the fans. We are defending the shock sale of Andy Cole to Manchester United.

So how did it come to this?

It was all to do with Kevin believing Andy had lost that little bit of drive.

It came to a head when we were in London preparing for a game against Wimbledon in November, 1994. Andy wasn't doing what he should have been doing in training and Kevin told him to buck up his ideas.

It didn't matter who you were and what you had achieved, Kevin expected 100 per cent in training. That was as important to him as the actual matches. I'm certain Kevin had never given less than 100 per cent on the training pitch when he had been Europe's top player. He wasn't going to let Coley get off with anything. You could see there was something up because he was just going through the motions. Kevin was seething.

"Coley you're no use to us like this. You might as well go and get changed," he yelled.

Kevin hoped that would shake him up, but when Andy was full of attitude there was no shifting him. Instead of coming back with a reaction, he just sloped off to the dressing room. This wasn't the Andy Cole we had signed and who had taken the Premier League by storm, scoring 40 league goals in our first season back in the top-flight.

Kevin didn't pick him for the game, preferring Peter Beardsley and Paul Kitson up front instead. We ended up losing 3-2, as Mick Harford scored what turned out to be the winner in just the 36th minute.

Coley wasn't happy about being dropped and went in to see Kevin who told him in no uncertain terms that if he repeated his sulky actions then he would stay out of the team.

I know that shook Coley up because, like all the players, he respected Kevin and also loved being a number nine who the Newcastle fans adored. "Okay, gaffer, I won't let you down," Coley told Kevin, although I don't know how convinced Kevin really was, especially for the long term.

Really we needed him back because he was our goalscorer. Kevin told him to show us what he was capable of in training and that he would soon be back in the side. Coley trained properly and, true to his word, Kevin put him back in.

Players shouldn't be able to dictate to managers. That happens too often these days. Some managers are too scared to fall out with their star players because it could cost them their jobs, but Kevin made certain he was always in control and the players knew that.

Even though Coley was brought back into the team, Kevin felt he wasn't the same player as the one who had caused mayhem in his early days on Tyneside. He thought he had gone a bit stale and he didn't have that spring in his step.

Was he being tapped? I don't know. Could he have been tapped? Probably. He wasn't the same Andy Cole anyway. He does have a dark, sinister side and he could be awkward, although on his day there were few better strikers. That's his make-up. Kevin never told me once that he wanted to sell him. But Manchester United came in with an offer in the January worth a British record £7 million which we accepted.

Kevin had told me the bombshell news before training and although there had been no rush to get him out of the door, it was good money, added to the fact that we had talked about trying to sign Les Ferdinand from QPR for some time. Coley's sale would arm us with the money to tie up Les, who was a fantastic striker.

If it had been my decision I wouldn't have kept Andy Cole either. As far as we were both concerned, he had lost something. Kevin always had the final decision, but I knew where he was coming from on this.

Kevin, though, wasn't going to let Manchester United have things all their own way in the transfer. The move came with a stipulation – Keith Gillespie would have to be included in the deal.

If Manchester United hadn't have agreed to that, Kevin

wouldn't have sold Andy Cole. I didn't know too much about
Keith but Kevin did and he had liked what he had seen. As far
as Manchester United and Sir Alex Ferguson were concerned,
he was one for the future, but they were prepared to let him go.

Even so, Coley's sale didn't go down well with the fans. The
announcement had been made that Andy was leaving the club
and Kevin and I were upstairs in the office at St. James' Park
when fans started gathering on the steps below. This could only
happen at Newcastle. The crowd was growing and growing.
What could we do? By about 5pm there were even more fans
there. People were finishing work and going straight to St.
James' Park, upset by Cole's transfer.

Kevin said he was going outside to talk to the fans. "You've
got to be joking," I told him. "What are you going to tell them?"

"The truth," he answered back. "They've got a right to know.
They pay good money to watch us."

Freddy Shepherd, who was with us, couldn't believe it but
Kevin insisted they needed to explain their actions. He told
Freddy that he and I would go down. I must admit I wasn't too
keen, but I admired Kevin. Only he would do something like
that. It's why most people like him. He's so honest. He's got time
for everybody. These fans were hurt and they couldn't believe
what Kevin had done.

He just said to the supporters: "Listen guys, you are going to
have to trust me. I've made a decision, it's not been easy." They
were yelling back 'why Kevin, why have you done this?' Kevin
replied: "I've done it for the benefit of this football club. I'm
prepared to take the flak. I'm not getting rid of someone I don't
like or anything like that. We just think it will be best for the
club in the long run. Just wait and see who we bring in."

He thought he would be able to go and sign Les Ferdinand from QPR straight away. In the end, he had to wait until the summer for Les so in the meantime we had players like Paul Kitson up front, which probably cost us because we ended up finishing sixth with Andy still finishing as joint-leading scorer with Peter Beardsley on 15 goals.

But name me another manager who would have stood on those steps, explaining a decision to the supporters? No-one would do it. It was brave of him, but typical of the man.

That season had seen us finish lower in the table than the year before but things were still looking up.

Les Ferdinand finally arrived along with David Ginola, but no-one could have predicted our stunning start to the 1995/96 season – one in which Kevin was at last able to answer the critics of Andy Cole's sale. We kicked off with four straight wins before a defeat at Southampton. Then we won another five before a 1-1 draw at White Hart Lane.

Les scored in three of the first four games and just carried on in great scoring form, ending up with 25 Premier League goals in his first season for the club. He was great in the air, quick for his size and knew where the net was. He was a magnificent person off the pitch as well.

We loved him even more because he brought fantastic women to the club! There was a conveyer belt of beauties, he was never without a Miss World type on his arm. Les was a charmer and women seemed to fall at his feet.

Although he had spent all his life in the London area, Les quickly fell in love with the North East. He admitted that he had never seen so much passion surrounding football. "Even the girls want to talk about football," he would grin. Les had come up the hard way through non-league and appreciated every minute as a top footballer. He was a hell of a player and although we had been forced to wait to sign him, it was well worth it.

We had a team who were virtually all talkers – leaders in their own right. Belgian centre-half Philippe Albert was one of the nicest fellas you would ever wish to meet, but as a player he was a man mountain. He reminded me of Ron Yeats at Liverpool, who Bill Shankly called his Colossus. We also had John Beresford, another positive person and Rob Lee who would do his talking on the pitch – a really important player for us week in, week out. Darren Peacock was another giant of a man at the back for us. And they were all in it together.

Peter Beardsley was teetotal, a drop of alcohol never touched his lips, but he would still join the other lads on an evening out, visiting a few bars or having a meal together somewhere. Once a week they would all go out as a big group. They did so with Kevin's and my blessing. "Right lads," Kevin would tell them if he knew they were about to go out. "Let's keep you on the back pages of the newspapers and off the front."

It was a great mix, you'd have David Ginola sat with a cigarette on the go, complete with a glass of nice wine, while Barry Venison would be knocking the pints back, often dressed in some garish outfit. There wasn't any trouble if they bumped into any fans around the Newcastle area because there was a great bond between the supporters and the players. The city was alive with football. Everyone lived and breathed it.

You can always tell a good team by the atmosphere of a dressing room. If you've got a good team allied to a good dressing room then you have a chance of winning things. We had a great dressing room, and I mean a *great* dressing room. I've never known anything like this team spirit – and I've known some good ones over the years, Liverpool in their heyday, for example. We knew during those balmy days at Anfield that we were going to win games and at Newcastle it was the same with this team. We believed that we were capable of beating anyone.

David Ginola was a great player who just glided over the pitch. I've never known anyone be able to turn both ways with the ball like he could when he was close to the by-line.

Normally, when a winger is close to the touchline, he's going to cut inside but David could turn on the proverbial sixpence and go down the line. I'd never seen anyone manage that consistently before. He would do it week in, week out.

I remember Kevin asking David to show some young kids who were watching us train how he did this trick of going on the outside when there was virtually no space. He asked David to show them.

Kevin knocked the ball up to him. He went to turn but David could only push the ball out of play. He went to do it again and failed once more. He just couldn't do it. David finally turned around to Kevin and said, "Gaffer, I can only do this successfully on matchdays."

So obviously it was intuitive.

For six to eight months, he probably played some of the best football I have ever seen. You knew when you had Ginola in the side you always had a chance. What better attacking option could you possibly have?

Typical of David, just before the 2016 European Championships, he had a serious heart problem, but after a quadruple heart bypass he was back on the telly a few weeks later, present-ing a show for French TV. Nothing seems to faze him.

After winning nine of our first 10 games to head the Premier League table, people were talking us up as potential champi-ons. At Christmas, we were still top, with a healthy lead over Manchester United. In fact, we were still in a good position in March, despite losing at West Ham and drawing at Manchester City.

When it mattered we suffered a lot of bad luck, hitting the woodwork and having shots cleared off the line. I've seen tapes of games and I'm in despair thinking how we did not win some of them. I know some people think it's a lame excuse, but I believe it 100 per cent.

For instance, we absolutely hammered our main contenders Manchester United at St. James' Park at the start of March but Peter Schmeichel pulled off save after save, many of them world class and we ended up losing 1-0 to an Eric Cantona goal early in the second half. It kept United in the title race.

I think the club was jinxed – and I wasn't the only one who thought that.

There was even talk at one stage of bringing in an exorcist to try and rid ourselves of the demons which we thought had invaded the club. I know Kevin was keen to look into it after lis-tening to some of the older supporters who swore that a curse had been cast over the club because the area, in centuries gone by, was supposed to be associated with the hanging of witches. Maybe this was now payback time.

As the season approached a climax, it was all about us and Manchester United – who was going to come out on top?

The irony has never left me that probably our dream of winning the Premier League faded with that famous 4-3 defeat at Liverpool at the start of April which I talked about earlier in this book. It was heartbreaking and the years haven't softened the hurt. It affects me today just as much as 20 odd years ago. We ended up being gutted but we should have been proud too after the performance we had put in.

As usual, our fans were unbelievable. They knew we had done everything possible to try to win the game.

At the final whistle, I shook hands with now Liverpool manager Roy Evans. Roy was a real diamond. There was so much respect between Kevin and Roy so even after what we had been through, there was no lack of formalities after the final whistle. We were suffering badly and really I just wanted to get away from it all as quickly as I could. I wanted the ground to open up so I could just disappear down a great black hole.

Kevin, meanwhile, admitted he had come close to punching Sammy Lee's lights out.

Sammy, who we both knew well, was one of the Liverpool coaches and went berserk after Stan Collymore's late winning goal. While we're both hanging over the advertising hoarding, he's doing a jig right in front of our dugout. He was beside himself, jumping up and down, which he often does but where he did it was completely out of order. If he had got any closer, Kevin would have knocked him out. Sammy is a smashing bloke but you don't do that. He was dancing in front of all of our staff. To be fair to Sammy, he rang Kevin the next day and apologised.

Losing 4-3 in the last minute of a game which has gone down in football folklore was gut wrenching, it left me sick in the stomach. Imagine your worst feeling and double it. Horrible.

Would we have won the Premier League if we had beaten Liverpool? Almost certainly, yes. You have to give some credit to Manchester United, though, as they kept doing what was needed. They kept winning games 1-0, usually in the 92nd minute, and they kept getting the three points.

Despite missing out on the title, we were still the best team in the country at that time. We were exciting and were quickly dubbed 'The Entertainers'. I don't think there has been a side since who have played the brand of buccaneering football we provided during this incredible season.

Every day, I couldn't wait to get to training and work with this group of players Kevin had assembled. It was just phenomenal. The camaraderie showed out on the pitch. Anfield aside, if the opposition scored two, we'd get three; if they scored three, we'd get four – it was magnificent to watch.

We had great players. I look back now at some of the goals we scored during this period and some of them are beyond belief.

I know when some people try to dissect the reasons why we didn't win the League they will point to the signing of Tino Asprilla, and to some extent that of David Batty, in February, 1996.

One hundred per cent, Asprilla didn't cost us the League title and it was the same with Batty. Some people were saying he wasn't the type of player we needed. Without a shadow of a doubt they were our best two players at the time. Maybe after that Liverpool defeat some players started having doubts about themselves for the first time because, remember, we didn't have many players with the experience of winning a League title – perhaps just Batty at Leeds United.

Tino was a real character, a lunatic, but a nice one. He was a fantastic addition to the dressing room. He was very funny, mad as a hatter. You just didn't know what he was going to do next. He used to rent a house in the Newcastle area and would have parties in it almost every night. When he finally left Newcastle and gave up the house, the owners discovered he had turned it into a disco, fluorescent lights, the lot.

We also found loads of his wage slips around the place. There was blood from cuts from parties, obviously people had broken glasses. We had to send people to clean the place up. The lads loved him. I saw him on TV recently. He's a lot bigger than he was. He lives in his native Colombia and has a pile of rifles in his house! He was always a bit different.

Kevin and I knew what he got up to. We knew what all the players were doing. Anyway, after what I had done over the years who was I to say *you can't do this, you can't do that?*

During my time as a player any Saturday was the most important day of my life. It was the same for a Tuesday or Wednesday night when we had a game. If I couldn't have performed like I did for Liverpool on those given dates, I wouldn't have gone out.

And I know some people will disagree but we could defend that season. Our record wasn't as bad as some people have imagined. We let in 37 goals, only bettered by Arsenal (32), Liverpool (34), Aston Villa and Manchester United (35) so, as you can see, we weren't that bad. But Kevin's philosophy was to attack and that season the football was, at times, breathtaking. I've never seen anything like it.

The defiant spirit amongst the squad was borne out in the coach journey back to the North East after that Liverpool loss.

Nobody was in a bad mood and the atmosphere was good. We felt there were still enough games to win the League and, as far as Kevin was concerned, they had given everything at Anfield so he didn't allow the performance to outweigh the result.

Normally, on the way back from an away trip, we would stop off at Wetherby, up the A1, for fish and chips. *The Wetherby Wailer* was our traditional port of call. Some of us, including Kevin, would take the orders and queue up amongst the locals. But by the time we reached Wetherby after the Liverpool game, played on a Monday night, the chippy was long shut.

At least it meant there was no interruption for the card players in the squad. They would often call Kevin up to the back of the bus for a game. They would shout 'come on gaffer do you want to play?' We were quick to have a beer with them and have a joke. Oh, and by the way, many a time it would be Kevin and me running off the coach and into an off-licence to buy the crate of beer. There was no demarcation, we were all in it together.

Everyone goes on about Kevin supposedly losing his marbles after our 1-0 victory at Leeds a few weeks later and giving Sir Alex Ferguson a psychological advantage. He famously told Sky Sports that "I would love it if we beat them" and that has gone down in folklore as evidence that Fergie had the upper hand psychologically on Kevin. Absolute nonsense.

We'd just won at Elland Road. Kevin came on to the coach to tell me he would be five minutes because he had to do something for Sky Sports. He was laughing. Suddenly when he was put in front of the camera he must have thought back to what Fergie had said in trying to motivate Leeds to beat us. But I've never known words from anyone score a goal or influence a game, so no matter what Fergie or Kevin said, it didn't make any difference during games. It's the players who make the difference on the field. None of our players had gone on about what Ferguson had said and maybe Kevin had just had enough of what he had been trying to do.

The first we knew about it was seeing Kevin on the telly while sitting on the coach. Hardly anyone made a comment. It's not something that we ever spoke about.

I know the main accusation from that season is that we bottled winning the title, which is a horrible thing to say.

Especially when it's not true.

In fact, we still had a chance to win the Premier League going into the last day of the season. If we had beaten Tottenham at home and United had lost at Middlesbrough we would have been champions. But the writing had been on the wall.

What lifted us was the wonderful reception we received from the fans on our end of season walk around the pitch.

There was now a determination to go again the next season. It might have knocked the stuffing out of us, but we soon got our mojo back.

My mate Kevin: We hit it off from the word go and so much of my career at Liverpool, England and Newcastle was spent with someone I've shared great times and had great laughs with!

Feel the force: I'm not normally one to hog the limelight, but when I'm with Kevin there always seems to be someone with a camera around!

Coaching career: I had two special spells as first-team coach at Newcastle, getting to work with Kevin twice more

Room for one more: We liked to include everyone on the Newcastle team photo – and my son Greg wanted to be in on it too

Promotion party: Kevin turned things around as Newcastle manager and we got the club back into the Premier League in 1993 after finishing as Division One champions

The entertainers: Newcastle won admirers for their style but couldn't quite clinch the Premier League title

Sinking feeling: Seconds after Liverpool made it 4-3 in April '96 and dented our title dreams

Wembley walk: I led the team out for the Charity Shield match against Manchester United in 1996

Still got it: At the training ground just after Kevin's resignation in 1997

Toon legend: When I joined Newcastle as a coach for a second time in 2005, Alan Shearer was still there

Old friend: I stayed on at Newcastle when Kenny Dalglish was appointed

Second spell: I served under Graeme Souness, Sam Allardyce (pictured), Glenn Roeder and Kevin between 2005-2008

Footballing journey: I've had coaching spells at Celtic, Huddersfield Town and Birmingham City – and folded my arms at every one of them!

Good times: Having a few beers with my brother Robert (above) and my father-in-law (below) at my 'second home', the Quarry Green Social Club

The great and the good: Outside football I've met some interesting people like Princess Anne, Wet Wet Wet's Marti Pellow, singer Kim Wilde and legendary jockey Lester Piggott

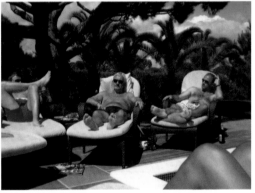

Sun, shades and Shearer: A bit of relaxation time away with the Newcastle boys

Feeding time: I was fond of horse racing as a player and have continued to follow it since

Real thoroughbred: Alan Shearer and I were part-owners of phenomenally-successful race horse Intersky Falcon, which won many big races including back-to-back Christmas Hurdles

A different paddock: Phil Thompson and the Liverpool boys join me at the stables

Friends reunited: With Kenny Dalglish and Alan Hansen (top) and Kevin Keegan and Alan Shearer (above)

Oh Carole: A recent photo with my lovely wife (top) and our three grown-up kids (above)

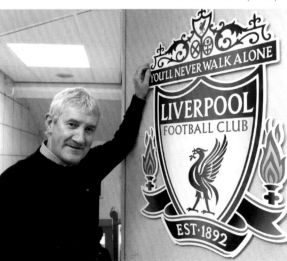

This is Anfield: These days you can often find me at the home of Liverpool Football Club, where I enjoyed my greatest successes as a player, telling my stories to the fans on legends stadium tours

CHAPTER 18

THE BLACK BOX

NY lingering hangover from missing out on the title was removed when we paid out a world record fee of £15 million to sign Alan Shearer from Blackburn Rovers before the start of the 1996/97 season.

To be honest, I couldn't believe that we had pulled it off – one of the best strikers in the world coming to Tyneside. The club even built a special stage just outside the ground so he could be presented to the supporters. There were about 10,000 fans flocking around Alan – just incredible scenes.

Douglas Hall had been the real instigator behind Alan's shock signing.

If he had something in his mind he would try to deliver. Sometimes his ideas were a bit over the top, but he would still try to go for it. He tried once to sign the top Italian striker Roberto Baggio. Kevin couldn't believe it when Douglas said he was going over to Italy to try and bring Baggio to St. James' Park.

I ended up going with Douglas and Freddy Shepherd. We arrived unannounced at Juventus and knocked on the door. Douglas said: "I'm Douglas Hall of Newcastle United in England. Who do I speak to in order to sign Roberto Baggio?" The Juve official told him there was no-one at the club available to talk about Baggio and, in any case, he was not for sale.

So Douglas and the rest of us had to slope out of the ground and head back to Turin Airport.

Not to be defeated, Douglas wondered whether we could now find the money to try to sign Alan Shearer. Kevin obviously wanted him because Alan was the best striker in the country. We knew we had to pay big money and Kevin found out that it would cost Newcastle £15 million to bring Alan to Tyneside.

Douglas told Kevin: "Leave it to me, I'll get it sorted."

Alan got in touch with the Blackburn owner Jack Walker and told him he wanted to leave.

The only problem we had was Manchester United were also desperate to sign Alan and had already met him. There was even talk of Alan looking at property in the Manchester area. Kevin moved in quickly and spoke to Alan himself and arranged to meet him. Even though he was on the verge of agreeing to join United, Alan changed his mind after listening to Kevin's plans. Being a proud Geordie and committed Newcastle fan, he also saw it as his chance to come home.

Even so, £15 million was a huge fee and there were some doubts that we could manage to find the money. Kevin didn't even think it was a possibility, especially when Jack Walker insisted on the fee being paid in one hit. Somehow we managed to meet that requirement and he was soon on a plane with Kevin to join the rest of us on a pre-season trip to the Far East.

Alan, being black and white through and through, had just one stipulation before he agreed to sign – and it had nothing to do with money. He wanted to wear the number 9 shirt. He wasn't coming unless that number was his. That left us with a big problem because Les Ferdinand was the proud owner of that iconic Newcastle shirt.

Not many people can carry that number, worn by legends like Jackie Milburn and Malcolm Macdonald.

Kevin had to call Les in and ask him to give it up. Les wasn't happy, but thankfully agreed, allowing Alan to carry on the tradition of great Newcastle number nines.

We now had attacking options of Shearer, Ferdinand, Ginola, Beardsley, Asprilla, Gillespie and Lee – simply mouthwatering.

Despite that, the season didn't get off to the best of starts as we lost 4-0 at Wembley in the Charity Shield against Manchester United, who had completed the Double in May.

At least I had the honour of leading out the side at Wembley. Kevin insisted I should do it. I normally wore a tracksuit for games, so I knew this time I would have to be booted and suited. Come the big day, I was at the front of the line but the only problem was I'd set off at quite a pace, waving to people in the crowd – when I finally looked around, the players were miles behind me! I felt like a big idiot yards in front of them, completely isolated.

As soon as the formalities were over I dashed straight back down the tunnel and changed into my normal tracksuit.

TERRY MAC

At least we gained some revenge for that day by thumping United 5-0 at St. James' Park in the October, Philippe Albert placing the seal on a wonderful performance with a fantastic chip over Peter Schmeichel.

It could have been 8-0. We hammered them. The game has gone down in Geordie folklore. Everything we touched that day turned into gold – and what an atmosphere. We might have had some fortune with the first goal because from Alan Shearer's knockdown Darren Peacock's header was scooped away by Denis Irwin, but the referee ruled it had gone over the line. Peter Schmeichel went charging towards the touchline pursued by David Beckham to remonstrate with the officials.

Manchester United couldn't argue with the next four goals. David Ginola has scored some great goals during his career but the one he struck to make it 2-0 takes some beating, curling a terrific drive around Schmeichel from outside the area – and with his right foot too, just to prove how good he was with both feet.

Before half-time we were 3-0 up with a goal owed to a fantastic cross from Alan Shearer who had selflessly burst down the right wing for Les Ferdinand to score with a terrific header which cannoned in off the underside of the bar, making it look even more dramatic.

"Same again please lads," Kevin requested at the interval. They were bouncing, sensing that it was going to be a great day in Newcastle's history. If United were going to make a fight of it they would have to score early in the second half but instead we made it 4-0. Alan Shearer hammered in the rebound after Schmeichel had somehow kept out a close range shot from Les, who had followed up a blocked effort from Peter Beardsley.

Then came one of the greatest goals I've seen, the audacious Albert chip. I probably got on Kevin's nerves because after every goal I was jumping all over him, but that was one to celebrate.

That performance has lived on in all our memories. It was the best game I was involved in with Newcastle. To say it was our turn against Manchester United was an understatement. It was the perfect game for Kevin because he has always wanted to win games, but do so in style. No-one could question those two qualities that day.

Alex Ferguson normally comes in after games for a glass of red wine but we didn't see him after the 5-0. I'm not surprised – it's not often they lost games by that scoreline. We've had some good conversations over the years after games, often talking about horses because, as everyone knows, he's a big horse racing fan. I don't think he was in any mood to listen to or give out any racing tips that day.

Little did anyone know that we were fast approaching the end of the Kevin Keegan era.

Just after Christmas we thrashed Spurs 7-1 at St. James' Park and, typical of Kevin, he ended up feeling sorry for Gerry Francis who was the Tottenham manager. Of course, he was delighted we had played so well, but there was no way he wanted to dance on Gerry's grave, especially after the two of them were once England team-mates.

Away from football, I knew Kevin wasn't happy with the club being floated on the stock market and he felt that it was starting to resemble a business rather than a traditional club.

It all blew up when Newcastle tried to persuade Kevin to sign a new 10-year contract in the January.

Kevin knew it was all tied up with the club flotation, it was all about proving to the financial gurus in London that he was part of the new-look football club. Despite starting to think about leaving, he agreed to attend a meeting.

The Newcastle hierarchy were there – plus a new financial man that Kevin had never met before in his life.

Within minutes, this bloke, who he never knew, pushed the new contract towards Kevin on the table and started taking over the talks, insisting to Kevin how important it was to sign this new deal.

Kevin told this guy, who was now seemingly in charge of the new contract, that he didn't know him. He also said he wasn't having it.

"You'll have to sign it," replied the financial man.

"I don't have to sign it," Kevin insisted.

That was it as far as Kevin was concerned. He didn't like what was happening and didn't want to be part of it.

He phoned me up.

"It's finished pal," he blurted out. And he meant it.

I was in the Swinburn pub in Stamfordham playing pool with a mate, enjoying a few pints. I couldn't believe it. We had unfinished business, a league title to win. I had been enjoying myself. Now I felt absolutely gutted. I knew he was upset and that there would be little or no chance of him changing his mind.

Later the phone went again and it was Freddie Fletcher, the chief executive, asking me to go to the ground.

I'd had a good drink and I could have done without this. At least this time I had a driver! So he took me to St. James' Park. Freddie asked me to take over. I told him I wanted to speak to Kevin first. He wanted me to explain what had happened to the players the next day in training. As I'm walking out, stunned, Freddy Shepherd – who had also been at the ground, came up to me.

"Terry," he said. "Can you get hold of Kenny Dalglish for me?"

I asked him why and Freddy stated that they fancied him as the new manager. "I can ask," I told him.

Kenny was out of work after leaving Blackburn, who he had led to the 1994/95 Premier League title.

I was still devastated at the news that Kevin had quit, but Freddy's actions showed that they weren't prepared to try to make Kevin change his mind.

I rang Kenny the next day. He was on his way to a funeral in Scotland. I asked him if he would be interested in taking over from Kevin and he admitted he would be, but couldn't meet them that day. They arranged to meet Kenny the next day in a hotel, The Tickled Trout, just off the M6 near Preston.

Obviously I knew Kenny well and got on great with him, but there was no way I was going to stay unless Kevin gave me his blessing.

"Kevin, I came in with you and I'll go out with you mate," I told him. Kevin, being Kevin, wasn't having any of that.

"No way," he said. "You love the club and you should stay." I told him I had been asked to ring Kenny and he was great about it, pointing out that I lived in the area while he would now go back to live in his Southampton home.

Kenny said yes to the job and immediately asked me to stay on because he wanted me on board. I agreed and we both signed contracts. He also brought in Alan Irvine on the youth coaching side and we still had first team coach and my old Newcastle boss Arthur Cox, who was great around the club.

Things didn't change drastically because, strangely, Kevin and Kenny are very similar in many ways. They share the same sense of humour. People can get the wrong impression about Kenny and can think he is a bit abrupt but in reality he's always winding people up through his humour. He can't tell jokes but his stories are good. I was lucky that Kenny had come in. It could have been anyone and I could have been on my way.

Once again I had survived, which was going to happen a few times at Newcastle – so much so that I got the nickname 'The Black Box' – nobody could get rid of me. I was indestructible.

After Kevin left, I had to tell the players. They couldn't believe it. Most of them just sat in the training ground dressing room looking down at the floor. They idolised him and obviously wanted to know what had gone on.

"Was there a chance he would come back?" one of them asked. "No, not this time," I replied. Alan Shearer looked particularly bemused and you could see the frustration and anger boiling up in him. He had only been at Newcastle half a season and the man who had persuaded him to sign on for a world record fee was gone. He asked if I was staying and I told him I was. The one big consolation for Alan was, of course, that he knew Kenny from their successful days at Blackburn together.

Kevin was a hard act to follow, but under Kenny we managed to finish second in the table again, which meant we now qualified for the Champions League after a change of UEFA rules.

We'd also reached the quarter-final of the UEFA Cup, losing to Monaco, and only been beaten twice in the Premier League after Kenny's arrival, but despite this he struggled to win the fans over. They had adored Kevin and it didn't matter who had taken over, they would not have been readily accepted after what had gone before them. If people are prepared to analyse Kenny's record as Newcastle manager it wasn't bad. Kenny also loved being at the club, but didn't have the best of luck.

Before a ball had been kicked the next season he had lost David Ginola and Les Ferdinand, who were both sold to Spurs.

Every time David, who was a good lad by the way, went back to France to visit his family, there would be a story saying he was leaving Newcastle for this club and that club. One time there was talk of Barcelona coming in for him. It was all over the papers.

At the training ground, we had a get-together on the pitch and the players were all sat down while Kenny and I are stood up.

He looked at David and said: "How come every time you go home there is a story saying you are joining another club?"

"I have nothing to do with these stories," David snapped back.

"It used to happen when Kevin was the manager – didn't it Terry?" said Kenny. I thought 'why has he dragged me into this?' But I had to agree with Kenny.

"No, Terry you are wrong," David moaned. Later, David pulled me because he was hurt at the suggestions that he had manipulated the stories. Just to calm everything down, we agreed it must have been his agent. But we knew that David was looking to get away. In the end, it was Tottenham and not Barcelona where he ended up.

Kenny was great at looking into a player's mindset and with David he knew what was going on, but tackled it in a fairly lighthearted manner. He wasn't one for big confrontations.

There was more bad news at the start of the new campaign when Alan Shearer got a bad injury in a pre-season Umbro Cup match against Chelsea at Everton. That was more than 30 goals gone in one go with Les no longer at the club.

Alan was devastated, especially with it happening in a game which really didn't matter that much. But he was a hardened professional and was determined to get back as soon as possible. He never cut any corners, listened to what people said and probably came back in record time for an ankle injury of that nature.

Another time he had a hernia and again was the quickest to return from that. The normal time a player would be out with a hernia was around three weeks. Alan was back in 10 days. He never liked missing games.

Amongst all this, Kenny still managed to record a stunning victory over Barcelona in the Champions League at St. James' Park in September, 1997. We won 3-2 with a hat-trick from Tino Asprilla. It was another night that has gone down in Geordie folklore, going 3-0 up before half-time with a Tino goal-show and then hanging on after the break. It was like the Alamo with Barcelona going for it, but we did it. No-one can take that away from Kenny.

We also reached the FA Cup final despite the set-backs which had played havoc with our performances in the Premier League, in which we finished a disappointing 13th.

The fans weren't happy with what was going on in the transfer market, believing that many of Kenny's buys were inferior to the players he allowed to leave.

Some of that was put to one side by reaching the Cup final, although along the way there was a struggle to beat non-league Stevenage in the fourth round. We drew 1-1 away before scrambling a 2-1 win on Tyneside. The semi-final at Old Trafford was tough against Sheffield United, who were a division below us, but a fit-again Alan Shearer scored the only goal.

We never looked like winning in the final against Arsenal and it was another Wembley disappointment, Nicolas Anelka getting the killer second goal in a 2-0 defeat. I suppose the writing was on the wall for Kenny with some of the fans chanting '*attack, attack, attack*', believing he didn't share the same sense of adventure as Kevin.

Within a month of the 1998/99 season, Kenny had been sacked. I wasn't too surprised considering something that had happened at the cup final.

Freddie Fletcher, the chief executive, had been talking to a group of people after the Arsenal defeat in the Banqueting Hall at Wembley. He was telling them that he didn't fancy Kenny as the manager and he would try to get him out.

Little did Freddie know that one of Kenny's mates was in the huddle and relayed the conversation to him. Kenny, of course, told me after confronting Freddie, who denied saying anything. He knew that Freddie was after him. We used to call him the 'Jockweiler' because he was very determined. To be fair, he was very good for the club, but never hit it off with Kenny. Maybe it was something to do with the fact that Kenny was very much Celtic and Freddie was of the Rangers persuasion.

Kenny also had a problem with Bob Cass, an influential football writer in *The Mail On Sunday*. I had a lot of time for Bob, but he was getting stuck into Kenny saying that he should be moved on. Kenny decided to invite him into his office for a frank chat. Kenny asked me to come in as well. I liked Bob, but I felt this time he had been out of order with what he had written.

I thought they were going to make up but the conversation got animated. They were having a real go at each other. Bob's final retort to Kenny was: "I'll get you out of this club." I thought that was a controversial thing to say to a football manager. Kenny just replied: "We'll see." Within a few weeks, Kenny was gone. The dice seemed loaded against him from all different areas.

I remember how it all happened. Kenny was staying in a house in Low Fell, Gateshead, owned by Douglas Hall. I got a call from him one Sunday evening asking if I fancied going for a Chinese meal. I declined as I'd just had a big roast dinner, but I could tell that something wasn't right, especially Kenny wanting to have a chat with me on a Sunday evening.

In the end, I decided to go. He told me he wasn't happy with the way things were going.

A couple of days later, Kenny was coming back up to the North East from his Southport home when he got a call telling him not to come in, the club were relieving him of his duties. So he turned back. I was also told not to come in, so I decided to get away from everything and stayed overnight at Richmond, where a mate has some racing stables. Being with horses is a great release from football for me.

Eventually, I got another call asking me to go and see Douglas Hall and Freddy Shepherd. They asked me to stay and look after the Academy. I said that wasn't for me. In the meantime, Ruud Gullit was coming in as manager.

It had been done so quickly that I imagined that they had sorted out Gullit before letting Kenny go. I turned down the job offer and sorted out my leaving terms, which were very fair. I'd been with the first team so I didn't want to drop down.

No-one likes losing their job, especially at a club you care about, but that was it. It was heartbreaking, to be honest. I could have carried on with the same money but I didn't feel it was right, especially after they had got rid of Kenny so soon into the new season. Kenny had known since May that his days were numbered once he found out his chief executive was gunning for him.

Kenny was criticised for bringing in players he knew from his Liverpool days, like Ian Rush and John Barnes. They were getting on a bit, but they were still special players. Stuart Pearce came in as well. Stuart was brilliant to have around the place. He would run through a brick wall for you. He would always be in other players' ears trying to gee them up. He was Mr. Motivator. There was some good experience at the time. Some people might have thought it was turning into an old people's home, but they were still good players. It was a good dressing room, but the results weren't brilliant.

We'd brought in French World Cup winner, Stéphane Guivarc'h from Auxerre, but it didn't work out for him. At Newcastle he couldn't hit a cow's behind with a banjo. It wasn't for the want of trying. A year earlier we'd signed Danish striker Jon Dahl Tomasson who didn't do a thing at Newcastle, but went on to star for AC Milan.

Kenny also signed Gary Speed in February, 1998. Speedo used to call me Postman Pat. I knew he was unhappy at Everton so I was ringing him up all the time telling him to hand in a transfer request. He said I was like Postman Pat asking him if he'd put his letter in yet!

We had a nucleus of a good team but Kenny wasn't given enough time to mould everything into place. I think he should have been shown more respect for what he had achieved in the game.

Kenny is a winner just like Kevin Keegan, but 18 months just wasn't enough.

He also got slaughtered by the supporters for selling Les Ferdinand, but that wasn't his decision. At the time it was kept quiet, but the banks were putting pressure on the club to raise some money and Kenny was told that they needed £6 million as quickly as possible from player sales. He insisted that he didn't want to sell any of his best players. There were players he would let go, but no-one had come in for them.

So Kenny was told in no uncertain terms that raising the money was the priority, not the good of the team.

He said the only way to do it was to let Les go. He knew Spurs were interested. They told him to do it, leaving Kenny to carry the flak. Les wasn't just a fans' favourite, he was a favourite of mine and Kenny's and he wasn't happy because he loved it at Newcastle.

He would have been at Newcastle for many years if the bank hadn't had their say. I know Les loves coming back to the area at any opportunity now and still enjoys a great rapport with the Newcastle fans.

After Alan was badly injured at Everton, Freddie Fletcher tried to stop the deal because Les hadn't put pen to paper on the Tottenham move, but Les said no, because Newcastle had originally been desperate to sell him.

That meant Kenny was now without both Alan Shearer and Les Ferdinand.

Not long after, he was without a job.

CHAPTER 19

BACKING
A WINNER

I T wouldn't be long before I was linking up again with
Kenny – this time at Celtic.

Danny Wilson had also asked me to join up with him at
Sheffield Wednesday and I went to meet him in Wetherby. I'd
known Danny for a few years and I was flattered but I already
knew that Kenny was trying to get me to Celtic, where he had
become Director of Football in the summer of 1999 with John
Barnes as the manager. Danny told me if the Celtic offer didn't
materialise there was a job for me at Sheffield Wednesday.

But the call came from Kenny to come up to Glasgow and join
him and John.

"Would you be interested in coming up?"

"Of course I bloody would. Celtic? It would be brilliant."

He wasn't going to beg me but posed the question. I immediately thought it would be a great club to be at, especially with 60,000 singing *You'll Never Walk Alone*!

So I drove up with my wife Carole and now three kids, Neale, Rachel and Greg. I wanted to move the family up there but Neale, who was 12 at the time, was crying his eyes out. He didn't want to leave his school and his mates. It broke my heart. I thought 'I can't put him through this' and so I decided to keep the family in England while I took a flat in Glasgow.

I loved the experience at Celtic even though there were some hairy moments. I was appointed assistant to John Barnes. I watched a lot of games, looking at players with Kenny or with Eric Black, who was also on the coaching staff, but things started going wrong on the pitch – not helped by the fact that Rangers were top of the League.

We were always playing catch-up, which is not what the Celtic fans want. One of the biggest blows we suffered was losing Henrik Larsson to a double leg fracture. Henrik was a superb player and a real loss to the side. Mark Viduka was also there. He really impressed me, scoring 25 SPL goals that season, and when I left Celtic I told Newcastle to try and sign him.

The Celtic fans certainly didn't expect to watch their team lose to part-time second tier side Inverness Caledonian Thistle at Celtic Park. After that 3-1 defeat in February, 2000, our fans went berserk. After the game, we went into the manager's room and looked out of the window to see thousands of fans demonstrating outside the main entrance.

I looked at Barnesy. "They're going to string us up," I said. I wasn't joking either. This was a club that had just suffered probably the most embarrassing result in its history – and with two former England internationals in charge. Not the place to be right now. "We'll be here all night," I added. "I'm not going out through that mob." What was worse was our cars were on the other side of the road. There was no escape. Take one step on the road and we'd be lynched.

We thought it would cool down but at 11.30pm they were still there in their thousands. George, the head of security who had been at the club donkey's years, told John and Eric to go to the side of the pitch, walk to a big gate in the corner of the ground and their cars would be taken around to meet them and off they could go.

I asked, "What about me?" He told me I would be alright to walk through the mob because they were 'just after Barnesy!' I told him there was no way that was happening. So he said he had another idea. I was to put on a bib and pretend to be a steward and walk to my car. I did as he asked and just about got away with it!

Kenny had missed the game. He was away in La Manga and got called back the next day. He was immediately given the job of going to see John Barnes and Eric Black. Kenny asked me to go with him. They were told that because of what had happened, their jobs were now untenable.

We all met at John 's apartment and Kenny told him and Eric they had to leave. He never said anything about me. When we got back in the car he asked me what did I want to do? He said that if I wanted, I could stay with him. I told him I couldn't because I had been part of it and would be liable for any flak. He thought I would be okay, but I declined the offer.

"Look, Kenny, I'm part of this, I don't think it's right that I stay on," I told him.

"I'm not telling you to go. I want you to stay. We can move on from this," he said.

"No, my mind is made up."

The next day, some people from Celtic came around to my apartment to sort out a settlement. I had my bags packed and was ready to go. Even then they tried to make me change my mind. I really appreciated that, but I stuck to my guns. I was soon on my way back to England.

Kenny took over until the end of the season and Celtic reached the final of the Scottish League Cup against Aberdeen. He invited me to the game at Hampden Park and so I went. Celtic won 2-0 and Jim Leighton, who I'd chipped at Pittodrie for Liverpool back in 1980, was still in goal for Aberdeen!

There had been a problem earlier with a Scottish newspaper accusing me of being a mole in the dressing room, telling tales on the players to Kenny. I was fuming. I've never ever been a spy in the camp.

According to the players in this article I was known as 'The Camcorder'. I consulted a lawyer to clear my name and sue the newspaper. This was an obvious slur on my character. I'd always prided myself as someone who would never let anyone down, who could be trusted. Now I was being cast as an unscrupulous low life who would sell my own grandmother. I was determined to clear my name.

I spoke to a number of the players; Paul Lambert, Tommy Boyd, Mark Viduka and Jackie McNamara, who were the main men, and asked them all if they had ever heard me referred to as 'The Camcorder'.

They all said it was complete nonsense. No-one had heard anyone ever say a bad word about me.

That was enough, so I went for it and won the court case, the newspaper having to make a financial payment. There was also an apology in the paper. So at least I can say I won something up there!

After leaving Celtic, it was the start of a life without football. I was back in Newcastle and I just did what I wanted to do. I went watching horse racing all over the country. I really enjoyed myself. I was doing things I hadn't had time for, like playing numerous rounds of golf. I was with my family which I loved. As well as the golf, there was plenty of socialising!

What started to take off was a horse racing syndicate we were running. A mate of mine had a company called Intersky which was in charge of hospitality at race tracks. We decided to start a racing club which involved jumpers and it went from strength to strength, so we started investing in bloodstock. I really got into it and we were going to all the race tracks. Cheltenham, Haydock, you name it, we were there.

We even ended up winning the Swinton Hurdle (which is a pointer to Cheltenham's Champion Hurdle) at Haydock in 2002. We won it with a small horse, giving away almost two stone, called Intersky Falcon.

It was a day to remember. I travelled down from Newcastle to watch Neale play for Newcastle Under-18s against Manchester United at Old Trafford. Straight from there I rushed over to Haydock to watch Intersky Falcon.

I was in my element because I was at the forefront of the club, following the horses everywhere. At one stage we had four or five horses owned by the syndicate. We also grew to more than 30 members.

Sadly, as it grew and grew, there were some people involved who wanted to make it into a business which would remove the fun side. They wanted to make more money. Before, it had been more pleasure than business, now it was the other way around.

We won a number of prestigious races including the Fighting Fifth Hurdle at Newcastle which landed us around £30,000, so we treated ourselves to a dozen bottles of champagne. Not everyone in the club could go to all the races and some started taking offence at spending money on celebratory drinks. They thought they were missing out. The fun was disappearing.

At least no-one could take away the joy we had with Intersky Falcon. He was a horse discovered for us by famous former jockey and now trainer, Jonjo O'Neill.

I had known Jonjo from his time as a jockey as he had come to Anfield one day for treatment on an injury and we'd always kept in touch.

We asked him to look out for a decent horse for the syndicate. When he rang to say he had found us something I went over to Cumbria to see him. A mate came with me and when we arrived, the horse was just lying there. He got him up and it looked a bit small. Jonjo said he had a feeling about it.

We paid £25,000 for the horse. We went on his word and, sure enough, Intersky Falcon never let us down. His jumping was outstanding and after he won the Swinton Hurdle at Haydock, I did an interview with the BBC's Richard Pitman who told me that we should now be thinking about entering Intersky Falcon for the big one, the Champion Hurdle at Cheltenham the following March.

I said we just do what our trainer, Jonjo O'Neill, tells us. Richard certainly thought we had Champion Hurdle material on our hands. He won a few more races before we did go for it. He actually ended up taking part in three Champion Hurdles and finished third in 2004. We were delighted with that as third place was big money.

As time went on, we ended up having horses with a number of top trainers including Nicky Richards and Nigel Twiston-Davies. They all had Intersky in their names, like Intersky Champagne and Intersky Native. When we got enough money in the coffers we would invest in another horse.

Things didn't always go to plan. We had Intersky Champagne running at Redcar in 2001 being ridden by a big pal of mine, Jonny Carroll. We fancied it strongly and wagered a bit of hard cash but in coming out of the stalls it banged its head, got covered in green paint and was suffering from the horse's equivalent of concussion. Safe to say, it came nowhere. But you have to take the rough with the smooth.

Intersky Falcon's success kept the club running. As well as Cheltenham, Intersky Falcon also ran in the Grand National meeting at Aintree on four different occasions.

For the 2002 meeting we took a coach down from the North East full of Newcastle United players. There were old mates like Alan Shearer, Gary Speed and Steve Harper there but they could only watch the Friday races.

I knew Intersky Falcon could be running the next day depending on the conditions but they had to go back on the Friday night and, after a few drinks, dragged me on to the coach to take me back to the North East.

I was a little uneasy because I didn't want to miss him running but in the end I was persuaded because I also knew Neale was playing in a Newcastle team the next morning. I went over to

Durham to watch him and then discovered that Intersky Falcon was going to take part in the first race on Grand National day.

I'm looking at my watch wondering if I'm going to get away from Neale's game in time to place a bet on our horse.

After the final whistle, I rushed to my car and intended getting back to Newcastle in time for the race. Within minutes I'm stuck in traffic on the A1. I had a brainwave and pulled off into Team Valley on the outskirts of Newcastle, praying I would see a bookies. Thankfully I spotted one with about five minutes to go before the start of the race. There was also a TV so I could watch Intersky Falcon run and placed my bet, £10 each way.

All my mates in the syndicate were there at Aintree, enjoying the hospitality and I'm stuck in a scruffy bookies on the edge of Newcastle.

I was as nervous as anything because this was a big race and I would have given anything to have been there. I felt a complete plonker for coming back to the North East, especially when he surged into the lead from the off and went around the first circuit way ahead.

He was going further and further ahead on the second circuit. I'm thinking he's going to nail this no problem and he jumped the second from last fence well clear. I thought it was too good to be true and he was going to blow up, but no way, he went on and on, finishing 15 lengths ahead of the nearest horse in a top, top race. When he crossed the line I jumped up and down like a lunatic. It had come in at 10-1, absolutely brilliant.

I'd only wagered £10 each way but I wasn't bothered about the money. It was just part of a great four years with this magnificent little horse. I've kept tapes of all the races, the wins all over the country. All this took me over, really.

Sadly his days as a top jumper were numbered when he suffered a breathing problem later in 2004, something which many race horses develop. He had an operation but he was never really the same horse after it. Jonjo admitted that he didn't know how the operation would go and he did win one more race, but only a minor contest at Newton Abbot.

The sport of kings has made me some great friends amongst the racing fraternity, some of them household names.

There's been no greater jump jockey than Tony McCoy, who luckily I've got to know. He's simply the best there has ever been National Hunt-wise, absolutely unbelievable. I've never known anyone to have so many broken bones, suffer falls you wince at when you watch them. Horses bounced on top of him. There's brave people and there's brave people. No-one is braver than 'AP'. He rode some of our horses and always had time to text you back if you congratulated him on a big win.

Jonjo O'Neill is the same, a fantastic bloke. When he wins a big race with one of his horses I feel part of it, having known him for some 45 years now. It's great when they combined because Tony would often race one of Jonjo's horses and if it won I felt as if I had ridden the horse myself.

The jump jockeys are a different breed. I remember seeing Tony at Wetherby one day and he couldn't get off the horse because of the damage he had done to himself the week before. His body had seized up after somehow persuading the course doctor he was alright to ride.

Tony's now a fantastic ambassador for the sport, but I'm sure he still gets aches and pains after everything he has gone through. He's a good guy.

TERRY MAC

I named my eldest son after another top jockey, Neale Doughty. He won the Grand National in 1984 with Hallo Dandy.

Neale was a huge Newcastle fan and would come and watch us train and travel to some matches with us. Sometimes he would actually sit in the St. James' Park dugout decked out in a Newcastle tracksuit a few seats away from manager Arthur Cox!

We were playing Swansea on the day of the Grand National and all the players had backed Hallo Dandy. As we were going out for the second half, someone in the St. James' Park crowd shouted to me that Hallo Dandy had won at 13/1. So that's why my Neale has an extra 'e' at the end of his name!

Although I enjoyed betting a bit too much when I was a young player, I've become more sensible over the years. I like a bet and in the past I've had £100, £200 on a horse, but now my maximum bet is usually £20.

I used to know Pat Eddery very well. He was flat racing's champion jockey on 11 occasions. I've even stayed at his house in Newmarket. After an England trip abroad we flew back into Heathrow Airport and I had made arrangements to go racing at Newmarket with Paul Mariner and Mick Mills. I was also due to meet up with a big racing mate, Mike Dillon, the main man at Ladbrokes and also a big friend of Sir Alex Ferguson. We'd been on the drink on the plane and carried on boozing at Newmarket, the champagne coming out at one stage.

By around 4pm I'm absolutely gone. I needed a sleep so I went away from the main area, found a field about a quarter of mile from the track and lay down on the grass in warm sunshine. In no time at all, I was fast asleep.

The next thing I know, it's 7.30pm and everyone had gone. I'm completely by myself with no idea where I'm supposed to go because I'm staying at Pat Eddery's, but I had no idea where that was.

I eventually hailed a taxi and told the driver 'take me to Pat Eddery's house!' Luckily, the taxi driver knew where he lived! When I got there they were all playing cards and the drinks quickly started again.

Another time, Liverpool went on a trip to Ireland and a group of us met the famous trainer Vincent O'Brien. There was Graeme Souness, Phil Thompson, Alan Kennedy and me. He showed us a horse he felt was good enough to win The Derby called Storm Bird. It was one of the greatest horses ever. Suddenly the horse took a fancy to Alan Kennedy, snuggling up to him. Alan responded by asking one of the greatest flat trainers in history whether Storm Bird was going to win the Grand National! We didn't know where to put ourselves. Here was a top flat horse which had never been near a fence.

On another occasion, after going for drinks inside Vincent's house, his wife Jackie came in with a few of her friends. Jackie turned the music on and encouraged us to dance. By now I wasn't too steady on my feet and ended up accidentally headbutting her! I love the racing people. They are very close-knit and love a good time. My favourite track is Cheltenham. So much so that when I was at Birmingham I even went to Prestbury Park when there was no racing on just to have a look around. That's how passionate I am about horse racing.

I've been numerous times to the Festival there. One of the best times was when I backed a 33/1 winner, The Drunken Duck, which is probably appropriate! We were in a private box and the snooker champion Steve Davis was in the room and we told him to back it as well. He was well happy.

Ascot was always a delight to attend. One time myself, Alan Hansen and Alan Kennedy went and I drove. We had a great time, but coming back the next day they fell asleep and the next thing I know, we're heading up the M62 towards Leeds, having missed the turning to Liverpool. You can imagine the abuse I got.

It reminded me of another Ascot faux pas. We stayed in a posh hotel for the five-day meeting one year and the food was very pricey so I told the lads that we shouldn't eat there, to save our money for betting purposes instead.

So we ended up living off sandwiches and snacks for five days only to discover at the end of the trip that the hotel was full board for Royal Ascot week! Jocky has never let me forget that either.

There is never a dull moment when racing is concerned!

CHAPTER 20

REVOLVING DOOR

I 'D stayed friends with Alan Shearer from our days together at Newcastle with Kevin Keegan and Kenny Dalglish.

Every summer, the same group of eight would get together at Alan's villa in Portugal. It was supposed to be for golf, but it was always five days of alcoholic poisoning. There was Alan, myself, Shay Given, Gary Speed, Steve Harper and three non-footballing mates. It was a war of attrition trying to stay on your feet. Everyone loved their golf, but maybe the drink just as much. I always thought after these trips that I needed to book myself into The Priory. I don't know how we did it.

Alan Shearer always takes great delight in reminding me of a couple of incidents from our golf trips. The first was after we'd been on the driving range before playing a round of 18 holes.

I hit a shot into the water and shouted over to Al to chuck me another ball from my golf bag. He opened it to discover it was filled with balls from the driving range. Who knows how they all got there?

We play on a course called Pinheiros Altos on the Algarve and Al also likes to remind me of the time I tried to adjust my angle to accommodate my natural slice. The ball slammed into a tree and my immediate reaction was to shout "who put that fucking tree there?" Alan and the lads all fell about laughing as the tree had probably only been there for half a century or so!

When Graeme got the Newcastle job in 2004 after Bobby Robson had been sacked, Alan suggested to me during the latest 'golfing' trip that I should ask Souey for a job. But I've never been a pushy person so it wasn't in my nature to do that. Alan went on to say I knew everything about Newcastle and that would be useful.

"It's a no brainer. You would be brilliant for Graeme," Alan insisted. "I don't know," I said, knowing deep down that I would jump at the chance of getting back into the game – and especially at Newcastle United.

For once, I plucked up the courage to make the telephone call. "You know where I am if you need any help," I told Graeme. He said to leave it with him. I didn't know at the time but Alan had also gone to Freddy Shepherd saying he had heard that I might be returning to the club in some sort of capacity. It sowed the seed in Freddy's head.

A couple of days later, I was playing snooker at a mate's house when I got a call from Graeme, asking me what I was doing the next day. He told me he would ring me then for a longer chat. I got really excited thinking I might be going back to Newcastle.

I went home and told Carole who agreed that it would be brilliant for that to happen. True to his word, Graeme phoned and asked me what I was doing that night. He was going to a reserve game and wondered if I fancied joining him for a Chinese meal afterwards. He said he would book a table and see me there.

I go there thinking it's just going to be me and Graeme and maybe his assistant Dean Saunders having a cosy chat. I walked into the restaurant and there's Graeme, Deano, Freddy Shepherd and Freddie Fletcher. I couldn't believe it. So we sat down for the meal and started talking, although nothing was mentioned about any future role for me. The main conversation revolved around Craig Bellamy. As usual with Craig, something had gone off.

There had already been a bit of a bust-up between Graeme and Craig. Graeme evidently had Craig by the throat against a wall at the training ground. I was asked what would I do about Craig Bellamy? There's only one thing you can do, I replied, get him out of the club – on loan if necessary. You can't have people like him questioning managers. Craig has had problems with loads of managers, including Bobby Robson. He can't help himself.

That was it, there was no talk of me coming back to Newcastle. I went away from the restaurant completely deflated. At least I had a free Chinese meal.

The next morning, Graeme rang and told me I had my dream – I was coming back to St. James' Park. I jumped off the ground in celebration and almost banged my head on the ceiling.

I reported to the training ground like a nervous kitten. I knew some of the players, but not all of them. I was shaking in my car thinking of what was happening because Newcastle meant so much to me. I had a bit of breakfast with Graeme and then I was introduced to the lads out on the training pitch. I'm glad he didn't ask me to say anything because my head was mashed. It was a dream come true. Surreal.

There was still the Craig Bellamy affair to sort out. Graeme wanted Craig to apologise in front of the rest of the players for his actions. Evidently he had called Graeme by the C-word. Not something you say to someone like Graeme who quickly had him around the throat. Craig can't help himself, he never shuts up. Another argument started between the two, ending with Bells walking out of the room and blaming Graeme for starting it. There was always a problem when Craig was around. He's grown up now and probably regrets some of the things he did, like most of us.

I was asked to do a newspaper article on coming back to New-castle for the local paper. At the time there were plenty of stories doing the rounds that Graeme Souness and Craig Bellamy weren't exactly bosom buddies. I thought I wasn't going to hold back because I felt that Bells wasn't good for the dressing room, so in the newspaper piece I mentioned what a disruptive influence Craig can be. He has caused trouble wherever he goes. I said that the club had to get rid of him. A few days later he was on his way, on loan to Celtic. He was a lucky boy to get up to Celtic because a few more incidents with Graeme and Bells might not have been able to walk for a while!

I never saw him again at Newcastle, but a couple of years later we played Liverpool at Anfield in a night game and Craig by then had signed for them.

After the game, I was walking down the stairs when someone at my shoulder calls me 'a wanker'. I looked around and it was Craig. I asked him what he had just said and he then followed that up by calling me 'a fucking wanker'. I got hold of him and yanked him over the bannister.

It was now bedlam and everyone was trying to cool things down. Jamie Carragher came racing over, but I'd lost it. "Come here again and say that and you'll see what happens to you," I shouted at Bellamy.

Eventually the security people released him from my grip and when he got to the top of the stairs he was at it again with his mouth calling me a horrible bastard. I told him to come down and say it.

Five months later we played Liverpool at St. James' Park and I'm ready for him, but to be fair to Craig, he put out his hand. At first I thought he was trying to punch me – but he wanted to shake hands and end the ill feeling between us. I shook his hand and everything was forgotten. He was mouthy, but Bells was a good player.

At Newcastle, he fell out with Alan Shearer and started sending him abusive text messages when he was up at Celtic. One day I was playing golf with Alan when his phone goes and I can hear Alan shouting, "You little shitbag!"

I asked him afterwards who he had been talking to. "That little runt Bellamy," he explained. Bellamy had said in the text messages that Alan's legs had gone, that he lived in a little North East house and that he was a sneak. The phone went again and it was Bellamy with more insults. It was the time when it had been reported that Craig had spent £20,000 on his teeth. I could hear Alan saying: "You come to my little house and come to my little door and I'll knock your bloody teeth out."

Like Kenny, Graeme wasn't really accepted by the Newcastle fans. He's a great fella and he is probably the best football pundit there is. I love watching him on TV with his observations of the game. He says what he thinks. Too many of them don't want to upset anyone. That honesty was reflected in his management. He's also great fun. I've always got on well with Graeme; it was a pleasure working with him, even if things didn't work out as planned.

At Newcastle, he was very meticulous in his planning. He always gave the players plenty of information about the opposition. Maybe the players just weren't good enough during his time on Tyneside. He was good enough. He understands players and was never afraid to kick them up the backside if it was needed. Some managers are too scared to do that. That's why they get trodden on.

Graeme's reign came to an end after we had played Manchester City away in February, 2006. Kevin Keegan was the City manager and I'd had a chat with him before the game. Jean Keegan was there as well, so I had a conversation with her too. Then the game started – but we didn't! We lost 3-0 and were very poor. It also meant we had only picked up one point in six Premier League games.

The next day, we were at the training ground going through the DVD of the game when one of the administrative staff, Tony Toward, who had been at the club years and is still there, came into the room looking ashen-faced. I'd known him for years and he's a great bloke. I could see he looked worried.

I said to him: "Tony, you're here to bring bad tidings."

He agreed and explained that he had letters to give out.

So he handed one to Graeme, one to Dean and one to Alan Murray, who was on the coaching staff, and one to the goalkeeping coach Roy Tunks.

Graeme calmly and slowly opened it and blurted out: "We've been sacked lads, we've been sacked." I asked Tony where was my letter? He told me I didn't have one. I didn't want to leave, but at the same time I didn't want to be separated from the rest of them, to be treated any differently.

They were asked to leave and I said to Graeme I was going out with them. He said I wasn't because I loved the club and it was part of me. "You stay here. This is your home. It's more than a job for you." I wasn't comfortable and part of me wished I'd been handed an envelope as well.

Next thing, my phone rang. It was Freddy Shepherd. "Terry, can you tell the players the news please? I'll be down at the training ground later to talk to you." I was getting used to this by now. Most of the players were gutted that Graeme had gone because they liked him.

Alan Shearer, for instance, loved playing for Graeme. In fact, if it hadn't have been for Graeme, Alan would probably have quit as a player by now. The previous season we had been in Dubai and Alan was talking about retiring as a player, but Graeme was desperate for him to stay and asked me to have a word with him.

The fact that Graeme thought he could still do a job was good enough for Alan, so he stayed on. If Alan hadn't have liked him that would have been it, but he ended up signing for another year.

Graeme was very popular. During his time at Newcastle he lived in a cul-de-sac where Freddy Shepherd's son Charles and Dean Saunders also lived. It was like Brookside.

Freddy came down to the training ground and had Glenn Roeder with him. Glenn had been working in the club's Academy just around the corner from the first team training ground. Freddy said that, for the time being, Glenn was going to take over the reins with Alan Shearer and me.

I'd bumped into Glenn for the first time in years when I went to Newcastle races not so long before. I had been invited to a get-together in a marquee and Glenn was there sitting at a table. He told me he had come back to Newcastle to run the Academy. Dean Saunders had asked me what Glenn was doing and when I explained about his new job he said to me that Glenn was here to eventually replace Graeme.

I said that I didn't think so, but he was proved right. I always invited him to our training ground to be part of Graeme's group and he started coming down to our building. I know Deano wasn't happy because he looked upon him as a danger to our jobs.

Glenn became caretaker manager, but I never seemed to be included in his plans. He always wanted to talk with Alan. Things went well for him for the rest of the season and he was given the job permanently.

We won a lot of games playing good football and so he deserved to lose the caretaker tag. But I started getting frustrated with not being involved 100 per cent. He'd also made Nigel Pearson first team coach. Things came to a head for me on a pre-season tour.

By this time, Lee Clark had also moved on to the coaching side after being a player. Glenn asked me to help Clarky with the reserve side, which at first I didn't mind. He said I would still be involved with the first team, but I felt a little uncomfortable. Maybe I was being paranoid, but I sensed that I was being squeezed out.

I asked Lee if he felt out of it, like I did, because Glenn wouldn't involve us in any of the planning. Nigel seemed to be his main man now, along with Alan. It wasn't the same for me and I thought I'd have to have a word with him.

"Glenn, have I done something wrong?" I asked him. "I don't appear to be part of the team discussions and I want to play a bigger part in the club." He denied there were any problems.

I was still talking to the players, although I imagine some people might have been wondering what my role at the club actually was by now.

People say someone's a coach because he puts sessions on, but that doesn't mean you're not a coach if you don't put on sessions. I thrived on helping players.

On one occasion, I got Jermaine Jenas into the office and told him he was a hell of player but he could be even better. "You can score more goals," I assured him and he left feeling 10 feet tall. That's just as important in my eyes as being able to put on sessions. Quite often it's what's in a player's head that can make the difference. I can't go up to Michael Owen and tell him how to put the ball in the back of the net, but I can encourage him by saying something like: "You score, we win."

I feel that what I had achieved as a player and who I have worked under allows me to give advice that players will listen to. It's harder when you haven't actually done it. There are good coaches and managers who haven't been great players, but I think initially it's harder for them. Some players could turn around and say 'look at him, he's given me advice and he's only played for Rotherham or Barrow.' Dressing rooms can be cruel. I don't think I upset too many players over the years and I hope they had respect for me.

TERRY MAC

When Glenn didn't enjoy the same positive results he had enjoyed as Newcastle caretaker manager, it started to unravel for him. In May, 2007, another one bit the dust. Once again, although I'd seen a lot of Newcastle managers depart, there was no clamour for my own departure.

The next man to take over the hotseat was Sam Allardyce. I knew Sam from my playing days. When I was playing for Bury years before, Sam was with Bolton. It's fair to say I didn't like going into a tackle with him because he was like a raging bull!

So, although I had once again earned my black box reputation by staying at Newcastle, it remained to be seen what he would be like to work under as a manager. My future wasn't clear-cut, but, to be fair to Sam, he wanted to see how things worked out between us.

CHAPTER 21

COCKNEY MAFIA

S AM was a very clued-up manager and he was a good guy to work for but once again I felt that, for whatever reason, the Newcastle fans didn't take to him.

It's too easy to give someone a label and in Sam's case it was that he was a long-ball merchant. That was a total myth. I never once heard him tell someone to stick the ball up top. It might have happened some time in his past, but not at Newcastle and when he was at West Ham, for example, the football was good on the eye.

Sam was a joy to be around. He may have brought a lot of his own people in, but still kept on people like myself and Lee Clark. He was big on socialising. He was a good listener even though he had his own ideas, but talking football over a good meal and a few beers was a fantastic way of conducting club business. There was immediate respect between the two of us, just in many ways two old down-to-earth football people operating in a changing world.

On a Friday night, before games, he would take some of the staff to a restaurant and have a nice bite to eat. Sam was always asking my opinion on players, I was always honest and he appreciated that. You should never be afraid of voicing your opinion. I was never frightened to tell Sam that, if it had been left to me, I wouldn't have included someone he had picked. That should be part and parcel of football chat.

Sam respected the past, but also wanted to move on. He was big on sports science and I lost count of the masseurs and nutritionists he had involved. I hate to think what the wage bill was. Sometimes there was no room to get changed because there were so many of them!

Most of the players liked him – apart from a Spanish player, Albert Luque. Sam wanted to keep the training ground solely for the players, so he erected portacabins to accommodate family, friends and agents where they could congregate, complete with refreshments. It meant that our area wasn't clogged up.

One day, Albert came storming into the coaches' room shouting at Sam. He wanted his dad to be allowed to come into the main building, but the security guy had guided him into the designated area for visitors. Albert went berserk.

Sam was sitting down and had to listen to Luque insisting he had been insulted by his father not being allowed into our area.

"Mr. Manager, he comes all the way from Spain and he can't come in here," he screamed. Sam explained the reasons why, but Albert was not having it.

"This is fucking ridiculous," stormed Luque. Sam said he could eat and drink and relax in the special area. "This is an insult to my father, you shit," Luque responded.

At this, Sam got out of his seat and went nostril to nostril with Luque before bellowing: "Fuck off. Get out!" I thought Sam was going to hit him.

On the pitch, the results weren't great in 2007/08 and there was a change of ownership with Mike Ashley taking over. I had no idea the club was going to be sold. I was told Freddy was lying flat on his back in hospital when the deal was done between Sir John Hall, Douglas Hall and Mike Ashley. There had been speculation about American or Asian investors coming in, but there had been no talk of Sports Direct owner Ashley. I'd never heard of him.

At first, you would see Mike at the training ground having flown in by helicopter. It would land on the side of the pitch. He seemed quite shy and certainly kept himself away from the media. He seemed to get on well with Sam. He also appeared to be loving his connection with the football club, joining some of the fans for a drink in the city's Bigg Market and necking down a pint at the Emirates, something that was picked up by the TV cameras. It seemed a marriage made in heaven.

I was disappointed, though, to have seen the end of the Sir John Hall era. I still see Sir John now. I was shocked he sold the club. He probably regrets what has happened since, especially with Newcastle suffering two relegations. It was sad to see Freddy Shepherd and Douglas Hall go, but there was excitement at the promise that Mike Ashley was going to invest big time in the club.

We played Stoke in the FA Cup in early January, 2008, and

ended up drawing. There had been speculation that Sam was under pressure. But in the changing room before the game, I saw Mike Ashley bear hugging Big Sam. I even told someone that Sam wouldn't be going anywhere – that everything was fine between the manager and the owner. We drew the game but, amazingly, before we got around to the replay at St. James' Park, Sam had been sacked.

The news that Sam was history at Newcastle came when I was watching Sky Sports. I couldn't believe it, especially after seeing the bear hug between Mike and Sam.

All the talk was of who was going to come in. Sam was upset because he obviously thought he was doing a decent job – and so did I. I was shocked at the news.

Believe it or not, Sam used to hate matchdays. He would openly admit to that because of all the nervous tension that surrounds a game. All the attention, the things that can go wrong played on his mind. He used to get so wound up. "It's a great job this – if there weren't any games," he would often tell me. He was completely surprised at the suddenness of his sacking.

I suppose, looking back, the writing was on the wall when a photo showed loads of Newcastle fans yelling: 'Get out!' and hurling insults at him when he stepped into the technical area during the home game against Liverpool, which we lost 3-0.

But I got on very well with him and I think he is a good manager. Getting the England job would have been the pinnacle of his career, so I felt for him when it was all over after just one game. I know that was his ultimate goal in management, to take charge of his country. Last time around, when it became obvious that the job was going to go to someone born in this country, he was really gutted when he lost out to Roy Hodgson.

Sam had been mentioned for the job a few times in the past and it was great to see his beaming face when he finally landed it. He is a proud Englander. It's a tough job, thankless at times but he was more than happy to take it on – and not for the stupid inflated wages the likes of Sven Goran Eriksson and Fabio Capello received.

The job he had worked all his life for was then taken away from him. I can only imagine the devastation he felt. To be caught up in a newspaper sting like that was a surprise to me. He was caught out trying to help someone else. Whether he deserved to lose his job over that is open to question.

One thing that is not in question for me is that the England job should always go to someone born in the country. Then it's a case of delivering in tournament finals. We don't generally seem to have much trouble in qualifying. It's all about the finals and our record has been poor. There was no way back for Roy Hodgson after the last European Championships when he couldn't even beat Iceland.

At least Sam was well looked after. I bumped into him a little while after he had left Newcastle and he told me the story that he was lying on the beach in Barbados drinking a bottle of champagne when he got a call from his agent who asked him what he was doing.

When he replied "drinking a bottle of champagne" the advice came back to get a few more bottles in because £5 million in compensation from Newcastle had just gone into his bank. You have to give Mike Ashley credit for that.

Mike asked Nigel Pearson to take over temporarily before he appointed a new manager. We had to play Manchester United at Old Trafford. The strong speculation was that Sam's successor was going to be Harry Redknapp. Graeme Souness rang me because he had spoken to Harry, who had indicated he was keen on the job and that he was going to keep me on.

I thought that was nice of him, but on the morning of the game Harry announced that he wasn't coming. It was all over the newspapers. He wanted to stay in the south – which was a big disappointment after what I had been promised. We went on to play United and although it was 0-0 at half-time, we ended up being stuffed 6-0.

I know Alan Shearer would have fancied taking over after Harry pulled out, but the club put out a statement saying he wouldn't be offered the job because of his lack of managerial experience. A couple of days later, Kevin Keegan rang me up just to talk about the Manchester United game, hardly believing the score.

He asked me what was happening with the manager's job and after telling him, I asked whether he fancied the Newcastle job again.

"Don't be silly," he replied. "I don't fancy that."

I told him that Mike Ashley seemed a good guy who was going to put in substantial money for transfers.

"Would you mind if I ran your name past someone at the club?" I asked. He told me not to, but when I asked him if he'd fall out with me if I did, Kevin said he would not. I got the feeling he hadn't completely ruled out the chance of a return.

I rang the chief executive Chris Mort. "I think Kevin Keegan might be interested in the job," I told him.

"If you or Mike get him in the room and persuade him then it would be the best move you ever make." Chris said to leave it with him. I didn't phone Kevin back because I had nothing concrete to tell him.

Next thing, we had the FA Cup replay against Stoke in midweek and when I was getting ready to go to the game I got a phone call from Ray Thompson, the kit man.

"Bloody hell, you know!" he shouted. "Know what?" I replied. "Put on Sky Sports." So I did and there running along the ticker tape was '*Kevin Keegan – Newcastle United manager*'. I couldn't believe it. I couldn't wait to get to the ground, I must've driven at 80 mph. How I didn't get stopped by the police, I will never know.

All the talk around the ground was about Kevin coming back. All those who knew him were excited, knowing the whole place would take off again with him in charge. In the end, the kick-off was delayed for 15 minutes because there was so much demand for tickets.

About 20 minutes into the game there was suddenly a crescendo of noise and the fans started going crazy. I turned around from the dugout to look up at the stand and there's Kevin making his way into the directors' box.

We won the game 4-1 and just as I'm going out, along the corridor outside the changing room there's Kevin coming the other way with the Newcastle hierarchy. I was buzzing. He told me we'd have a chat later.

He rang me the next morning and I went to pick him up at the Gosforth Park Hotel, where he used to stay. He told me he hadn't said anything to anyone about taking the job. He hadn't even told his two daughters, just his wife Jean. He apologised for not ringing me, but I didn't care – he was here. His return gave the whole area a massive boost and I couldn't wait to get up in the morning and start work. It was exciting and you also knew you would have a laugh when Kevin was in charge.

I remember we always used to play head tennis before and after training. Take it from me, Kevin and I were the best and I think we only ever lost one game. We were the kings. One of the first things we did on his return was to mark out the court to resume the games. It was like old times. A lot of the players started coming in early so they could play before training – then they would play again afterwards.

We would take on all comers for money and even the staff would join in – it was an obsession. Anyone wanting to play us would have to put down a fiver or a tenner.

One day, Michael Owen and Nicky Butt decided to challenge us. We kept on hammering them but they wouldn't give up and the money would keep increasing until this day it got to £80.

We hammered them again which saw us pocket the money but just to rub it in, Kevin went on the computer and drew up some great posters boasting of our win and mocking Michael and Nicky. He told them to bring the £80 the next day and they were really peed off. The next morning I bumped into them and they asked me if I'd been into Kevin's office. I hadn't because Kevin hadn't arrived yet, but they mentioned that it might be worth popping in for the money.

When Kevin turned up I told him our money was waiting for us in his office. We opened the door and there was £80 worth of penny pieces piled up on the desk! They had gone into two or three banks to get all the coppers. I think in the end we gave it all away to the dinner lady.

Kevin put all the posters on the walls for the rest of the players to see.

"Right, lads, take us on if you dare and prepare to meet the fate of these two!" Kevin crowed.

The players laughed their heads off. That's what Kevin is all about. It's why it's a joy to be around him.

Michael Owen, who was signed from Real Madrid by Graeme Souness in 2005, really loved his time with us. He once told me that being at Newcastle with Kevin was one of the best periods of his career. I know that will surprise a few people who thought he wasn't happy in the North East.

Michael also gets stick from some Liverpool fans who say he rejected them to go to Newcastle from Real Madrid and then later, of course, to Manchester United. But it was only because Liverpool didn't want him – I know he was desperate to go back but Rafa Benitez, who was the manager at the time, said no. That's why he came to Newcastle.

Graeme and I rang Michael lots of times and we spoke to his agent on numerous occasions too. Once he knew Liverpool wasn't going to happen, he was okay.

"You'll love it here. This club idolises goalscorers and there aren't too many better than you," we told him.

I don't think coming to Newcastle was ideal. He would travel to and from his home in North Wales by helicopter which didn't go down too well with the Newcastle fans who thought he was just using the club. He wasn't – he could get to Newcastle as quickly as someone trying to beat the traffic from Durham.

It was big money to bring him to Newcastle – the signing caused almost as big a stir as Alan's. The fee was £16.8 million, over £1 million more than we had paid for Alan.

Not living in the area probably made it harder for him to endear himself to the Newcastle fans. He was also unlucky with his injuries, suffering a broken metatarsal and a few hamstring problems. But I can assure you that he did care about the club. He wanted to score loads of goals for Newcastle to justify his fee. In the end, fans really turned against him when he ran his contract down in the season Newcastle were relegated – not the best thing to do if you want to be liked.

The results didn't go in our favour as soon as Kevin came back in 2008. He was never going to change things overnight and we played eight games before we grabbed our first win. We were going to need a long-term plan in place if Newcastle were to get back to where we had left them 11 years earlier. Many of the top clubs were stronger and, if I'm honest, we both had uneasy feelings about the future from early on.

It wasn't like the last time when we had close relationships with Sir John Hall, Douglas Hall, Freddy Shepherd and Freddie Fletcher. Owner Mike Ashley had surrounded himself by what the fans eventually dubbed 'The Cockney Mafia'. There was Dennis Wise, Director of Football, along with Tony Jimenez, the vice-chairman plus Derek Llambias, who was effectively the chief executive, and Jeff Vetere, who was the chief scout.

During Kevin's short time back at Newcastle we didn't see too much of Mike Ashley. Early on, he did invite us down to his huge Sports Direct factory in Derbyshire. We drove down because he wanted to show it off and have a chat.

It's a gigantic building, unbelievable – one that employs thousands of workers. We were really optimistic after the meeting because here was someone with millions to his name promising to invest fortunes on the team. He wanted to take the club back to where we had managed to propel it to the first time around.

It seemed that we could be heading in the right direction. In those first few weeks after training we would go into Kevin's office, where the club would put a lunch on for us. We would sit around the table with Dennis and his mates and discuss targets. They would suggest players which we didn't have a problem with. That's their job and it's how things should work, providing the manager has the final word on any signings.

Sadly, it didn't work out like that – and it still doesn't work like that at some clubs today. The manager is left out of discussions and players suddenly arrive who he doesn't know too much about. This started to happen at Newcastle which, as you could imagine, quickly unsettled Kevin. Again, the job was nothing like the advert in the brochure.

What was equally frustrating was that we would put together a list of players we would like to buy, but nothing came to fruition.

In the first few months, Kevin informed them he would like Luka Modric, who was at Dinamo Zagreb, and Jonathan Woodgate, who was down the road at Middlesbrough.

We even thought we were getting Modric. We had a meeting in Kevin's office with some of his agents and representatives of the club. The player was definitely interested in coming, but one of the agents pulled me to one side after the meeting. "This has to be settled today," he said. "Tottenham are also interested and they are in a position to move, today. If you want Luka, it has to happen now. Any delays and the chance will be gone."

I let Kevin know, but it did us no good. We found out that Newcastle had offered Modric a ridiculously low wage offer. Spurs offered at least twice the money and so he went off to White Hart Lane.

Over the months, we had our suspicions about what was going

on behind the scenes because Jonathan Woodgate also ended up at Tottenham. Were there close links between some of the 'Cockney Mafia' and Tottenham? There was no proof of that but who knows.

I can say that Mike Ashley wasn't involved in any of this because he left all the transfers to the people he appointed when he bought the club.

Again – I repeat – I don't have a problem with anyone recommending their own players as long as they are good, but they weren't. And with Kevin not seeing his own favoured targets coming in, there was quickly tension growing behind the scenes.

Dennis Wise came in one day and said that he was confident they could bring in two top Argentinian centre backs. One was Fabricio Coloccini and the other was Nicolas Burdisso.

To be fair, Kevin was given the choice and went for Burdisso who was playing in Serie A for Inter Milan. They couldn't get him and instead landed Coloccini, which was fine – that's the way things should work.

Sadly, that proved an exception because in the following months Kevin seemed to be less involved in the transfers with Dennis and his men trying to force players on him. There were players like Nacho Gonzalez, who came in on loan, and Xisco who were nowhere near the standard Kevin was looking for.

Kevin was well and truly cheesed off. "We can't go on like this," he told me. I agreed, but hoped he could sort the problems out like we did when we came to Newcastle the first time around and promises weren't being kept. All this led to some heated meetings with Derek Llambias and Kevin. Kevin put forward his potential signings, only for him to discover that no-one had bothered to move a muscle to try to meet his requests.

If they did go through the motions, they would either offer the club or the player a stupidly low amount of money so that any negotiations didn't even get off the ground. They could then turn around to Kevin and say they had tried, but couldn't conclude the deal.

The last person you try to pull the wool over the eyes of is Kevin. He's seen it and done it at all levels of the game and he would find out they were trying to bring in players he knew nothing about. It doesn't need a rocket scientist to tell you this relationship wasn't going to work.

During his first spell at the club, Kevin had virtually run Newcastle United with the backing of Sir John Hall. There was mutual trust.

There was definitely not the same rapport with the characters involved at the club this time around. The fans quickly latched on to the unease and, as I say, it was the Toon Army who first came up with the phrase 'Cockney Mafia'.

To be honest, it doesn't matter where you come from – London, Liverpool or Timbuktu – as long as you do your job properly. In my view, the correct way with transfers is to name the players to the manager and discuss them, leaving him to have the final decision.

One time we flew to France to watch the striker Bafetimbi Gomis. Kevin and I went on a private plane to run the rule over him following a recommendation by Dennis Wise and Jeff Vetere. After about 20 minutes, Kevin had decided he wasn't for him. He wasn't able to trap a bag of cement. He looked behind him and around five rows back were Dennis and Jeff and, to be fair, they held their hands up because Gomis was having a shocker.

At least they all agreed not to pursue the move – that's how it should have been – but get-togethers like that were a rarity. Gomis has since gone on to be a decent player who had a spell at Swansea but, at the time, he wasn't for us.

Over the months, Kevin's distrust of Dennis began to grow. Rightly or wrongly, he didn't think Dennis and the rest of them had any passion for Newcastle, that it was merely a job. They were just passing through and they didn't feel for the area like he and I did.

It's not their fault they were born in London, but in our eyes they weren't doing a good job and it seemed to us that they didn't really care. It all had to come to a head, which, eventually it certainly did.

CHAPTER 22

IT'S FINISHED

I USED to pick Kevin up every morning for us to travel in together for training.

Obviously we would talk about how things were going and it was clear he didn't have the same spark as before. He wasn't buzzing – and that's not like Kevin.

You sensed it was all going to end in tears, there was no question of that. Kevin, for instance, didn't have any time for the vice-chairman Tony Jimenez at all. That was virtually from day one. Rightly or wrongly, Kevin just didn't think he was that bothered about Newcastle United.

Kevin was prepared to stick at it because he still loved the club and especially the fans but things really came to a head as he prepared for only the third game of the 2008/09 season, a trip to Arsenal after we had drawn 1-1 at Manchester United and beaten Bolton 1-0 at home.

Kevin got a call from Tony Jimenez to say the club had received 'a magnificent offer' for James Milner from Aston Villa. There had been speculation about Milner leaving, but Kevin didn't want to lose him. He was a good player who could do a job in a number of positions. Evidently, Villa had offered £10 million, but Kevin insisted James was staying.

We were flying down to London for the game when Kevin took another call from Jimenez saying the Villa offer had been increased to £12 million. It was a decent offer so Kevin asked who would they get to replace him? When we got off the plane, Kevin couldn't wait to find out who they had come up with. Kevin knew it would have to be someone really good because Milner was a crucial player.

Jimenez told Kevin they had accepted the bid and added that it looked like they could sign Bastian Schweinsteiger from Bayern Munich. That excited Kevin because he was some player. Kevin said it was a no brainer – just do it. Jimenez then said that as Kevin knew Karl-Heinz Rummenigge, who was on the board at Bayern, could he give him a ring?

"What for?" he asked. "To ask if Schweinsteiger would be interested in coming to Newcastle," he was told. Kevin couldn't believe it, he was incensed. We were losing Milner but in reality had no-one definitely coming in.

I told him it was a joke and Kevin replied, "the swines have stitched us up." There was only one thing for it – Kevin would have to ring Rummenigge.

I knew an agent mate of mine who also happened to be Arsene Wenger's advisor and I knew he would have Rummenigge's number. Luckily he was due to come to our hotel that night before the Arsenal game. He came into the hotel and I took him into Kevin's room so we could relate the story about Schweinsteiger. The first thing he said was that he didn't think they would let him go. I asked him to go ahead and speak to someone there and then hand the phone to Kevin. He ended up getting Karl-Heinz and switched it to speaker mode. He said that a good friend was waiting to speak to him, Kevin Keegan. Kevin started chatting away in German and English.

In English he explained the reason why he was ringing him – that he had been told by his club that they might be able to sign Bastian Schweinsteiger. Karl-Heinz immediately started laughing. He revealed that Bayern had received an email that morning from Newcastle offering five million euros for him. "Kevin, we couldn't stop laughing," he added. "If you had offered 50 million euros we still wouldn't have sold him – but five million?!"

After the conversation ended, I looked at Kevin and he was ashen-faced. He knew we had lost a very good player with no suitable replacement. The club had hoodwinked him.

The next morning we were out for a walk in the Canary Wharf area, where our hotel was situated, and his phone went. It was Tony Jimenez. He asked him about Schweinsteiger and then, of course, it all went off.

The air was blue now with Kevin letting Jimenez know what he thought of him. I've never seen Kevin so incensed. He was blazing mad. He knew then that was it.

Kevin also found out that the club was trying to sell other players behind his back, like Michael Owen and Joey Barton. In fact, they tried to flog Joey on transfer deadline day. I went to watch the reserves play and Joey was also there, watching the game five or six rows behind me.

The actual transfer deadline was 11pm that night. It's now about 7.30pm and Joey rang me from where he was. His first words were: "Hey, Terry lad, are you trying to get rid of me?" I didn't know what he was on about. Joey explained that he had been informed that Newcastle had accepted a bid for him from Portsmouth. I couldn't believe it. Joey still thought I had known about the offer. I assured him I didn't.

I rang Kevin and asked him if he knew what was going on with Joey Barton. He said he didn't and what was I getting at? He couldn't believe it. No-one had told him. Joey rang me again and now said that Newcastle were trying to get him out on loan. He told me he wasn't going anywhere. I rang Kevin again to put him in the picture that the club were doing all they could to get rid of Joey.

Neither I nor Kevin wanted Joey to leave. I had got to like him and had supported him when he found himself in jail not long after Sam Allardyce had brought him to the club. Joey, being Joey, got into bother on a trip home to Liverpool and eventually ended up in clink. Newcastle weren't happy but they stuck by him. I got on well with him and I was set to go and visit him when he was in prison but for whatever reason I didn't. Maybe, with my past, I thought that they might have kept me in with him! I kept in touch through one of his big mates. We had a good relationship. He is a very bright guy and a likeable fella, but he had that little self-destruct mechanism inside him which would cost him dear at times.

When he first came to the club he was a bit lonely. His girl-friend was still living in the Liverpool area so he would often come to watch matches with me. I took him to Carlisle once and he would come back to my house, have a chat and my wife Carole would make him chip butties. He loves his football. Inside, he's a good fella. I've kept in touch with him. He just has to grow up at times. He was good in the dressing room, very vocal and at times demanding, but that was him – he wanted to be a winner. Sometimes he went over the top with players. On the pitch you had to be wary when he snapped because once that happened, there was no stopping him.

After we lost a game, he wasn't frightened to call people out. You would hear him say: "You lazy bastard!" to anyone who wasn't prepared to run hard enough or put a decent shift in.

He had a fall out with Emre, the Turkish midfield player. It happened on the training pitch. He yelled: "Get running, you lazy bastard!" Emre didn't take too kindly to Joey's blast and it carried on into the dressing room. In the end, they had to be separated. Both had a bit of passion. I think that can be good, as long as it doesn't boil over.

"Let's sort this out here and now," Joey yelled. Well, we didn't let them and eventually peace was restored. I'd rather have players like that, ones who care, rather than ones who just pick up their wages without any feelings for the club they represent. The Newcastle fans liked him because he would always give 100 per cent.

I think one of the problems for Kevin was that Mike Ashley wasn't involved enough. For instance, after the row with Jimenez over the Schweinsteiger business, I suggested to Kevin that he ring Mike and tell him what had happened. Kevin did and again I could hear the conversation because it was on speaker.

"King Kev, how are you?" were Mike's opening words. He always called Kevin 'King Kev'.

Kevin asked him if he had known what had gone on with Schweinsteiger. Mike replied that he hadn't known about all this and he would give Derek Llambias a ring. That was it, he never heard from him again about that.

Then they were letting it be known, again without Kevin's knowledge, that they would accept any decent bids for Michael Owen. Nothing transpired over Michael but it was another example of Kevin having no say in the transfer dealings. There was only going to be one ending after all this had gone on.

I had just finished my Sunday roast at home the day after the Arsenal game, which we lost 3-0, when the phone went and it was Kevin asking what I was up to. He asked me to pop around to his house. He was home with Jean and I could see he was annoyed. He told me that he had heard that two players were having medicals at Newcastle. One was supposedly having a medical in Newcastle and the other in London. I rang the club doctor and he was in London.

"What are you doing there?" I asked him.

"I'm doing a medical with Nacho Gonzalez," he said.

At the same time, there was a player, Xisco, having a medical in the North East. We didn't know anything about it. Our physio, Derek Wright, then confirmed everything.

Sure enough, a little later, Dennis Wise rang Kevin and told him the club were signing both players, Xisco for over £5 million and Gonzalez on loan. Kevin said he hadn't sanctioned the deals and so how could they sign them?

Dennis asked him to have a look at them, insisting they were good players.

Kevin made the reasonable point that he could hardly look at them now, right at this minute, could he?

"Yes you can," Dennis said. " Take a look at them on YouTube." That didn't go down well.

"They expect me to sign two players through this?!" Kevin shouted. "You can hardly see them. How can the club spend over £5 million like this?"

He wondered what to do. I told him he had to speak to someone because he couldn't allow this to happen. I said: "Why don't you get on the phone to Mike Ashley?"

He phoned him again and put Mike on loud speaker so I could hear as well.

"Hello King Kev, how are you?" Mike answered.

Kevin told him he wasn't feeling too happy. "Well, what's the matter King Kev?" Mike went on.

Kevin asked him if he knew of any players Newcastle were signing that day. Mike said that he couldn't say he didn't, but would get back to him.

The phone went down and he didn't come back to Kevin. Instead, it was Derek Llambias. Kevin immediately told Derek that Newcastle were signing players he didn't want, and that he had been asked to watch two new potential signings on his laptop. He told him he wasn't sanctioning the signings. Derek said they were still signing them. Kevin insisted he wanted to put it on record that the two new players had nothing to do with him. He would also tell the fans what had happened.

Llambias told him he wanted a meeting with Kevin the next day. Kevin agreed, thinking it would be about 9am, 10am. Derek said it would be at 5.30pm.

The reason, we found out, was that Derek was in London.

The transfer deadline was fast approaching, we're trying to get players in and he's away in London!

Kevin asked him what he was doing in London so close to the transfer deadline. Kevin then said he wasn't going to the meeting.

Llambias got all heavy-handed asking for confirmation that the Newcastle manager was refusing to meet the Newcastle chief executive the following day. Kevin couldn't answer him – Kevin was heartbroken, he knew the end of his Newcastle return was looming.

The next day was the episode with Joey, the club trying to sell him behind our backs, but come the closing of the transfer window Joey was still with us. Within another 24 hours, Kevin wasn't.

In a desperate attempt to sort things out, he did agree to go to a meeting at St. James' Park the day after the transfer window had closed – one which ended in a blazing row between Kevin and Llambias, Kevin leaping into his car and leaving the ground for the last time.

The media soon got wind of what had happened and reported that Kevin had either been sacked or had walked out. He quickly issued a statement saying: 'A manager must have the right to manage and clubs should not impose upon any manager any player he does not want'.

The balloon went up, the Newcastle fans couldn't believe what had happened and the protests soon started.

Mike Ashley knew he had to try to rescue the situation – the supporters were not having the fact that Kevin Keegan was no longer manager of Newcastle United. He asked Kevin to meet him in London and Kevin went down hoping to resolve things because he loved the club and knew what he could achieve if it was run properly. Some people have accused him of being moody if things don't go his way. That's rubbish, it's because he cares so much for the football club.

He had settled back into managing the club and had bought a house on Tyneside because he intended being at St. James' Park for a considerable amount of time. The atmosphere amongst the players was building again and he was excited about the future until the problems over transfers began.

On the way down to London I know that, despite everything, Kevin was still confident that he would return as Newcastle manager. That's what everyone wanted. I was anxious, hoping the meeting was going to go to plan. Kevin told me it did at first because after a long chat between the pair, everything was agreed. It all seemed hunky dory.

But Kevin then insisted on just one stipulation – he could no longer work with Dennis Wise and Tony Jimenez. Get rid of them and Kevin would willingly continue as manager. Mike said he couldn't do that, he couldn't agree to the request. So that was it. Kevin reluctantly gave up his favourite job in football.

"That's it. It's finished," he told me. I could hear the devastation in his voice. He wasn't the only one.

"Is there nothing we can do?" I implored.

"No, nothing, unless Mike Ashley changes his mind over Dennis Wise and Tony Jimenez," Kevin replied.

His heart was saying 'stay', but with everything going on around him, his head was saying 'go'. I've never seen him so gutted, so low and so really beside himself.

He took himself off to Florida with his wife Jean. He just shut himself off across the Atlantic and licked his wounds. I didn't have any contact with him for a few weeks. Although he locked himself away from the rest of the world, he did ask my wife Carole to look after his house in the North East for a while.

Ironically, a few months later, Jimenez left and that was followed by Wise going too. You just felt it was such a waste, Kevin leaving after just eight months back on Tyneside.

I thought that with Kevin going, that would be it for me as well. Kevin told me to keep going in to work otherwise I would lose out on any future financial compensation. "This is your club, don't do anything stupid. This is now about looking after yourself. Forget me," he said.

The protests from the fans mushroomed – there were banners everywhere calling for Kevin to return. Everywhere you went in the city, fans were absolutely devastated, calling for the Ashley hierarchy to bring back 'King Kev'.

Not being from the area and not having been involved for too long, I'm certain the people in charge didn't realise what Kevin meant to the Newcastle supporters. He was more than their manager, he was their Messiah.

To be fair to Mike, he was a brave man because he kept on turning up for matches, taking the flak for allowing Kevin to slip away from his grasp.

With Kevin gone, despite what he had advised me, I didn't want to be there. There were still backroom people I knew involved and I loved the club, but there was no Kevin. I was deflated. Chris Hughton was placed in temporary charge. He had been part of the coaching staff and was a good lad.

Kevin spoke to me again and told me not to walk out, but for the first time in my life I didn't want to be at Newcastle.

It was a Sunday night and I was due to go in for training the next morning, yet I didn't really want to go to work. I'd never ever felt like that before, no matter what had happened. I decided to follow Kevin's advice and go in but as I'm getting ready the following morning, Lee Charnley, who was on the administrative staff, rang me and said he had bad news, they didn't want me to come in.

He didn't ring me too often so I guessed what was coming.

"You know what it's about, don't you? Please don't come in this morning. Can you come in instead during the afternoon?" he asked.

"Well, okay, but I'd have liked to have said goodbye to the players."

"No, come in the afternoon when everybody has left."

They had also, for some reason, told Adam Sadler, who had been in charge of the reserves since Lee Clark left to work with Glenn Roeder at Norwich, not to come in for work either. He was just a good young kid learning the game. Why they got rid of him, I don't know.

Later, they asked me to report to the training ground after 2pm when everyone else would have gone home. I turned up and there was Tony Toward, who I knew well and got on with, so we had a chat. Adam joined us and that was it, we were officially finished. I felt terrible, horrible. The dream was over, but that's life.

What rankles me more than anything is that, as I've said, just a month later Jimenez left and Wise followed him out of the door in April, 2009 with the club deep in the relegation mire. It could have been so different if that had happened when Kevin asked for it.

I've seen Dennis since and shook his hand, but there's no friendship there. I know he was just doing a job but, in my opinion, he did it badly.

Another Londoner, Joe Kinnear, ended up taking over from Kevin, but results were poor and in the February he ended up in hospital needing a heart operation. Chris Hughton took charge temporarily, but then Dennis Wise went and Alan Shearer was brought in to manage the team for the final eight games of the season.

Unfortunately, Alan was unable to keep Newcastle up and they were relegated to the Championship on the final day of the season following a 1-0 defeat at Aston Villa through a Damien Duff own goal. It was gut-wrenching to see the club Kevin and I had brought into the Premier League in 1993 go down after 16 seasons, but things had gone so wrong off the pitch that perhaps such an outcome was inevitable.

By then, I already had another job. In the same week I received my pay-off from Newcastle I had joined another club to work with a familiar face from my days at St. James' Park.

CHAPTER 23

A FINAL FLING

L EE Clark had joined Huddersfield Town as manager in December 2008. After finishing playing, it was always his ambition to go into coaching or management. When we were together at Newcastle under Sam Allardyce, he had mentioned to me that he would like me to be his assistant if he ever broke into management. "I fancy that," I told him. "If I'm not working with Kevin then I'd love to."

Well, with Kevin gone, the call came from Lee asking me to join him at Huddersfield, but to hold on a bit because the chief executive was trying to push his own candidate on to him. It was the former Wales international Barry Horne. When that didn't materialise, I eventually agreed my terms and couldn't wait to get started.

Although Huddersfield were in football's third tier, they were ambitious and hopefully had the owner's money behind them. Dean Hoyle had just sold his successful Card Factory business for millions and millions, so it felt that the club would be on the way up with his investment.

The start of life at Huddersfield was a bit of a culture shock. For training we got into our cars and drove around 20 minutes away from the ground to this run-down dump of a place. The best I can say is at least it had a football pitch there. There was nothing else – no changing facilities, nothing, not even any toilets. You would often be soaking wet after training and you'd have to get back in your car and shiver all the way to the ground, where you could get into a welcome shower. There would be four or five of us sharing cars. Despite this, I still enjoyed it. We had a good set of lads.

The owner was true to his word, putting money into the club, meaning we could buy some decent players. We were paying £250,000, £300,000 for players which was good at that level. We signed Anthony Pilkington from Stockport in the January for decent money and the next summer bought Jordan Rhodes from Ipswich for £350,000, who we sold later to Blackburn for £8 million. Lee knew a player alright and he bought wisely.

In our first full season in charge, 2009/10, we finished sixth, which meant we had qualified for the play-offs. After a goalless first leg semi-final at home, we lost 2-0 to Millwall at The New Den, so that was the end of our promotion hopes for that year.

We went one better the following season. We finished third and faced Bournemouth in the play-off semi-final. We drew 1-1 away in the first leg and then brought them back to our place for what turned into a memorable game. It was 3-3 on aggregate after extra time and we progressed to the dreaded penalty shoot-out. Fortunately, things went our way and we won 4-2 to set up a play-off final against Peterborough. We really fancied our chances after clocking up a club record 87 points that season. But we were star-struck and froze on the big stage, losing 3-0 at Old Trafford.

The next season, 2011/12, we had to go again. I was staying in a flat just around five minutes away from the ground which was difficult because I couldn't always get home to the North East. I could go two or three weeks without seeing the family.

Despite the progress we were making, the football side could also at times be a little exasperating. Dean was the chairman as well as the owner. He was also a big fan and on one occasion, his enthusiasm got the better of him, which caused a few problems. Against our advice, he wrote an article in the matchday programme before we played Exeter City criticising the team, saying there had been a lack of effort, a lack of this, a lack of that. You can imagine what the players thought of it.

We ended up losing that game 1-0 and we had a meeting on the Monday involving all the staff plus Dean and Chief Executive Nigel Clibbens. In front of the players, Dean came out and apologised for his outburst in the programme. "Look, lads, I've let my emotions run away with me. I've learned my lesson, I won't do anything like this again," he said.

Suddenly, Steve Black, who was our fitness coach and psychologist and someone who has worked with a number of clubs and high profile individuals like rugby union star Jonny Wilkinson, spoke up. He said: "The person who wrote that is not the person I know. The person who wrote that is a twat. The person I know would never have done it."

The rest of us now have our heads down, not knowing where to look or what to say. To be fair, the chairman took it without saying too much. But not long after, they wanted to see Blackie in the office. I knew then he was going to be history. Sure enough, the next day he was gone with the chief executive telling him the club couldn't have people disrespecting the chairman. We lost a little bit of spirit with Steve's departure because everyone liked him.

The next game, I asked Lee if I could speak to the players after the coaching sessions had finished. I got them in a huddle on the pitch and told them to ram the words the chairman had written right down his throat. We won the game 4-1. A few days later, Dean must have heard that I'd spoken to the players and asked me what I had said to help turn around their fortunes. I told him I couldn't honestly remember. He looked at me and asked whether I had mentioned his programme article in any way? "Now, why would I do that Mr. Chairman?" I answered, laughing my head off.

The pressure was on now because he wanted promotion.

We responded with a fantastic unbeaten 43-game run which set a League record, overtaking the one set by Brian Clough's Nottingham Forest. Ironically, it was Liverpool who brought the Forest run to an end when I was at Anfield. We won 2-0 and I scored both of the goals. Now it was Huddersfield eclipsing the great Forest side.

That run had begun in 2010/11 and went on until November 28th in the next campaign, when we lost at Charlton.

Travelling down on the coach to London before that game, I got a call from Alan Shearer.

I took the phone towards the steps where you get on to the

coach so I could talk to Alan in private. "Are you sitting down?" he asked me.

"Yes mate, why?" I said.

"It's Gary Speed. He's dead."

I couldn't believe it. I was told that he had hung himself. I went and sat down next to Lee and delivered the sickening news to him.

"You've got to be joking?" he said.

"Lee, you don't joke about things like this. Look mate, I'm sorry but it's true. I just feel numb and sick."

The next night we lost 2-0 and that brought the record to an end but, to be honest, I wasn't that bothered after the news.

Speedo was such a great lad. I loved him to bits.

He had been a big part of our social life, playing golf in Portugal every summer. I had only seen him a fortnight earlier. Lee and I were watching Cardiff in South Wales and Speedo was there watching players as the Wales manager.

We were in the stand and he grabbed me for a chat. He seemed in a great mood, his normal jovial self.

What a waste of a fantastic life. I can't understand it to this day. I still miss him. We all do. He was the last person I could think of that would do what he did. He seemed to have everything going for him. He had adulation from players and fans, a lovely family and everything to live for. It's hard to believe.

As far as Lee's job was concerned, there were no signs that he was in danger, especially after claiming the record. We only lost one more game before playing Sheffield United at home on St. Valentine's Day. We lost 1-0, although we had been outstanding and Danny Wilson, who was the Blades manager, came into the office after the game saying: "How did we win that? You were brilliant. You should have won easily." Even so, we were still up there, very much in the race for promotion.

The chairman had missed the game because he was off skiing. The next morning, I went to the ground for our usual debrief. Some of the staff like Paul Stephenson and Steve Watson were already there and I was bright and breezy as usual, saying good morning to everyone. The two of them looked at me and said: "You haven't heard have you?"

"Heard what?" I replied.

"Lee's been sacked," Steve said.

I couldn't take it in. Lee was out on the pitch on his phone and after a little while he came back in and passed me without saying a word. He was devastated.

I went back into the building and the club secretary came in and told us that we were meeting the same fate as Lee. "I'm sorry, but he wants everyone out. There's nothing I can do."

I thought what they did to Lee was disgusting. Dean Hoyle's reasoning to Lee was that he didn't think he could take the pressure. He had seen Lee become animated on the touchline but that was because he had passion. It was a poor excuse in my eyes. He couldn't have Jurgen Klopp as his manager judging by that argument and as for David Wagner's touchline celebrations when Huddersfield beat Leeds in February, 2017…

I thought Lee has always had it in him to be a top quality manager. He's got a lot of good points. He has his faults, as I have mine. If he had been losing games week in, week out, he would have accepted the sack, but this came out of nowhere. Good people from inside the game said they'd do anything they could to help, including Sam Allardyce and David Pleat.

Simon Grayson took over in February, 2012, and a few months later, Huddersfield were in the Championship. They finished fourth in the table and beat Milton Keynes Dons in the play-off semi-final. Promotion was secured after an 8-7 penalty shoot-out win over Sheffield United at Wembley. We can't have been doing too much wrong if the team went up in the same season Lee was sacked.

I was on holiday in Tenerife that summer and saw that Chris Hughton had left Birmingham City to go to Norwich City.

There was turmoil at the time at Birmingham with the owner Carson Yeung having his assets frozen and being in trouble with the football authorities. Even so, Lee fancied the job and asked me to give Chris Hughton a ring. Chris told me that despite all that was going on, there were good people running Birmingham. I asked if he could put in a good word for Lee, which he did, and he was given an interview, which went very well.

When I got back to England, Lee rang me to say that he felt he had a good chance of getting the job. Sure enough a couple of days later it was his and he asked me to join him along with Derek Fazackerley, who was part of the Huddersfield staff.

We all had a meeting in a room overlooking the St. Andrew's pitch and quickly had our contracts sorted. With Carson Yeung unable to come to England – he was later sent to prison – it was his right-hand man Peter Pannu who was running the show.

Despite the club having financial problems, the atmosphere amongst the workforce was good. There was a transfer embargo in place which was going to make it more difficult but we were all up for the challenge, especially Lee, who felt he had things to prove.

Lee's first season in charge saw Birmingham finish 12th in the Championship. That summer, the club's financial situation meant that we were forced to sell players to raise money. Players like Curtis Davies and Nathan Redmond left for decent money and we were also told to get rid of the higher earners like Marlon King and eventually, Peter Lovenkrands, which obviously made the squad weaker. Jack Butland had already gone to Stoke. All the money went to reduce the debts.

Lee used the loan system brilliantly. We brought in players from Manchester United, Federico Macheda, Jesse Lingard and Tyler Blackett. Macheda ended up scoring a few goals for us while Jesse's start was incredible. He scored all four goals when we beat Sheffield Wednesday 4-1. No-one did us more favours during that time than Sir Alex Ferguson at Old Trafford.

I think maybe that was helped by our mutual love of horse racing. "Can we borrow a player Alex?" He would reply: "Aye, well, what about this horse? What do you think his chances are?" The loan system can often depend on favours, on how well you get on with the manager of the club which has the players you want.

Lingard was a good kid and he's doing very well now at Manchester United and has played for England. I'm really pleased for him. What I love about the players who want to get better is they will ask you to put on extra sessions for them, a bit of shooting, some passing, crossing, things like that. Tyler Blackett was one of those. Macheda was also a great talent. I've been a little surprised how his career has not hit the heights. During his time with us he certainly knew where the goal was. Most people can still remember that fantastic goal he scored against Aston Villa in his early days at Manchester United.

One interesting player was Ravel Morrison, who we got in on loan from West Ham in 2012/13. I think Sam Allardyce, who was manager at Upton Park, felt he couldn't handle Ravel. He was a strange lad but I've got to say Ravel had a good heart. You just didn't know what he was going to do next. You didn't know what mood he would be in each morning. At times he could be a bit dour and then on other occasions he looked happy.

I took him under my wing because I liked him. "Have you had a good night Ravel? Is everything okay?" Little chats like this make a player realise he is cared for and there is interest in him.

I've always been drawn to what we call mavericks – those with great skill, but also those who don't always conform. I never wanted to be a manager, but if I had been I wouldn't have been put off by flamboyant players. As a manager, you do have to be more ruthless than when you're a coach. I like to be liked and that's easier when you're a coach and you're not picking the team, but I still feel I could have handled mavericks well as a manager. I'm somebody who finds it hard to fall out with people, I always give somebody an opportunity to redeem themselves.

Me and Lee Clark sat Ravel down one day and gave it to him straight. "If you put your mind to it, you could be as good as Paul Gascoigne," I told him.

"You can go past people, make killer passes and score great goals." He looked back at me with a vacant expression on his face. "You know who I'm on about, right?"

Turns out he didn't have a clue who Paul Gascoigne was.

We knew he was getting mixed up in things he shouldn't have and there was talk of him having a gun when he was in Manchester. I don't know how true that was – at least we didn't spot any firearms at the training ground!

Ravel was an absolute diamond and we sent him back to West Ham as a better player and, more importantly, a better person.

"What have you done to him?" Sam asked me on the phone one day. "He's a different fella." Coaches just have to spend a bit more time trying to understand him.

There's still time for him. Sir Alex Ferguson once remarked that Ravel was the most talented player to come through the ranks at Old Trafford, but even he couldn't handle him which says it all. I think we came the closest to sorting him out.

I was starting to find it a struggle as the season went on because things weren't the same between Lee and myself. I felt my input wasn't what it was. I didn't have the same influence on things.

We were falling out over team selection and Lee seemed to be confiding in me less and less. I found out that he was talking to other people. I wasn't enjoying it and that made me lose that bit of spark. I didn't feel wanted and I confided my observations to Derek Fazackerley because we shared a flat during our time at Birmingham.

When we played our old club Huddersfield at St. Andrew's, it was agreed that those who lived outside the area like myself could go home after the game to spend the Sunday with their families. I was especially looking forward to that because I'd been in the Birmingham flat for almost three weeks non-stop. We were due in on the Monday, so Sunday was going to be special.

We lost the game 2-1, equalling a club record of 11 winless home games, and Lee told everyone, the staff and players, that he wanted them in the next day, the Sunday. That was his pre-rogative, he's the manager but I just felt that in the knowledge that some people had made plans to travel the extra miles to go home for one day, he could have left everything to the Monday.

Derek and I went to the flat and then went out for a Chinese. The next morning, Derek said he was still going to go home to Blackburn, where his family were based, after training. I wasn't going to do that because my family was almost three hours away in Newcastle. I followed him to the training ground, got changed and then heard a commotion which seemed to be coming out of Lee's room. When I got there, the pair of them were having an almighty row. As soon as I walked in, Lee turned on me. "And you're just as bad. You two piss in the same pot."

I thought 'that's it for me'. I hadn't been enjoying it and this confirmed to me that if our friendship had any chance of surviving, I had to leave. I had treated him as my little brother and although we are friends now, I didn't speak to him for months. I didn't tell him I was leaving the club. I just walked out of the room, collected my belongings and headed for my car. I passed the fitness coach who was coming the other way and he asked me where was I heading? I told him I was going home.

I got into my car and headed straight to the flat to start packing up my stuff. As I'm finishing off, Derek arrived saying he had walked out as well. Neither of us had planned it. It just happened. We had both had enough.

We later got the call from Birmingham that they wanted to meet us. So we met them in a hotel in Stafford and they were brilliant, sorting out our leaving terms after we made it known that we didn't want to return.

I was bitter at how it all ended. I had guessed it was probably going to be my last job in football and there's no way I wanted my career to finish like it did. I had enjoyed working for the people at Birmingham who, despite all the troubles, were great to be around.

In the end, I had walked out on a manager, not a friend.

I didn't speak to Lee for around 18 months. We bumped into each other at a golf club in the North East, we said hello and shook hands. I've seen him since, in a garden centre of all places. That's when we had a longer conversation and I told him what I thought. I said he has the credentials to be a top manager, but he has to surround himself with the right people.

There had been a chance to see Lee earlier when we had both been on holiday in different areas of Marbella, but at the time I couldn't bring myself to see him. We're alright now and we've put everything behind us. I'm glad we're friends again but, for a time, I didn't want that. Now he's like my little brother again and I wish him the best of luck in his new job with my former club Bury.

I left at the end of February and just two months later Birmingham were fighting for their lives under Lee to try and stay in the Championship. They went into the last game at Bolton knowing if they didn't get a point and other results went against them they would be relegated. It was an incredible game – one which I watched at home.

Birmingham looked dead and buried, 2-0 down with 12 minutes to go. Nikola Zigic got a goal back and Paul Caddis equalised with a 92nd minute header at the back post – and he was the smallest guy on the pitch! He's a good lad Paul, a Scot who is still at the club. I was delighted for him.

It was a funny feeling because I wanted the club to stay up, but was sad I wasn't there. I would have loved to have joined in the celebrations at the end.

If Birmingham had gone down it would have been a disaster, similar to when Kevin and I returned to Newcastle and we just managed to make sure they didn't drop into the third tier. Neither club, quite probably, would have survived relegation.

I knew that was it as far as jobs in football go.

There will be no going back on that – unless Kevin Keegan suddenly returns to the game. It's absolutely criminal that Kevin is not involved in football in some capacity. He's still sprightly and bright enough to be a manager. It's beyond belief that his knowledge isn't being tapped into. Look at the Football Association for instance. Surely this organisation would be enhanced with Kevin's input? He has played at the highest level, managed at the highest level, played for England.

Kevin is so honest, he says and tells it as it is. Look at him resigning as England manager. Some people say he wimped out, that he spat his dummy out. Believe me, no-one else would have had the courage to do what he did. It takes a brave man to admit he wasn't good enough for the job. Most other managers would be thinking they didn't want to miss out on two or three million pounds. He just walked.

I can't believe that any of the new owners who have invested fortunes in football clubs haven't considered using Kevin's knowledge. He's the perfect man to be involved and, as I say, the only one I would return to football for. I would go anywhere for him if he called. Afghanistan, anywhere! Whether there is another football club in him I really don't know, but you can still dream about a last hurrah.

Another man who is a big loss to football is Arthur Cox. I still talk to Arthur. Even though he is past his prime, he would still be of use to any club in the country with his knowledge and passion. He really cares and when I worked with him, he gave absolutely everything. Football was, and still is, Arthur's life. You couldn't find anyone more committed and that's why I put him right up there as a top manager.

Bobby Robson was another great manager and came closest to bringing back the Kevin Keegan glory years. Bobby came in after Ruud Gullit. Ruud made the fatal mistake of taking on Alan Shearer, leaving him out of the derby at St. James' Park against Sunderland. Within a few days of that demoralising defeat he was gone. I have a chuckle when I see Ruud and Alan sitting next to each other on BBC TV's *Match Of The Day*. Alan didn't used to like Ruud, but now they are big mates!

Sir Bobby had special qualities. The fans loved him. He's got a statue outside the ground. Not many others have one. He had the common touch and being from the area, knew what made the football club tick. One of the saddest things was seeing him sacked and I believe that Freddy Shepherd, chairman at the time, now regrets that decision.

Bobby's legacy lives on in the North East with the Sir Bobby Robson Foundation which has raised millions. Apart from Kevin I would say he was the most revered manager that Newcastle have ever had.

You look at the list of Newcastle managers over the years and it's pretty impressive. It makes it even harder to stomach that they haven't won anything for years and years. Yet a club like Leicester City have won the Premier League!

Newcastle might still not be able to win the Premier League but surely a cup success isn't out of the question?

CHAPTER 24

HEROES

WHEN I think about trying to compile a list of the best-ever footballers, it takes me as much time as anyone else because of the quality around today, but also the amazing stars of the past.

For me, Lionel Messi and Cristiano Ronaldo are modern day greats. There is always a lot of debate about who is the better player, but I would go for Messi.

Messi just glides past people. I've never seen anyone score goals so frequently and often effortlessly. His awareness of players around him is incredible. Messi also renders statistics meaningless; he probably runs less than any other player on the pitch, but his impact is far greater.

Looking around at the greatest ever, Pele and George Best are up there for me, while Kevin Keegan and Kenny Dalglish aren't too far behind either.

Don't ask me to separate Kevin and Kenny. Everyone asks that and I can't give an answer. They played in the same position but were different types of players. Kevin was all-action, buzzing around everywhere with fantastic pace. He was brave, could go past players and was also brilliant in the air for his size. You don't win two European Footballer of the Year awards if you're not a special player. He was something special.

Kenny, of course, went one further than Kevin at Liverpool and became manager. Kenny's six years in charge undoubtedly continued the Anfield success story. It's hard enough being a player at a big club like Liverpool never mind being a manager on top of that. It didn't seem to bother Kenny. He even scored the title-winning goal at Chelsea on the last day of his first season in charge as player-manager – absolutely typical.

Kenny, of course, took over from Joe Fagan after the 1985 European Cup final at Heysel against Juventus. The night impacted on Joe a lot, although he had already decided to step down as Liverpool manager. It must have been horrendous for everyone involved that night. How a football match could ever take place considering what had just gone on before is completely bewildering, but I know that the decision was made to try and avoid further problems with 39 lives ultimately lost.

Joe's anguish was there for all to see when you saw him crying on the shoulder of Mary Evans, Roy's wife, on the tarmac at Liverpool Airport. Football had never been meant to spark a terrible tragedy. Sadly it was to do that again just four years later at Hillsborough when 96 Liverpool supporters lost their lives on the Leppings Lane terrace before the FA Cup semi-final against Nottingham Forest.

I was amongst the Liverpool supporters at Goodison Park

in 1991 watching what turned out to be Kenny's last game as a manager, the 4-4 FA Cup replay draw with Everton. You couldn't have wished to have seen a more exciting game, but within a few days, Kenny had resigned.

Nobody saw his resignation coming but I believe that he was still suffering from the effects of dealing with the aftermath of Hillsborough. I know that one day he went to five funerals. That's how much he cared for Liverpool and its fans during the club's darkest days. He would go to the houses of people who had lost their loved ones, spending time talking and comforting them. It must have taken its toll – who was comforting Kenny? Nothing prepares you for what he had to go through. Everyone wanted a piece of him and by the time he quit Liverpool he was absolutely shattered.

I went with Phil Thompson to a number of funerals. It affected everyone connected with the club, myself included.

My elder brother Peter went to the game and I have since seen footage of him outside the Leppings Lane entrance with his father-in-law amongst the crush of fans. Luckily, he never went through the gates and was thankfully spared.

On that April day in 1989, I had gone to an open day at Jonjo O'Neill's stables in Cumbria. On the way up, I heard what was unfolding and I phoned home, praying that Peter was alright. Eventually we discovered he was safe.

It must have been horrendous for him, but I can't imagine the hurt of the families left devastated by losing loved ones who had gone to watch a game of football.

Afterwards the whole city came together to grieve, to try to help the sufferers. I decided I wanted to help in any way I could after going down to Anfield with Phil Thompson and seeing the rows and rows of wreaths, scarves and photographs placed in front of the Kop. There were some of the relatives who had lost people there. The least we could do was to give our support at some of the funerals. If events had been different, I could have been attending Peter's funeral.

What has followed in the years since has been an incredible fight for justice from the fans, battling to clear the names of people who perished on that Saturday afternoon. If I had lost someone on that day would I have let go of the campaign? No way. The hurt never fades. After more than 25 years they have finally got the truth. No-one should ever forget that day.

There have been many memorable Liverpool games since Kenny's first spell in charge, but I suppose it is the events of May 25, 2005, that will most be remembered from recent history.

The manager on that famous Istanbul night, of course, was Rafa Benitez. Rafa got a bit of criticism before he wrote himself into Anfield folklore by winning the Champions League. Before then, I spoke to him after a game and asked how he put up with some of the flak he was getting. "Not a problem Terry," he said as he waved his arms in the air. He pretended he didn't know what the fans had been shouting.

I must confess, like most people, I thought we had lost the final against AC Milan. I was watching at home on the telly and at 3-0 I had lost interest, turning the sound down. I thought that was it, game over. One of the kids came in and said that Liverpool had scored so I started watching the game again, turning up the volume. What happened then was beyond belief, especially with that late save from Jerzy Dudek to deny Andriy Shevchenko – but if your name is on it…

I believe that game surpasses anything that we achieved in terms of drama. Many people say that the first European Cup win was the outstanding European night, but in terms of sheer excitement you've got to go for this comeback – you won't see another game like that. Jose Mourinho goes on about how he is 'The Special One', but you've got to put Rafa in that category. He is a great manager. I'm delighted he is now at Newcastle. The fans love him because he connects with them.

It was great to see Steven Gerrard lift the European Cup on that famous night in Istanbul, but the big pity for me is that, as one of Liverpool's greatest ever players, he never lifted the Premier League title. The absence of a League title winner's medal will always sting for him and no doubt it will be the same for another fantastic Liverpool servant, Jamie Carragher.

It's easy to describe Steven as a player: he is simply one of the best midfield players I have ever seen. I am astounded by the amount of goals he has scored from that position. Try to find some faults in his game. I can't. He scored goals, he made goals, he took penalties, he could tackle, he was good in the air, he was as tough as nails and he was someone who could put his foot in when it was needed – a real leader of men. At his peak, he was the best I have witnessed and I've seen some good ones as well, including my big mate Graeme Souness.

I was with Graeme at Newcastle when someone posed the question who was the best Liverpool midfielder and I answered, "Stevie G." Graeme looked at me and said: "Are you sure?!" He added: "Steven Gerrard better than me?" I replied: "Only just!"

Souey was a fantastic player. The two of them were special. One thing they shared was they could both be nasty bastards when necessary, which was great for the players around them. Steven has to be up there with Kevin Keegan and Kenny Dalglish as Liverpool's best ever players.

I met Steven for the first time in Portugal. He was there with Joey Barton. I've seen him since at Liverpool games. It was a thrill to meet him and it's nice that he has spoken about me being a Liverpool legend. He is certainly one and he's even working in Kirkby these days at the Liverpool Academy.

You idolise people when you're younger, like I did as a Liverpool fan in the 1960s – players I was watching like Ian St. John and Roger Hunt. But I would have Stevie G in any team. He would, in fact, be one of the first names on the teamsheet. He is a proper legend and deserves all the accolades he has received.

I've talked a lot about football heroes and another very special person I'd like to pay tribute to was my dad.

My dad was a huge influence, not just on my career, but my whole life. He sacrificed so much for the whole family. He watched as many games as he could from me being a kid, going to Bury, Newcastle and of course the club he supported all his life, Liverpool.

When he became ill and eventually died in 1989 it was just horrible and something which still hurts now because we were a close family and had already lost my mum in 1977. My dad survived a heart attack, but sadly couldn't beat cancer a couple of years later. When we received the gloomy diagnosis, we advised the doctor not to tell him because we felt that would have given him literally nothing to live for. It was confirmed he was suffering with cancer in the June and by the end of November he was no longer with us.

At the time, I wasn't in football and the one consolation of not having a job then was I could spend more time with him, heart-breaking as it was, during the last weeks of his life. He would go past my room to the toilet many times during the night and when I was lying in my bed, I could hear him shuffling along the corridor. Then there would be this terrible cough which went through me. I knew he was in pain and it was just awful. The worst thing was knowing you couldn't do anything about it. You didn't have a magic wand to make things better.

When my dad eventually passed away, we had the funeral in a church just 500 yards from his house. It took place a few weeks before Christmas and the service was wonderful. The church was packed with family and friends. Suddenly, as the coffin is being taken away out of the church, you heard *Jingle Bells* coming over the sound system.

Someone had put the wrong tape on! It should have been *You'll Never Walk Alone,* but being so close to Christmas the tapes had been mixed up and my dad was leaving the church to *Jingle Bells* instead.

That brought the house down. The tears and sniffles turned to smiles and laughter because we knew my dad would have seen the funny side of things.

My dad was one of the nicest fellas you could wish to meet, there was no malice in him, he was just a lovely bloke who loved his family. He was always calm and collected, worked hard at Tate and Lyle and was a massive supporter of my football.

I used to love going down to the Tate and Lyle factory to pick him up in Liverpool because normally he would have to get a bus to get there and come back. Most of his workmates were mad-keen Liverpool fans, so there I'd be in my Ford Capri waiting for him and you could see the pride in his face that here was Terry McDermott, Liverpool footballer, giving him a lift home. If you had a Ford Capri in those days you weren't doing badly. Now it's Bentleys, Hummers and all that.

My dad was fantastic to me and it left a big void in my life. I think losing your parents hardens you up for everything that follows in life. I know losing my mother when she was relatively young made me go off the rails a bit which I've spoken about. I suppose in a way that prepared me more for my dad going, although it was still hard.

Family was the most important thing in my dad's life and I'm the same. I love having my family around me. There's nothing better than when we are all together. Usually, the kitchen is a hive of activity with all the banter. My dad loved a busy house and I'm no different. There were never any fall-outs and that's the same at my home now.

It was a bonus for someone who played for Newcastle United to see both my sons, Neale and Greg, in the famous black and white stripes. The pity is neither quite made it into the first team.

Neale had a great start in his football life playing for England Schoolboys at the same time as Wayne Rooney. He became friends with Wayne. I once watched the pair of them against Wales Schoolboys and even then Wayne looked a real player and looked like a man. You couldn't knock him off the ball. He was strong, determined and had a football brain. Neale was taken on as an apprentice by Newcastle and ended up playing regularly for the reserves. It was a real disappointment when things didn't work out for him there. Neale was a midfielder and a good player, he could run all day – like his dad! – and he cared about his football.

At least I got the chance to watch him in action at St. James'

Park, something which filled me with tremendous pride. Neale later joined the agent Paul Stretford's business, which set him up for a move to Adidas, so he is still involved in the game.

Neale's younger brother Greg started going to Newcastle from the age of six or seven. I would drive him everywhere. It could be horrendous trying to get through the traffic, dealing with all weathers, but that's what parents do as they look to help their kids. Alan Pardew called time on Greg's career with the Toon. Alan told Greg he needed to be playing first team football and there was a big road block with established midfield players including Yohan Cabaye and Cheick Tiote ahead of him. He said he would try to help him get a club. I have no qualms with that and trying to help players find another club is what every manager should do if they are letting you go.

Greg ended up at Gateshead and hopefully now he is on the road to being a coach. He has taken some of his coaching badges and has been taken on by Liverpool to travel around the world promoting the club by putting on training sessions for local youngsters. He's excited about that and so am I. He is keen and very knowledgeable about football. It's nice that both my lads are making their way in the game.

I've given both of them advice, but they don't take any notice! After watching them play, I would say things like: "You've got to get forward." Or "your passing has got to be a bit better." Usually it's met with: "It's alright you saying that, but the coach has told me to sit and be a holding midfield player." I suppose that's fair enough, but I'm just trying to help. Maybe it doesn't work having a former professional player as a dad when you're learning the ropes yourself.

Then, of course, I've got a lovely daughter, Rachel. She always says that people express surprise when they discover she exists. Like all women, she has a naughty streak, but is the life and soul of the party and she loves a good night out, just like her dad.

The other lady in the house is my darling wife Carole, the best thing that has ever happened to me. I could have gone off the rails without Carole. Arthur Cox told me to get her married and it's the best piece of advice I've ever been given. She saved me, she hasn't got a bad bone in her body. I've been with her since 1981. We've been in the North East since 1992 and we love living up here, but we go back to Liverpool a lot.

I'm also lucky enough to reveal that I've never had an argument with any of my brothers or sisters and we have always been close. None of them has been jealous of me as a footballer. My eldest brother Peter has always followed my career closely and knows more about what I've done than I do!

While I've had a great life, been idolised as a footballer, earned decent money and brought up a wonderful family, the spectre of my younger brother Charles never leaves me. Even now I ask 'why did something as cruel as this happen to him?' Horrible to say it, but what was the point of his life?

I am someone who prays, but looking at Charles it did make me question my religious beliefs. It's the same when you see someone who is blind or who is deaf. Why is this allowed to happen to them? It seems so cruel. In a family of six, Charles was the odd one out and it's hard to accept even now.

I have decided to sell my football medals – but I won't take a penny from the proceeds.

I know this might surprise some people but, for me, it's 100 per cent the right decision. I hope fans don't think badly of me, but I'm doing it for my three kids. The money will be divided between the three of them to help them get on the property ladder. I won't be touching any of it.

You have options about what you do with your medals. I put them on display for years, loaning them to the club museum, but I've now got them back again. I put them in a bank for safe-keeping, but I'm not seeing them, so what's the point?

I've come to the decision to help their futures. Even though I might not have the medals, I will still have the memories.

At my time of life, it is also important to maintain my health. I had a reputation for being able to run for ever as a player so it might be hard to believe that I've had a few scares with the old ticker over the years.

Everyone knows when they are not right and at times I have felt my heart was beating in a strange way. So much so that I decided to have things checked out.

I went for tests on a running machine but the specialist couldn't find anything untoward, although I was prescribed some tablets. Now and again I still have some twinges in the same area, a reminder that we are vulnerable and that I won't be around for ever.

One thing that has improved is my knee pain – and it's all thanks to magic potion that was prescribed by Kevin and Jean Keegan!

It's a teaspoon of cider vinegar mixed with a teaspoon of honey, taken before you have anything else in the morning.

Kevin and Jean told me to try it and, all of a sudden – and I don't think it's a coincidence because I don't normally believe in things like this – the pain has disappeared. Carole takes it and I've told a few people like David Johnson and Ian St. John about Kevin's special brew. It might not work for everyone, but it seems to have done the trick for the McDermott family!

I'm still involved with Liverpool. I sometimes do tours of the ground or question and answer sessions with the punters at Anfield. It's always very entertaining.

The most common question is: "What's your favourite goal?" I've been lucky because I've had a few. That comes out in the conversation we have because the fans seem to have differing opinions over my goals as well. Bob Paisley always says that the header against Tottenham in the 7-0 at Anfield was the best goal he had ever seen. Then the odd punter might say: "What about the goal against Aberdeen?" I've often forgotten about that. They have to remind me. But then I think to myself, well there's been quite a few good goals.

One of the questions which sometimes crops up is do I still speak to the nurse who unfortunately was on the wrong end of a shower from the St. George's Hall balcony!

I've found the Liverpool fans very knowledgeable. It's similar with the Newcastle fans. They know what the game is all about and appreciate their football. As I said at the start of this book, neither set of supporters will accept a lack of effort from a player. They know when players are pulling out of tackles.

They absolutely love their clubs and they can't get enough stories. That's why I still love being involved.

Sometimes I'll do a tour of the ground on a Sunday, the day after a game, and it's like a matchday with so many fans milling outside Anfield. They come from all over Europe and they are so fanatical, it takes me aback.

Obviously the young kids won't know much about me, but the dads and granddads do and they are usually more excited than the youngsters. I also do the occasional talk for charity, which I love doing, and again it's great to meet those who attend.

I love every minute of these activities because it often gives me the chance to meet up with so many players I shared a dressing room with at Liverpool. It's wonderful how the players from the Seventies and Eighties are still idolised.

I suppose my only regret is that my kids haven't really seen me play. There's the odd feature on TV about my career, with all the goals and trophies and everything else, but they don't really take much notice because they weren't involved then!

That's the way the young generation are. It's all about the here and now.

I've had a great career. I would have loved to have won the FA Cup as a player and a trophy with Newcastle in later years, but I can't argue with everything else I have achieved.

It has been a fantastic adventure – one that I hope you have enjoyed with me. And who knows, if Kevin Keegan ever gets the call from Newcastle again…

ACKNOWLEDGEMENTS

It's been fun sharing the stories in this book with my ghost-writer John Richardson. Of course, he's had to be indoctrinated into the McDermott way of life with a few good nights of liquid refreshment to help oil the memory cells. I've known him for a good number of years and that has helped in putting all this together.

The most important people in my life are my wonderful wife Carole and my children Neale, Rachel and Greg. I love Carole dearly and she has been the major driving force behind me putting pen to paper about my life. The three kids who I adore have also pushed me to write my book.

There's also my mum Maggie and dad Peter, sadly no longer with us and my brothers Peter, Robert and Charles, who tragically didn't really have a life as I have explained, and sisters Mary and Irene who have always stuck by me through thick and thin. There's been good times and bad times but they have always been there for me. My father-in-law George, who sadly died just over a year ago, and Carole's mum Geraldine have also always been there for me

At times, I probably didn't realise how proud they all have been of me playing football at the highest level, how they felt as they watched me play for their beloved Liverpool. When it's happening, you don't really think about it but now, looking back, I realise what it must have meant to them.

A big thank you goes to older brother Peter who has come to my rescue many times during the writing of this book, when I've had trouble recollecting exactly what went on, involving

Liverpool games especially. Luckily for me, he possesses an encyclopedic memory. The only problem is he's always thought he could play a bit. Just stick to watching Pete!

As well as my immediate family, I must have thousands of relations all around Liverpool which should help the book sell (although many of them will be after a free copy!) Some used to go to games to watch me, which was fantastic. My brother-in-law John and his son John were regular supporters.

Luckily, as a player I made some fantastic friends. As I've said, one of my closest is The Doc, David Johnson. We've known each other since I was 11 when we played against each other in various teams. We've always had a special rapport and still have today.

I'm still close friends with Kevin Keegan too. He didn't hesitate when he was asked to write a foreword for this book. He's one of the nicest people you could meet and myself and Carole, together with Kevin and his wife Jean, still enjoy the odd break together or go out for a meal. He is such a genuine guy.

Another former Anfield team-mate I love bumping in to is Kenny Dalglish. He is so similar to Kevin in many ways with his sense of humour. They both love wind-ups, jokes and football stories. They are also the two best players I've been fortunate to line up alongside.

Then there's other some real characters I'm close to; Liverpool greats like Graeme Souness, Alan Hansen, Phil Thompson, Alan Kennedy, Jimmy Case, Phil Neal, Ian Callaghan and David Fairclough.

I am also in regular touch with Arthur Cox, one of the best managers I've known and one of the funniest – even though he doesn't know it.

TERRY MAC

I would also like to mention a great friend, Alan Stockton, who I lost just over two years ago, someone I miss terribly for his companionship and his great sense of humour.

Finally, I would like to thank Steve Hanrahan, Paul Dove, Chris McLoughlin, Roy Gilfoyle and Chris Brereton at Trinity Mirror Sport Media for all their help and guidance and allowing me the platform to write the book.

Thanks, Terry

POSTSCRIPT: CAROLE

Recovering from the stroke was one thing – discovering just a few months later that my wife Carole had cancer was another.

Carole is someone who has always been vigilant in checking her body and over Christmas (2016) she discovered a lump in one of her breasts. She knew something wasn't quite right because around the area where the lump was she had been experiencing some sharp pains.

Typical of Carole, she didn't want to spoil Christmas and also wanted me to fully recover from my problem before she sorted herself out. With Christmas over and me on the road to recovery, in the middle of January Carole went to see the local doctor who told her that in her opinion there was nothing to worry about – there was nothing untoward and in any case she was due a mammogram in 12 months' time.

At first that was good to hear but she was still uncertain. There was still something niggling her, she felt there was something not quite right. A couple of months later she decided to see another doctor for a second opinion. This doctor was also quite casual but at least she decided to send her to hospital to see a consultant, though her case wasn't to be considered urgent.

The appointment came through for the April but Carole and I had arranged to go to Majorca in the week she was booked in. Because it hadn't been considered an urgent consultation we went ahead with the sunshine break. Another date was pencilled in and she finally went and had a mammogram, a scan and biopsies taken.

The end result was simply horrendous. Sitting there together after being called in to discuss the examinations, you hear the horrible word – the worst one you can ever hear – CANCER. She was diagnosed with stage one, grade two cancer. I just went cold inside. Carole was a little tearful.

The consultant Henry Cain was magnificent. I said to him 'Will she be okay?' He said: 'We'll look after her Terry, I'm sure she will be okay.' That was all I wanted to hear. I had been dreading him saying there was nothing they could do for her.

If it had been a negative response I would have probably collapsed on the floor. He couldn't have been nicer. You hear some people having a go at the NHS but when you see close up what goes on, you see what a great job they all do. One moment you're on the floor then after what he said you are suddenly lifted.

And the good thing about Carole is that she is strong mentally. Everyone who met her during this nightmare period or who spoke to her on the phone or sent messages couldn't believe how strong she appeared. She believed she was going to beat it.

When it was me and my stroke I was able to cope better than when Carole was dealt her blow. When someone you love is going through all this you feel absolutely powerless. When she started her chemotherapy, I would have done anything to swap situations and for me to be going through it rather than her.

It was really tough at times. We slept in separate bedrooms because it was important Carole had the best night's sleep possible. At times she was tired, in pain, looking completely different to the Carole I knew. The worst thing for her was losing her hair. She couldn't get to grips with that. She didn't want anyone to see her without her wig. We had gone out and bought a couple of wigs once her hair started dropping out.

Sitting on the edge of the bed with her one day she just said 'this is going to be a long haul isn't it?' But she wasn't going to let it beat her. I suppose then you are just wishing time away for when she would be back to normal. For those six months of treatment – she was having bouts of chemotherapy every three weeks – you've still got to put on a brave face, taking her a cup of tea or dinner to her bedside. Sometimes she would come downstairs to eat. It was horrible.

After I think the third lot of chemo, she was told that the tumour had shrunk which was great news. Carole's friend from Liverpool, Sharron, came up for Carole's first bout of chemo. She stayed with Carole while I went off for a walk, struggling to get my head around what was happening. I was in a daze most of the time. I didn't know what I was doing or where I was going. I was just thinking 'Christ she's got six months of this.'

I couldn't face going to any more sessions. Instead, Jane, a friend of Carole's from Newcastle, accompanied her for the remaining sessions. Also, another Jayne, from Liverpool, was fantastic, driving up from Merseyside, spending a few hours and leaving at 5am to get back to work.

From the first day we found out about Carole's diagnosis, the house was inundated for the next six months with flowers, gifts, hampers – beautiful ones sent by Angie – other friends and family coming up from Liverpool just for the one night.

Kevin Keegan and his wife Jean were brilliant, very support-ive. Then, of course, there was Kenny Dalglish and his wife Marina who has gone through the same thing as Carole and was fantastic in offering advice after her own experience. On Liverpool match days, the former players who like me did the hosting were great, asking all the time how she was getting on.

Finally, after all the treatment we had to see the consultant. It was nerve-wracking for both of us. You didn't know what to expect. Has everything worked? Has it partly worked? Or it hasn't worked, there's nothing more they can do. All these thoughts were going through my mind.

I was looking for any signs when Dr. Cain walked into the room. How did he look? Was he smiling? What if he just comes in and sits down with a stern face? He walked in, said 'Hi Carole, Terry, everything okay?' I knew then it was going to be good news. He said everything had gone great. Well, I could have jumped on his back as if we were celebrating the scoring of a goal – except this was far more important. We were so relieved.

I discovered that when you finish your treatment in a cancer hospital, the tradition is you ring a bell. I couldn't wait to get to that bell. There was the three of us; Carole, me and Jane. We almost tore the bell off its hinge and we were singing. What a feeling! To think that I could have lost her – my most prized possession. I can't really put into words the feeling of relief that a most horrendous period was at an end.

Just a few weeks later we became proud grandparents with eldest son Neale and Erika producing a lovely daughter Darcey. That was another thing that kept Carole going. About half way through her treatment, Neale told us that Erika was expecting. That was one of the goals for Carole to get back to full health.

Carole loves babies. In fact, she would have loved to have been a midwife. Now she was holding a newly born baby which was lovely to see – a far cry from those sickening moments as she fought cancer, a word I never want to hear for a very long time.

Terry McDermott, 2018